Reflections on a Puerto Rican Life

What Reviewers Are Saying

"Wonderful."—*Newsweek*

"This book is intended as a positive alternative to much testimonial literature about Puerto Ricans/Neoricans in which they appear as passive victims.... The sad absurdity of racial and cultural prejudice is illuminated.... Highly recommended."—*Library Journal*

"Benjy is a good antidote to those who believe that the culture of poverty concept is all but divinely inspired.... Valuable research, excellent writing."—Raymond E. Crist, *Latin America in Books*

"Bringing to Lopez's story advanced instruments of social science, an effective interpretative scheme, and a solid sociological background, Levine has rescued Third World man from indignity.... Few works will better demonstrate the circumstances of the Puerto Rican in New York than this one by Levine."—Miguel Barnet, *Caribbean Review*

"I applaud his attempt to give a different picture of Puerto Rican life, one not ridden with despair and resignation like many other writers ... have done."—Helen I. Safa, *Caribbean Review*

"Acaba de aparecer un estupendo libro.... Tras esa historia aparentemente vulgar, se esconde algo realmente conmovedor: la lucha de un imigrante de origen hispano para ser respetado y apreciado.... La labor de selección de información hecha por Barry Levine puede considerarse ejemplar. Ahí estan en ese magnífico libro todas las luchas ... de miles de puertorriqueños."—Carlos Alberto Montaner, Spanish International Television Network

"A rare work about the Puerto Rican diaspora that leaves the reader on the whole more cheerful when he finishes reading than when he started."—*Américas*

"Benjy's story is much more interesting and refreshing than the countless one-dimensional sociological studies of Caribbean and Latin American emigrants to the U.S., or Mediterranean emigrants to Western Europe."
—*Times of the Americas*

"[Benjy's life] opens the reader's eyes to the problems and challenges, the pain and frustration of life as a Puerto Rican in the big metropolis."
—*Contemporary Sociology*

"An attempt to redress the balance in the sociological literature about Puerto Ricans. . . . providing a more balanced view of Puerto Rican migrants and of the acculturation process."—Frank Fernández, *Revista/Review Interamericana*

"A good read."—*Caribbean Studies*

"Stupendous. A very human document about a very human being."
—*Bijdragen*

"Levine's simpatico study reveals unique kinds of resourcefulness and suffering that elevate Benjy from a 'type' into a subject of human concern."—*Choice*

"What Levine seems to be pointing out . . . is that the migratory experience . . . sharpens the migrant's ability to deal with life situations successfully."—Eugene Mohr, *The Nuyorican Experience*

"Ojalá que Barry Levine, quien con tanto acierto ha sabido comunicarnos la personalidad de este hombre puertorriqueño de nuestra época, ofrezca en algún momento nuevas noticias que vayan completando esta apasionante 'historia picaresca'."—*El Mundo*

"Barry Levine has that increasingly rare gift, the sociological ear. In this book we have the result of his listening—patiently, sensitively, with a fine feeling for nuance to what I'm sure must be one of the most colorful characters in sociological literature."—Peter L. Berger

"Great book, very well written. A mind-blowing book. I want to find more books by this author."—Anonymous, London, UK, *Amazon.com*

Markus Wiener Publishers
Princeton

Reflections on a Puerto Rican Life

Benjy Lopez: A Picaresque Tale
of Emigration and Return

Barry B. Levine

Second printing, 2010
Copyright © 2009 by Barry B. Levine
First Markus Wiener Publishers edition, 2009, including two new essays
Benjy Lopez was first published in 1980 by Basic Books, Inc., Publishers, New York

Cover design by Juan de la Rosa, copyright © Blue Mango Creative

All rights reserved. No part of this book may be reproduced or transmitted in any form or by any means, whether electronic or mechanical—including photocopying or recording—or through any information storage or retrieval system, without permission of the copyright owners.

For information, write to
Markus Wiener Publishers, 231 Nassau Street, Princeton, NJ 08542
www.markuswiener.com

Library of Congress Cataloging-in-Publication Data
Levine, Barry B., 1941-
 [Benjy Lopez]
 Reflections on a Puerto Rican life : Benjy Lopez : a picaresque tale of emigration and return / Barry B. Levine. — 1st Markus Wiener Publishers ed.
   Originally published under title: Benjy Lopez. New York : Basic Books, 1980. With new introd.
   Includes bibliographical references.
   ISBN 978-1-55876-483-5 (hardcover : alk. paper)
   ISBN 978-1-55876-484-2 (pbk. : alk. paper)
 1. Lopez, Benjy, 1922-2007. 2. Puerto Ricans—New York (State)—New York—Biography. 3. New York (N.Y.)—Biography. 4. Puerto Rico—Biography I. Title.
 F128.9.P85L676 2008
 304.8'747107295092—dc22
 [B]   2008034589

Markus Wiener Publishers books are printed in the United States of America on acid-free paper and meet the guidelines for permanence and durability of the Committee on Production Guidelines for Book Longevity of the Council on Library Resources.

Contents

Prologue, by Robert Farris Thompson ix

Introduction: Reflections on a Puerto Rican Life 1
   Metamorphoses of a *Jíbaro* 1
   In Search of Dignity 6
   From Testimonial to Testament 10

In Benjy Lopez's Words 13
   1. *Salpicar*: The Splash 15
   2. My First Growing-Up (1922–1940) 18
   3. I Became Such a GI (1940–1943) 28
   4. My New Way with the Army (1943–1945) 43
   5. We Conquerors (1945) 55
   6. The System Is Upstairs (1945) 63
   7. Marine Tiger, or "500,000 Came for
      Dinner" (1946–1951) 72
   8. A *Jíbaro* in a Goddamn Place Like That (1946) 78
   9. What the United States Was All About (1946) 86
   10. Forced to End Innocence (1946–1947) 91
   11. B-29s (1947) 96
   12. Marriage by Proxy (1948–1950) 101

13. Every University Has a Dubinsky (1950–1951) 109
14. How Eisenhower Ruined the Neighborhood (1947–1952) 117
15. These Cubans, They Were All My Friends (1952) 122
16. Don't Use That Goddamn Word "Crime"! (1953) 129
17. Trip Guy (1951–1953) 133
18. The Hacking Deal (1952–1956) 139
19. Turning Points (1955–1961) 148
20. My Exile from Puerto Rico (1961–1965) 157
21. The Waterfront Deal Was Dying for Me (1961–1965) . 163
22. Even Inside Puerto Rico (1966) 171
23. If I Keep on Thinking... 177

Afterword: Changing the Story 183
    Inconvenient Individuals 188
    The Sad Tale of the Puerto Rican Testimonial 190

Notes to the Introduction 195
Notes to the Afterword 203
Acknowledgments 209

Prologue

ABOUT FIFTEEN YEARS AGO, searching for sources on mambo in New York, I came across Barry B. Levine's wonderful testament to the life and times of Benjy Lopez, Puerto Rican migrant and existentialist extraordinaire. I thought I might find a few references to Benjy at the Palladium, the great dancehall where Puerto Rican New York flaunted mastery of mambo before thousands of admirers. Instead I found myself confronted with something richer, a hard-won philosophy of survival and continuity, born of cross-cultural challenges and brilliant responses.

This book is a classic, not only of the picaresque genre, a modern rival to *Lazarillo de Tormes,* but also one hell of an insight into the sharpening of mind and spirit that results from constantly improvising under pressure in a multicultural world. Levine has pulled off a genial masterpiece.

Benjy was a Puerto Rican in heavily Jewish New York. He learned from the Jews. He said that the Irish settled matters with their fists but that Jews called in lawyers, or not infrequently adjudicated matters themselves. This Puerto Rican's admiration for M.O.T.s (Members of the Tribe), as they called themselves in the fifties in New York and the Catskills, would be reciprocated in the world of New York Puerto Rican mambo. Larry Harlow, on the way to temple to train as a cantor, passed a Puerto Rican dancehall and was immediately captured by the staccato incandescence of the mambo. He walked in and passed through the door of his destiny. He is today one of the legends of salsa. (Benjy ends his account of his life story in 1965, just before mambo morphed into salsa.)

So some of Benjy's adventures run parallel to the blends of the world of New York *latino* popular dance music. I am haunted by one of Benjy's friends, a Puerto Rican who lived very simply in a rundown tenement, armed only with a record player and a pile of records. Outwardly poor, he was inwardly rich, presiding over a miniature acoustical Alexandrian library including, I would guess, 78 rpm disks of Noro Morales and Alberto Socarrás and other innovators who all eventually led us to mambo. Levine informs me that Benjy himself liked to dance to *música romántica,* that is, the close-in, embrace dance, *bolero.* Later, after 1970, he let himself go to the beat of Dominican *merengüe* and of course New York *latino* salsa.

Shifting from music to sociology, we discover so much lifemanship coded into Lopez's life and times. Benjy's adventures in the United States Army, for example, could be studied with profit by anyone contemplating a military career. The way in which he turned that institution around to his and his buddies' benefit is an exemplary tale in and of itself; it is a jewel of a narrative of self-realization. How he practiced leniency with his men, knowing that when inspection time came they would fall to and help him with incredible energy, is a wonderful lesson. I have actually practiced another one of his strategies: live simply but every now and then splurge.

What this wonderful book boils down to is the power to shape one's life the way one wishes. In the process you become, as Saul Bellow put it near the end of *The Adventures of Augie March,* an *animal ridens,* that is, a person of poise and inner resources who laughs at vicissitudes, who refuses to suffer (the very definition of humor). Levine himself calls this remarkable quality "the final resistance." By this he means refusing to lead a disappointed life. In this book, the portrait of Benjy, as he turns his life into a self-fashioned epic, is total. He is given full voice. When you reach the last page you feel as if you had actually known him.

Benjy leaves us with an abiding insight, learned on the run and from living among Anglos, Jews, Italians, and Irish. He did not see different cultures as predicaments. He saw them as opportunities. He saw them as grounds for the deepening of self. Summarizing all this, he says something extraordinary: "Imagine if you were twenty years old and didn't feel inferior to anybody or better than anybody. When you treat everybody the same, people open up to you." Amen.

Robert Farris Thompson,
Professor of Art History, Yale University,
and author of *Tango: The Art History of Love*

INTRODUCTION

Reflections on a Puerto Rican Life*

PUERTO RICO is a society caught in an untimed transition—a society between tradition and modernity, belief and secularization, rural life and urban life, poverty and wealth, Spain and America.[1] Benjy Lopez (1922-2007), our protagonist, spent his life traveling back and forth between the extremes of that transition: migration to and from the city, to and from New York; wandering between social classes; passing through political ideologies; journeying from one worldview to one not quite articulated.

Metamorphoses of a *Jíbaro*[2]

Lopez was born into Puerto Rico's modest agricultural middle class. During his earliest years his family lived relatively well, but during the 1930s two disastrous hurricanes and the worldwide economic depression crippled the Puerto Rican economy.[3] Fallen from their more comfortable rural life, the Lopez family was forced to move to an urban slum. Although careful to point out that those were not his earliest beginnings, Lopez seemed proud to recall his past days of poverty, a poverty that he both hated and overcame.

At the age of seventeen—by simply lying about his age—Lopez joined the National Guard to obtain a pair of shoes.[4] Soon thereafter, when the Guard was nationalized, he had his first sustained experience with Americans from the United States: monolingual, blond-haired, blue-eyed officers training unsophisticated Puerto

---

* The notes accompanying this essay begin on page 195.

Rican peasants to become efficient United States soldiers. Lopez initially took these Americans to heart and learned to be a good soldier by following Army rules, but he rapidly realized that breaking the rules was an even more effective way of achieving results. Promoted to sergeant, Lopez became an expert in strategic leniency,[5] relaxing some rules to induce compliance with other more strenuous dictates. Eventually, he became disappointed with the United States Army and no longer paid heed to any constraints.

The Army became the means by which Lopez engineered his emigration from Puerto Rico. He worked ingeniously (outrageously, some might say) to set things up in such a way that he would be discharged on the United States mainland rather than back on the island. Puerto Rico meant poverty to him; it meant suffering and a hard time. He hated the island and was determined to leave it. Thus, even given his resentment of Americans, migration to the mainland seemed to him more promising than returning home to Puerto Rico.[6] To his mind, Puerto Rico offered little support in his efforts to achieve a decent kind of life.

When Lopez got to New York, his struggle took on a different character. While work was available, employers discriminated against Puerto Ricans and attempted to restrict them to low-paying menial jobs. The Puerto Rican male was viewed as cheap labor and stereotyped for the least satisfactory work situations: washing dishes or operating elevators at thirty-five or forty dollars a week. Lopez pointedly refused to take on any such assignments. He refused two other options of a more entrepreneurial nature. Although tempted, he was not willing to go into the rackets (drugs, prostitution, minor crime), no matter how potentially lucrative. He feared being apprehended by the authorities and avoided any long-term involvement with such activities. Nor would he settle for a *bodega*,[7] which would have required many hours of hard work each day for a steady income that offered little possibility of significant economic success, no matter how respectable.

Lopez exhibited neither the extreme asceticism of the work ethic nor the equally extreme lethargy of the welfare ethic. During the time that he spent in New York, Lopez was a student, a pimp, a house painter, a rental agent, a taxicab driver, and a merchant seaman. His early years in the city illuminate a drama between the competing alternatives of pimping and schooling. Pimping was a way to get to the good life; schooling, a way to do what one was supposed to do. But eventually he followed neither path, finding in driving a cab and shipping out as a merchant seaman work that would allow him the independence that he sought. In both cases, he carved out areas of freedom subject only to his own control, chunks of time defined mainly by his mostly self-sufficient imagination.

Lopez often expressed the wish that he be treated as an individual, that he be recognized for what he wanted to be. But off the island this never seemed to be the case. For one thing, many people simply knew nothing about Puerto Rico or Puerto Ricans and would, without realizing it, try to assign Lopez identities that were not his. Many times, for example, he had to protest that he was a Puerto Rican and not a Mexican or a Cuban or a something else. Consequently, location between patently wrong identities and a not-too-well understood Puerto Rican one presented Lopez with frequent opportunities to practice the art of juggling masks. Though never quite a con man, he cannot be faulted for lack of cunning.

However, once the Puerto Rican migration to New York gained momentum, and the Puerto Rican population in the city became more visible, Anglos reacted by classifying individual Puerto Ricans as members of an undesirable social group. Their different language and life style were taken as proof of both their homogeneity and inferiority. Differences in status among Puerto Ricans that Lopez had learned to recognize in Puerto Rico (though not necessarily to take seriously) were invisible to the Americans. Where Lopez saw differences—pretentious or otherwise—between rich and poor Puerto Ricans, black and white Puerto Ricans, respectable and unrespectable Puerto Ricans, and island-born and mainland-born Puerto Ricans, for example, the Americans saw only Puerto Ricans.

Moreover, the Americans did not approve of what they saw. Puerto Ricans, then the newest and poorest group to immigrate to New York, were viewed as intruders in the normal life of the city and were looked down upon as people unable to understand what life in New York was all about.[8] Lopez experienced slurs, was refused service at eating establishments, and got into fights. Taken together with his fear that he would not be able to communicate well enough in English, Lopez often claimed to feel, especially in his early years in the States, particularly vulnerable around certain Americans.

This vulnerability was exacerbated by the conflicting ways that Puerto Ricans and Americans treated race. Race prejudice in Puerto Rico took the form of social exclusion. Blacks—identified as those with "bad" hair—were denied access to specific clubs and social situations. Though insidious, such prejudice involved nothing like the personal vehemence and organized violence of race prejudice in the United States. Most Puerto Ricans wanted to consider themselves to be shades of white. Americans, in contrast, wanted to consider most Puerto Ricans to be shades of black.[9] Somewhat in reaction to this attitude, Lopez absorbed this argument and defiantly took the position that all Puerto Ricans, including himself, were at least part black. But when he was off the island he was never quite sure what others would consider him to be. He sometimes passed for white and sometimes was put down for being black. But he never accepted skin color as a determinant denying mobility and he voluntarily passed into and out of black and white identities. The essential ambiguity of such situations caused him moments of anguish but also allowed him to be creative. Thus, when assigned to Benjy Lopez, color, as well as other aspects of personal identity, became elements for strategic use rather than for passive acceptance.

Upon his arrival in New York, Lopez learned that survival meant mastery of the city's ethnic geography, and he quickly familiarized himself with it. He learned to distinguish between Puerto Ricans and Americans, white and black; Puerto Ricans and Irish, Italians, and Jews; Puerto Ricans and Cubans, Mexicans, and Mexican-Americans; Puerto Ricans and Neoricans.[10] He was further practiced in ethnic geography by virtue of his travels both in the Army and in the merchant marine where he had known nationals from all over the globe. This skill was reinforced by his great capacity to differentiate himself from others, a differentiation that often took the form of a countervailing prejudice. Like others in his situation, Lopez was capable of some outrageous and terribly prejudiced views. The sheer diversity of Lopez's experiences makes it hard to describe his life as culturally deprived.

Lopez's capacity to differentiate was matched by his capacity to identify. He frequently expressed a community of feeling with other Latins, with blacks, or with Jews. But his most vivid articulation of ethnic relations is his simultaneous identification with and differentiation from the Cubans, a love-hate relation shared by many Puerto Ricans and Cubans that began with their intertwined histories in the Caribbean and has continued ever since.[11] Asked to identify himself, he would say, "I'm an international."

Lopez reflected on his time in New York as a period during which he developed sophistication in dealing with the modern world, especially with the instruments of bureaucracy. Any naive acceptance of organizational imperatives ended early in his career in the Army. From then on, his attitude toward bureaucratic demands was what sociologists like to call "aim rational"[12]—a fully calculating attitude by which an actor attempts to maximize personal gain while paying little attention to any ideological justification offered for such demands. Yet it was not until he got to New York and witnessed the paper world of the GI Bill, visas, licenses, and so forth, that he developed a finer appreciation of bureaucratic workings. He learned how to fill out papers, the when and where of tips and bribes, the importance of contacts and lawyers. That kind of knowledge, he claimed, would give him a comparative advantage back home among the uninitiated.[13]

But while he garnered some control over his working life, and though he was better off in the big city than he had been on the island twenty years before, he was never quite successful in New York. By the end of his stay there, Lopez concluded that he had not accomplished much, that, in fact, he was leading "a lousy life." He had become more callous than he had been when he left the island. He had not continued his education. And hacking and shipping out were dead-end jobs. He realized that he was not going to make it in New York. Again he had to engineer his own migration, this time to return to Puerto Rico.

In Search of Dignity

Back home, many of the things he had learned in the States were of great value to him. He had had some schooling and had done a great deal of reading. He was able to speak English easily, if not flawlessly. He was able to interact with educated people. He was better able to see through pretension and prejudice. He knew how to work bureaucracies. He understood how to think on a grand scale. He was familiar with the "things" of modern America. Most important, he had developed the social skills necessary to preclude the recurrence of economic and social deprivation. Unlike the myth of immigrant success in the United States, Lopez did not come to the United States and make it. Rather, he went there, learned how to make it, and then returned home to claim his reward.[14] In fact, it was only when he returned to Puerto Rico and applied his street smarts and New York knowledge on his own turf that his story became one of ethnic success. Back on the island, Benjy Lopez earned a comfortable living as an imaginative if unorthodox salesman and entrepreneur.

I met Lopez while teaching at the University of Puerto Rico. By then he had been married, was the father of twins, and was making money. Despite the fact that we started taping our conversations five years after his return, this book tells little about his life on the island. He didn't want his two lives connected publicly for fear that it might affect the new identity he hoped to create. The first edition told us little about life with Celia, his wife of 40 years, and even less about his family (his children are today in their late 30s and both have teenage children of their own). When he was in New York, he had no lasting relationships with women and had no family of his own. But with Celia, he surrendered a lonely autarkic existence and partnered with her in search of opportunities. His family pulled him in from the margins. She has the same analytical powers, and as strong a will, as he did. His life back on the island had more continuity and was less episodic but no less adventuresome.

When they met, Celia was an elementary school teacher. Her original impression of him was that he was *un americano* who knew little about Puerto Rico and whose English was better than his

Spanish. She would correct him and in time he dominated Spanish once again. Lopez was a tolerant agnostic; one of their twins is a practicing Catholic, the other, a practicing Evangelical. Politically, he held onto the ideal of independence for the island but concluded that it was not a realistic goal, so he became involved with the governing Popular Democratic Party (PDP). Politics for him on the mainland was at arm's length, something to talk about only, but on the island, he could actually get involved with politics and politicians. In 1980, Celia ran for representative as the PDP candidate from the small town outside of San Juan where they lived. Benjy was the campaign manager; he rented a truck with loudspeakers and paid a songwriter to create a jingle using cash he had accumulated in a safe deposit box in the bank (a habit he picked up in New York). Celia lost by 100 votes. So they went on to something else. In the early 1980s, Celia started a small business importing inexpensive items from China.

Benjy's first serious job on the island was selling advertising space for a throwaway magazine distributed on a Caribbean regional airline. He took the job with little knowledge of what it entailed—when it was offered to him, he turned to a friend and asked, "What's a column inch?" He took advantage of free flights, targeted a hotel and car company on each island with whom he would trade space for services, and devised a strategy for each island. Merchants unhappy with the service the airline was providing their island resisted his entreaties. Advertisers unhappy with the irregularity of publication tried to withstand his offers. He would persist. In some cases, he would appeal to potential advertisers' sympathy for another working man trying to earn his "rice and beans." In other cases, he would figure out who ran the island, cozy up to him, and use their relationship to get merchants to advertise. As difficult as the getting of the sale was getting paid; advertisers figured that all they had to do was stall and the salesmen would have to return to their home base empty-handed. His store of free stays allowed him to outlast and outwit that tactic. He was quite successful at the job; for him selling became a competitive sport with each sale a verbal conquest.

A friend of Lopez's had moved to New York and published a book about Puerto Rico. Lopez decided he wanted to see his friend. He invented the "Traveler Awards" to get his friend's publisher to pay for his trip to receive the "Traveler Best Book on Puerto Rico" award. Lopez then got a hotel to host the awards at no cost (they received the "Best Hotel" award), a caterer to provide food and wine, etc., etc., until he got to the poor commercial artist who was designing the awards and who wondered how *he* was going to get paid. Lopez calmed his fears: "Put your name in for the 'Best Commercial Designer' award." Lopez knew how to cash out status pretensions. At a party to welcome his friend back to the island, Benjy told about his experiences in the United States Army. As Lopez related his tales, I thought I was witnessing a Puerto Rican version of the 1970 film *M*A*S*H*. When the party broke up, I grabbed his arm and cajoled him to meet with me every Saturday over a bottle of rum to record his stories. Slowly but steadily, the rest of his biography leaked out; his story was much more than *M*A*S*H*, it was *Augie March*, a plea to the active life.

When the regional airline was bought by a national airline, the magazine closed. Lopez then proceeded to buy a farm in the center of the island—this despite knowing almost nothing about agriculture. At the time there was a scarcity of plantains on the islands, and they were selling at a premium. For him, it wasn't a romantic return to the land but a business venture, one he optimistically believed had a low knowledge threshold. He also planted squash. When unanticipated rains destroyed that crop, he got the federal government to give him $5,000 for crop loss and the Puerto Rican government to give him additional monies for crop damage. He didn't get back all he had invested, but he knew how to minimize his loss. With one of his workers, he would load a truck with plantains and two folding chairs and park in front of a Pueblo Supermarket. He would sit in one of the chairs, reading the *New York Times*, while his worker proceeded to sell plantains to Pueblo's customers. But the farm required lots of physical exertion and so exacerbated his disc problem that he had to spend months in Veteran's Hospital.

In the early 1970s, the U.S. government transferred to Puerto Rico the old Naval and Coast Guard base in the Isla Grande section of San Juan. The Puerto Rican government then moved its driver's license bureau there. Lopez instantly realized that thousands of drivers on the island had to renew their licenses every four years, and that each time they would need new photos to do so. He approached a friend, a celebrity photographer whose studio was across from the new bureau. The friend had taken portraits of the island's governors, done shoots for top advertising agencies, and photographed top models and artists. Lopez suggested they go into business together to take driver's license photos for the thousands of applicants who would need them. The famed photographer's response was, "No, no, no!"—in his mind that would be beneath him. But reluctantly he agreed under the condition that nobody knew about their arrangement.

Lopez bought a $600 Polaroid camera, one that displayed four shots at a time, 2 by 2, and became a photographer of sorts. He hired a physician to test eyesight and a lawyer to attest for a violation-free record, both of whose signatures were required as part of the application. He hired street hustlers to flag down motorists and have them enter his ill-lit and unadorned shop to prepare the necessary documents. After several months, he turned the camera over to his stepson and let him run the daily activities. Lopez would open the business at 10:00 in the morning, set it running, take off for the spa to get a massage for his bad back, have lunch, and return just before 4:00 in the afternoon to count the money and then pay the doctor and lawyer in cash for their professional services, the famous photographer for the rent, his stepson and the runners for their efforts. A chunk of bills went into his pants pocket. Despite its very ragtag appearance, he had created a cash cow.

The photographer lost his lease on the space for the 2 by 2 shop because the landlord was tired of perpetually waiting for late rent money. Lopez then negotiated a lease directly with the landlord. When the fashion photographer realized this, he set up an operation next to Lopez's in an unsuccessful attempt to compete with him. Benjy saw what his sometime friend could not. His ability to shrug off conventions and see through pretensions allowed him to envision possibilities.

There was a small wooden house on a big piece of land overlooking a sugarcane field about an hour outside of San Juan. When the owner died in an accident, the widow needed to sell the little house. The Lopezes bought the house, fixed it up, and moved in with their children. Lopez then used all his bureaucratic savvy, persistence, and contacts to buy the 5.5 acres from the Puerto Rico Land Authority. Over time, the Lopezes built a large concrete house that they kept adding to; in front of the new house was a long veranda; alongside it, a large swimming pool. He converted the small house into a stable where he housed *paso fino* ponies for a time. Once a new expressway opened, the trip to San Juan was shortened to about a half hour. Lopez had figured out how to earn his comfort relatively easily. But to achieve these ends would not have been for him worth the expense of a life of self-denial; as he put it, "the idea is to live like a rich man without being rich." So he did, and that is how he lived.

Benjy Lopez was a friend, but I wasn't the only one of his friends who, when in a tight situation or in a bureaucratic squeeze, would ask themselves, "What would Benjy do?" To ask that question was to burrow an exit out of a trap, to discover an option when one thought there was none. Benjy's life demonstrated that there were always options.

From Testimonial to Testament

Benjy Lopez was no ordinary individual. His life demonstrated the resiliency and the resourcefulness of those human beings who have learned to beat the system—a testimony to human intelligence and the will to resolve problems, no matter the disadvantages. During his life, Benjy Lopez proved practically indomitable. His vision of New York was of the underside of city life, and his pose was that of the survivor; but it is clear that he was a survivor who was not consumed by the process of survival.

Living across cultures allowed Lopez not to take cultural matters too seriously. More than most people, he was a liberated man—liberated from the fears, customs, conventions, and rules that normally keep us in our place. The human constructions of the social world never achieved such a dignity in his eyes as to render them immune from his examination and skepticism. The world of Benjy Lopez was not chiseled in stone. It was a world that announced humanness, that was open and malleable to his gaming mind. Indeed, the world to him remained fresh, something always to marvel at, something to manipulate and not be manipulated by.

This is a book about doing. Being, life, action, and social action are steps in the flowering of doing. We are what we are not yet unable to do—and at a certain level we all know this. Biological deficits define part of what we may be unable to do (and even then compensations are possible[15]), but social deficits are of a different order. By accepting the social world as given and by not using our abilities to confront the obstacles it places before us, we are complicit with whatever it is that threatens to hem us in. In that sense, we are reduced to what we will allow ourselves to do, and that becomes our story. Benjy Lopez understood this better than most. His life was defined by what he was able to do, and this was considerable. He overcame poverty, prejudice, and bureaucratic stumbling blocks, all of which he encountered both as a child in Puerto Rico and as a young man trying to make his escape by migrating to the United States. But biology did to Lopez what society could not. Biology began undoing him; in 1995, he had a stroke and was disabled.

At first, he lost many of his abilities. A fan of Frank Sinatra and Tommy Dorsey—what his wife called "that old music"—he forgot their songs and gave up listening and dancing to any music at all, no *bolero*, no *merengüe*. A committed reader, he gave up his daily *New York Times* and no longer listened to shortwave radio from overseas. A great talker, he no longer wanted to speak. His wife thought his old fear of being unable to communicate had returned, this time in two languages. He had always expressed to her a desire to live a long life but one with full faculties at his disposal. The stroke encaged him, much like New York had tried to; recovering from the stroke was a struggle, just as his days in New York were. But it was a different kind of struggle. He somehow knew that he wasn't going to beat *this* system. Still that didn't stop him from trying. He believed that if he swam and exercised everyday in his pool it would help him recover abilities. And in time, he was able to function much better, although it was easier for him to recognize those things that were brought to his attention than to recollect any such things without external clues. Indeed, he was able to communicate, but he was without *ánimo*, without *gusto*, without the "splash" that he had loved to project about, without the internal fire that had made him so vibrant. He was no longer the old Benjy. One time, after the stroke, when he and his wife visited their son who had come to South Florida to work, I went to see them, bringing with me copies of the first edition. When his son saw the books, copies of which had been in their house on the island, he said to me, "*Papi* told me most of the stories in the book, but I never read it; I want to read it now." Then, unexpectedly, Benjy said to me, "I want to read it too." He had forgotten much of his life. This book was to become his memory; no longer a sociological testimonial, it has now become a testament to his life and vitality. In 2007, at the age of 85, he had another stroke; this time he was "un-abled"; that's what death is: the end of the story—but what a story.

In Benjy Lopez's Words

— 1 —

Salpicar: The Splash

I HAVE BEEN PUSHED. I have been knocked down. I have taken the blows for more than twenty years all over the world, especially in the greatest city in the world where the *buitres,* the vultures, are.[1]

On this whole planet I don't think there is a place where they are so able to destroy the feelings of human beings as in New York City. In Buenos Aires, for example, there's all kinds of people, there's Italians, there's Germans, there's Spaniards, but it's not the same as New York.

I know New York is a place where somebody can hit the right trail, can get a break, but to me it was zero. I was a prisoner mentally for all those years in New York. Not in the beginning when I got out of the Army, but then that prison started coming around me, those *rejas,* those bars, started coming up slowly, and as the years went by, I was on guard all the time. I'd go out on the street expecting all the time to be whipped somehow or other. You can't get a drink here, you can't get in there. I was like something out of this world. It was like I was in the lower depth, and I can't understand how—I feel like vomiting every time I think about what I did with Marta.

To the white people, the upper ones in New York, I was just like one of those guys, those stereotypes, in Aldous Huxley's *Brave New World.* I'm driving a cab and I'm singing. Now I love music and I like to sing. I've always been crazy about it. I'm not singing because I'm

---

[1]. When a Spanish word is followed by its English equivalent, there will be no translation in a footnote. Except for the names of people in the public arena, all names have been changed, including that of the protagonist. When a Spanish name appears without its customary accent mark, it is because Lopez (no accent) emphasized its American pronunciation.

Puerto Rican or Latin American or Indian. I'm singing because I love to sing. And a woman gets in the cab and says, "You Latins, you always sing." In other words, I don't think, I don't have a brain, all I can do is sing. The world is a singing world for us. That's the stereotype.

So after all those years I was going nowhere in New York, and I decided to return to Puerto Rico. I realized that I had been living in a different world completely. It took about three or four months after I got back before I started feeling the bars going off me. I began to lose the feeling of lousiness from the lousy life I had up there, with the whoring and the Cubans and stuff like that. I found I was actually a human being. I could begin to respect myself. I could go anywhere, and nobody would look at me bad. I was like everyone else. For me, and I guess for most Puerto Ricans, the feeling that one is somebody becomes possible when we get back to our country.

Still, however bad the United States is, it is a more advanced society, that's definite. And New York, with all its defects, is the most. When you get out of New York and go to some small country, you're way ahead of everybody because you've been living with the media and the technology. No matter what situation you're involved with, it reflects. All of today is there in New York. Even the guys who don't know how to write, the guys who have no head at all, feel the effects of this tremendous technology.

So the ones that go to the States, when they come back they have an advantage over the ones who never left. They can see more, they can see the opportunities.

Like the Cubans say, it's *salpicar. Salpicar* is when you throw a stone in a small pool of water, and it splashes, and just one little bit of water can get you wet.[2] In New York it's the same. No matter how

---

2. Lopez's use of the term *salpicar* derives from the Cuban usage. José Miguel Gómez, president of Cuba from 1909 to 1913, often justified his corruption by remarking, "*El tiburón se baña pero salpica.*" The literal translation is, "When the shark dives, he splashes." Gomez meant that when the big boss does well for himself, everybody gets a piece of the action. Lopez here means simply that some of New York rubbed off on him and in that sense he got a piece of the action.

little you're there, you're never the same afterward. It touches you. Even laborers are splashed—by the people, in the movies, for example, on the television. I ran into bankers. I overheard guys saying things like "I'm gonna lose a hundred-thousand-dollar job, but I won't give in to the son of a bitch anymore." This really happened. I was driving a hack down 34th Street, and a young fellow in the back, about thirty years old, was telling another guy, "Fuck him, fuck the hundred thousand, I'm going home to my wife, I don't want the job." How can anyone living in a small country like Puerto Rico—one hundred miles long or even three thousand miles square—listen in on a deal like that?

It's *salpicar*. I got splashed more than most because of the way I did things. Some guys, they lie with the vultures but they never mingle with them. They're dishwashers, they work in a factory, they push a button for eight hours, they take the subway, go home. They don't speak a word of English, they don't see anybody, and they don't get too much pushed around. They just get in the subway, get out at the stop, go home, go on Sunday to see a Mexican movie, back home, back to work, back to the subway, get forty bucks a week, then come back to Puerto Rico. "Oh, yeah, I lived in New York," they say. I have met people that lived in New York twenty years and still don't know what New York is.

Like Ovid[3] used to say, "You have hooks all over the body." That's a philosophy. I got that book on 50th Street in Manhattan for a dollar. The seamen played cards, and I read that kind of stuff! Tough books. I didn't get it all, but something was left there.

---

3. Publius Ovidius Naso (43BC–17AD) was a Roman poet who wrote on love and transformations.

— 2 —

My First Growing-Up (1922–1940)

MOST PUERTO RICANS—not only Puerto Ricans, most human beings—are afraid of talking about their past. They want to think they've always been living nice. If they were poor, they don't want people to know it. They never say they were peasants, or that they lived in a lousy neighborhood. They try to look like a *blanquito*,[1] like they never went hungry and never had to go to the outhouse and get the mosquito in their asses.

When I was growing up, most of the roads in Puerto Rico were not paved. Muñoz Rivera Avenue around the *plaza de recreo*[2] up to the university was, but the rest wasn't because there was no money in the *municipio*[3] to pave the roads. At that time they didn't have any money to pay the government people—not even the teachers. The government would owe three, four, even five months pay. But everybody I talk to who is more or less my age still claims he was fine and that nobody used to be poor in Puerto Rico.

I ask them, "How come you went into the Army?" "Oh, I was drafted." "But in those days there was no draft, you were in the National Guard." "Well—" They don't want to say they volunteered because they were starving.

It's not only the Puerto Ricans who won't admit they were poor.

---

1. A pejorative term to describe an upper-class person; literally, "whitey."
2. The town square.
3. Municipality; the specific reference is to Río Piedras which prior to 1951 was independent of San Juan.
4. A society of zoot suiters, of street-corner cowboys hanging out all the time.

For example, my Cuban friend José was a *chulo,* a pimp. He didn't know better. I mean, Cuba as a whole was a *chuchero* society.[4] He told me he was lucky because he was the youngest, but his older brothers had to work the *guataquear*[5] to make the holes in the ground for the sugar cane. And even he didn't like to talk about being poor.

There was one period when I was a baby and my father was in charge of two farms, and those were good times. In those years Puerto Rico was all sugar cane—even the hills were planted with it. The guys made sixty cents a day, and they worked from when the sun came up until the sun came down—twelve, thirteen, fourteen hours a day.

My father had only gone as far as second grade, but the population was maybe 90 percent illiterate. There were hardly any schools. No one knew how to write. The *mandarines,* the people with the money, had a couple of schools in San Juan, and the government even fewer. My father knew how to write, and he was making twenty-five dollars a week. In the 1920s and 1930s that was more money than a thousand a week is today. You know what you could do with twenty-five dollars a week? In a restaurant you got a piece of meat, rice and beans, bread and coffee, for twenty, twenty-five cents. A pound of ham cost about ten cents; a pound of rice, two cents; a pound of bread, four cents. Five dollars would cover the shopping for a whole week. In those days we weren't really poor.

When I was in the first grade, I must have been about seven years old, we were living in Sabana Llana,[6] in what I would say is Campo Rico[7] today, near where El Comandante race track is. They took me to Rivera School of the Church of the Capuchinos. The first day I got there my mother was so mad she hit me because the priest was taking my name and I started cursing, *"¡Me cago en Dios!"*[8]—which was very bad in those days. So they threw me out. Eventually I wound up in public school. It was one small room built of wood like a peasant hut,

---

5. To hoe the ground to prepare for planting.
6. A *barrio* ("neighborhood") in the southeast section of Río Piedras.
7. A suburban housing development in the Sabana Llana area; known as Country Club.
8. "Fuck God!" —literally, "I shit on God."

on the old road near El Comandante. Another day they called my mother to school because I was being bad, saying bad words and things like that. There was one teacher there, her name was Peña. I grabbed her dress, and my mother whipped me in front of everybody.

My father was a man I respected. He had a lot of authority over me. Not that he hit me or anything, but whatever he said, that was it. My mother never questioned my father either. She always stayed home. She wouldn't even go to the store to buy food. My father would send somebody to the store with a list, and he would bring the stuff to our house. That's the way it was in those days. The Puerto Rican women would stay home and never even go shopping except for clothes.

Anyway, what my mother did was cook and wash clothes. Even in the good times she was not a fancy woman. Sometimes she walked barefoot around the house. I loved her very much but lost respect for her somehow. I just started disobeying her. My father, I never did. He used the whip on me five or six times in his lifetime. And when he whipped you, he used the horsewhip, no bullshit.

When I was very young I really didn't have it too bad. And because of that and my respect for my father, later on I always tried to avoid being a disgrace to him. Even though I have done some things I shouldn't have, it could have been worse. I could've wound up in Riker's Island or Sing Sing. I could've become a drug addict in New York and died of an overdose. Plenty of guys that were with me did that. But those early years gave me strength.

From Sabana Llana we moved to Carolina.[9] There was an *ingenio* there, a sugar mill. We lived in a little house, about three rooms, and I went to second grade in the public school there, close to the river, by the bridge. One thing in our house, school was very important. Not one of the seven of us made it through the university on account of money, but all of us had to go to school. I used to walk all the way across the town to school every morning.

---

9. A municipality east of San Juan, today considered part of the metropolitan San Juan area. In 1940 it had 24,000 inhabitants.

In second grade a funny thing happened. These things you don't forget even if you're eighty years old. I was sitting in school and I had to go to the bathroom. I was afraid to ask the teacher. I did it right there in the room. When the teacher noticed she said, "O.K. you can go home," and I walked home with all the flies buzzing around me. Eight years old, and that's how much respect I had that I didn't even dare to ask the teacher. . . .

My father lost his job in Carolina—I really don't know why, maybe the farm wasn't doing good. He was without a job for a few months, and that we all felt, right away. During the time my father was without work I used to go to the movies. The movies didn't have air conditioning, so at night they used to have the doors open, with a fence to keep people out. I didn't have any money, but at night all the kids in town used to jump that fence.

From Carolina we went to Fajardo,[10] and the farm my father worked there had one thousand to twelve hundred acres. The owner was the brother of the man who owned the farm my father worked in Río Piedras. Their name was Crespo. We lived in a big house with about six rooms and an inside bath with a tank. It was the owner's summer house.

In those days a trip to Fajardo was a full day, so sometimes this guy wouldn't go to see his farm for months. When he did come, he always had a new Buick and it was always dark blue like a limousine. He also had a horse and a saddle for himself that nobody else but my father could use.

In the beginning we walked to school. Some mornings when it was raining my father would have five horses going to town to take us. Sometimes he would take us to the road, then he would have Don Julio bring the horses back. From that point it was about five miles to town. Don Julio was an old man with a beard—ninety, eighty, something years old. He had lived during the time the Spanish controlled

---

10. A municipality on the east coast of Puerto Rico. In 1940 it had 20,000 inhabitants. Fajardo is the port from which travelers depart for Puerto Rico's offshore islands of Vieques and Culebra.

11. A jitney taxicab.

Puerto Rico, that old man. He looked like a phantom from the past. After a while my father got a guy in a *público*[11] to go all the way out to the farm in the morning, drive us to school, and pick us up when school was out. I think the guy made two dollars and a half a week for doing that.

We had a lot of fish because fifteen or twenty acres of the farm bordered on the sea. We also had lots of coconut trees around, and we'd go for picnics to the beach, and the guy who lived there would bring us coconuts. There, too, we lived pretty good.

In September 1932 the hurricane, San Ciprián[12] came. The night of the storm a lot of people came to our house. It was about the best house on the farm, so everybody came to us. The storm took all of the tops off the other houses. Our house was shaking. My father kept watching the corner of the house because it had a piece of steel that held two beams made of that good wood. He kept saying, "That's the one that's saving us." And the house held on. I remember my grandmother in the hurricane. She had all white hair, but the rain stirred up the bats, and her hair turned black with bat shit.

¡*Coño!*[13] then the bad times came, and we lived like they did in *La Vida*[14]—or worse, since those people didn't care. The depression hit the sugar cane industry in Puerto Rico. I was in the fifth or sixth grade. The farm didn't work anymore. The owner of the farm laid everybody off, including my father. But he didn't kick us out. We could stay in our house, even though there was no income. My father went on looking after the cows and horses, but no sugar was being produced. My father had an *hortaliza,* a vegetable garden, with tomatoes and *berenjena,* eggplant, on about half an acre. One of the tenant farmers worked it for him. We had milk free, all the milk we wanted; the farm had about fifty to sixty cows. For a while our main dish was *funche,* a porridge of corn and milk.

---

12. The hurricane, San Ciprián, hit the island 26 September 1932 and was named after the saint on whose day it occurred. It caused an estimated $30 million damage and 225 deaths.
13. Damn!
14. Oscar Lewis's *La Vida: A Puerto Rican Family in the Culture of Poverty, San Juan and New York* (New York: Random House, 1966) was a first-person sociology about a family of prostitutes.

I don't know, I think my father wasn't smart. If I would have been in my father's situation, I would not have gone broke in that depression. My father had had a job for twenty-five dollars a week. In those days land used to sell for fifteen or twenty dollars an acre. He should have got a farm of his own instead of working all those years for this big rich man. I know of people who once worked under my father and became millionaires from selling their land. There is a guy called Camacho, he's a millionaire. All the land near Country Club, he bought all that for twenty-five bucks an acre. That guy used to work under my father. But my father, couldn't he have saved twenty-five dollars every two weeks and buy twenty-five dollars worth of land? He could have had a big farm when the bad times came, and by now we would all have been rich. When I think about him, I think what a fool he was—too good, too honest.

My bad years really began with the crisis of the sugar cane. My father called my mother's brother in Vieques[15] and said, "O.K., let's send Benjamín to school over there." My uncle was a carpenter, he had his own house and four kids. He was better off than we were, he had a job. They all knew my father and mother, but they didn't know me and I didn't know them. I stayed there a year in the seventh grade.

Finally the worst of it came, and we moved to the city. That's where *La carreta*[16] starts. A guy moves from the country to the road, from the road to the city, from the city to San Juan, from San Juan to New York. (Lately it's been from the country directly to New York.) But we moved to a worse place, Buen Consejo[17] in Río Piedras, up from the old hospital. It was close to where good people lived, but it was the beginning of the slum. My father was without a job then, because all he knew was how to take care of farms. Our food was low.

---

15. An island municipality off the eastern coast of Puerto Rico. In 1940 it had 10,000 inhabitants. Lopez was born on Vieques.

16. The reference is to a 1951 play by René Marqués (1919-79) about migration from rural Puerto Rico to New York City. An English translation of the play, *The Oxcart,* was performed off Broadway in the late 1960s.

17. A slum in the Pueblo section of Río Piedras. In 1950 it had 8,000 inhabitants. *Buen Consejo* means "good advice"; in reference to the neighborhood by that name, the "good advice" was not to go there.

My mother was a good friend of the town judge. His wife was a *madrina,* a godmother, to one of my sisters. My mother used to take the *fiambrera,* the dinner pail, and come with food from the judge's house. And I used to get hand-me-down clothes from the judge's son. The judge had a good job, and the depression wasn't hitting them too hard.

Later on, when Roosevelt came with the PRERA and PRRA[18] to give the country a lift, my father got a job. He was building roads. I think he was in charge of about twenty men; he had had experience in giving orders so he got that kind of job.

Most of the boys in Río Piedras didn't go to school, but this time I went to a school near the university. There was a sugar mill not far away, and I used to walk around there with the other kids. There was a lake there with dirty water. Around Easter time it's hot, and once I jumped into the thing and got sick. I came home with a fever. I was sick for three months and almost died. The doctor came over and said, "Well, he's gone." They almost gave up on me, but the judge got me a place in the hospital. It is hard enough to get a place in the hospital nowadays—it was even harder then. You needed political pull. And a judge in those days was more powerful than he is now. He was second to the mayor.

They say that when I had the fever I used to hit everybody.

I kept seeing this train loaded with sugar cane coming that was going to run over me, but it didn't run over me because I kept moving off the track. After a few days I passed the crisis and my delirium went away.

I returned to school. I had missed about three months. I was always a good student, I always had good marks in school, and even though I lost three months, I still finished eighth grade and got my diploma.

The next year I went to University High School. Mr. Mullen, an American, was the principal. Now my troubles started. At that time

---

18. The Puerto Rico Emergency Relief Administration (PRERA), established in Puerto Rico in 1933, was a federally funded agency promoting many direct- and work-relief projects. It was replaced in 1935 by the Puerto Rico Reconstruction Administration (PRRA) which was more active in development projects.

you had to pay eleven dollars and a half for each semester. When my father was working, it was all right. The first year, I paid my tuition, but the second year my father lost his job. They finished the road he was working on, and again he went without work for a while. I must have been about sixteen or seventeen. I didn't have the eleven-fifty for the tuition, so I had to drop out. That's something that doesn't happen nowadays. Nowadays a guy can go to school without having to pay tuition, right? At that time if you didn't have the eleven-fifty, it didn't matter if you had good marks, if you were still a kid, or anything. I guess the government didn't care—no eleven-fifty, no school. So I couldn't go to high school. I cried, because I used to see the other kids going to school and I wanted to go and couldn't.

What did I do? I started hanging around Río Piedras. I used to go to the *plaza del mercado*[19] and do odd jobs here and there. A guy would say, "Do this for me," "Do that for me," and I would pick up a quarter. For a quarter I used to get steak, potatoes, bread, and a slice of tomato—a feast. Every time I landed a quarter I did that. And then it got so I didn't want to go home. Because though I never talked about it and my mother and father never talked to me about it, intuition told me not to ask for anything. I couldn't go home and say I'm hungry, because I knew I would only make them feel desperate. So I just went out to the *plaza del mercado* and did odd jobs here and there.

Next we moved from Buen Consejo to Capitillo Abajo[20] where the buses go now. There was no pavement. When it rained you got all dirty. My mother died there—of suffering. I know that was the cause because she died at forty-nine years old. A lot of people were in the same boat. It wasn't my family alone that was living through this kind of thing. As a matter of fact, there must have been a lot of people who were a whole lot worse off than we were at that time. Still, my mother died, and I know it was of a broken heart. She was buried in the *Cementerio de Río Piedras*.[21] When they buried her, she was at the

---

19. The central market.
20. Another slum in the Pueblo section of Río Piedras. In 1950 it had 4,800 inhabitants.
21. The Río Piedras Cemetery.

end of the *cementerio*—now she's almost in the middle.

That was when the family split up. We had to, because my father couldn't play mother to us children. I went to live with my aunt in a little house at Stop 26[22] in Santurce.[23] In Puerto Rico at that time there used to be the paved street with a nice house in the front facing on it, and then in the back there would be a little house built by squatters—that was government land. My aunt lived in one of those houses behind. She wasn't even a squatter. The squatters had more money. They would build houses on this government land and then rent them to the poor people. She was renting from a squatter who might have been a rich guy. Or maybe not a rich guy, but someone with three or four houses like that on public land. Someone smart with a few bucks would come along and be able to build because he had the money to buy the material, the wood, and the zinc for three, four, or five houses. Then he would rent them for ten bucks a month. Maybe he would be someone who had a racket, or maybe he would be working for the government, or something.

So there was this small house, with about one, two rooms, a living room and a kitchen. And there was my aunt with five kids. And then along I come with my brother and two of my sisters! I had no job and I wasn't going to school either. If I got home early enough in the night, then I would make a bed in the living room. Sometimes the entire floor of the living room would be covered with bodies, and then I would make my bed in the kitchen. If I came late, and everybody was sleeping, I would sleep underneath the house. I used to come at night after everybody ate, they always put something on the side for me to eat, and then I would go out under the house. Actually I didn't sleep right on the ground—there was the box spring left from my mother's. So that is how I slept, on a box spring standing in the dirty black sands under the house my aunt rented in the slum.

Later on when I was in the Army I said I would never come back again to this crazy island, because this is what I remembered, this

---

22. The bus stops along the Río Piedras–Old San Juan bus route are numbered, and residents of the city typically indicate addresses in terms of particular stops.

23. An urban barrio of San Juan.

rough time. You can live like a king as a baby, but if when you get to fourteen, you're hungry, that's all you're going to remember. When I left the island, I wanted to forget all about Puerto Rico. My idea was to never come back. And I stayed twenty years without returning. Even in New York when I was working and had money, I went to Cuba for vacations, not to Puerto Rico.

But if you think about it, during most of my childhood I was better off than the middle class today. In those days—1929, 1930, 1931—I was almost rich the way I was living. I had horses—that's like having cars now. We didn't have trouble with food—there was ample milk. I could go over to the coconut guy and say, "Listen, I want coconuts," and I could have coconuts. I could have anything I wanted. I'm not talking about luxuries, I'm talking about the basics of life that the middle class nowadays can't have even if they have a nice house and a television. They live worse than I did then even though I didn't have a nice house and a television.

Even the guys that were in New York or in the Army with me, American GIs, or the people I met in the streets, a lot of them must have been worse off than I was in my early years. I was living like a king here in Puerto Rico in the years of the sugar cane, while they were over there fighting in the streets and walking around like Charlie Chaplin looking for something to eat.

That's why when I got to New York I was lost for a while. I didn't know a whore before in my life. I didn't know how to do anything because in my early years I didn't do anything but just go to school and do what I most wanted to do—walk around the country, ride a horse, stuff like that. Really, my second growing-up didn't come until the city of New York, starting when I was twenty-three years old.

Anyway, in Puerto Rico in those years those things happened. Still I don't know why I didn't end up a bad boy, stealing and stuff like that. I think I didn't get really lost in those years, because I had a strong base to start from. A strong family. The house. The farm. Because of that I didn't become a thief.

— 3 —

I Became Such a GI (1940–1943)

IN 1940 I was not doing too well. My shoes were all broken, and my mother was not around to get the clothes from the judge like she used to in Río Piedras. I felt bad because there was a girl I liked but I didn't see myself walking around to meet her with my toes sticking out of my broken shoes. My father was staying somewhere or other. I was at my aunt's, and he would come once in a while to see us. He didn't have a job then, so I went to work.

They were building a house. At that time they used to build concrete houses in Puerto Rico by pouring it out of buckets. You would get a bucket full of cement and hand it to the other guy. The other guy would grab the bucket and hand it on. That's the way it went—another bucket and another bucket, until you got to the top of the house. I almost died because the buckets were so heavy and I wasn't too strong. I was big, but still I was dying from that work. They paid me a dollar and a quarter a day. I worked one day, two days, then I figured I had enough.

At that time the United States was getting ready in case they would have to go to war. Hitler was already invading Europe. So I said to myself, O.K., I'll go to the National Guard. I went to Stop 3, in Puerta de Tierra,[1] where they were taking down names. They were taking boys from eighteen up. I told them I was born in 1921—that made me eighteen. My birth certificate says I was born in 1922, but the Army didn't seem to care. I was big enough, and they didn't want to investigate.

---

1. A neighborhood on the eastern end of Old San Juan.

When I got sworn in to the National Guard, some guy lined us up, gave us shoes, GI shoes, and a uniform. The captain said, "These shoes are to come for training in. These shoes should not be used for extra hours." But I didn't have any other shoes. Every morning I put on my GI shoes and walked around. Training was on Sundays from eight o'clock until noon and then on Tuesday nights from eight to nine or ten, in Puerta de Tierra. We used to make one-two-three, one-two-three. I wore my shoes all week. One Sunday during inspection the captain came with the baton and hit my shoes. "Those were new shoes. We gave them to you only two weeks ago. How come they're all worn out?" He was mean.

I enlisted at the end of July, and on the fifteenth of October Roosevelt called the National Guard to active service. It was about a year before the United States went to war. October fifteenth was the day I really started getting the benefits of being in the Army—from then on I didn't have to take off my GI shoes. We didn't go to camp right away. We were all still living at home but had to report to San Juan every day at eight in the morning and stay until five. This went on until they got the camp ready for us. But even though we went home every night, they still had to feed us.

Each day they would march us to a different restaurant in San Juan. They took us to the *Casino de Puerto Rico* (that's the Institute of Culture now), to *La Vizcaina,* a restaurant for lunch, and other places. The Army must have arranged for the quartermaster to pay the restaurant. Now that I think about it, that food was always at the top of my mind. I had missed a lot of meals during that year. The way things were with me, I couldn't ask anybody for food. I just went without. The human being can take a lot—a piece of bread and a cup of coffee, and he can stay the whole day. But suddenly there I was having three hot ones!

They decided to send us to an army camp in Cayey.[2] There was already a regiment there, the 25th Infantry, an all-American outfit. They lived in the barracks where the University of Puerto Rico is

---

2. A small town south of San Juan, not too far from the island's southern coast.

today. On the other side of the Cayey Road there was a little ten- or fifteen-acre field where they put up a bunch of tents for the Puerto Ricans. Now we had everything—uniforms, boots, pack, canteen, and all the rest of the Army gear. We slept on cots with two blankets, one to be a mattress and one to be a cover. We were put to work to build a road in the camp. We also painted the stones and fixed up the camp. But mostly what we did was drill, drill, drill. There was no equipment, no rifles, no nothing.

We were under the supervision of the Americans. There was an American captain, he was the executive officer of the 25th Infantry from the other side of the road. And he would come over to us. We were the 162nd Field Artillery Battalion. The Ricans, we used to laugh that our commander was a captain. The regular grade for a battalion commander was supposed to be a lieutenant colonel, but we had a captain—after about five months he became a major.

We had to get up every morning at five, Army style, with the reveille. It was cold in Cayey. We used to come out for roll call with the blankets wrapped around us. At five in the morning it was dark, you couldn't see. They would say, "Report." And we would answer, "Lopez here." "So-and-so here." If it had been daylight, we would have been some sight with those blankets on our heads.

They were looking for guys to make corporals, and after we were in Cayey about a month or so they made me a corporal. That changed me immediately. I was just as cold in the morning, but I would come out dressed like a soldier. "Come on"—I used to push the others out of the tents—"Line up." In the beginning I had been one of the ones they had to drag out in the morning. Because I became such a GI, the guys called me "GI."

About a month later they came with an IQ test. All the grades were very low. One of the things to start with was that the test was in English. Imagine! You can give a genius a test in Russian, and even if he is a genius he isn't going to understand Russian! Anyway, I made a hundred on that test because the questions weren't too hard. But I still don't know how I did it. Most of the guys got fifty, twenty-five. Some guys didn't even turn the paper in. A lot of people handed it in blank because they couldn't understand what it was. Some guys answered one or two easy questions they could understand like "Do you like rainy nights?" Later when I became a sergeant, they gave me a test in Spanish. In that test I had the second highest grade.

I became a sergeant, a buck sergeant, three stripes. And then I became even more GI. They had inspections every Saturday morning, and I had my tent clean, my shoes clean, my mess kits clean, everything was shiny. I used to work at night. Friday nights, everybody would go to the town, I would get my things ready for inspection the next day.

We were only two hundred, three hundred guys, so after about six months in Cayey they recruited more Puerto Ricans to bring the battalion up to full force. In that new group of recruits came a lot of different types. The first group, most of them had been from San Juan. Now there started coming people from the country. And in this group was a guy named Camilo. He was a very goodhearted fellow, but to start with he didn't have too much education. And second, he was a little retarded. As a sergeant I used to drill the platoon, and every time I was drilling I yelled, "One-hup-three-four! ¡*Camilo cambia paso!* Camilo, change your step!" He would try, he would run, jump, anything, and still he would be out of step, "One-hup-three-four, *Camilo cambia paso.*"

It wasn't only me who said that, it was the other sergeants and corporals, too, and even the captain. When the battery was in full force and ready to go on parade, the captain used to say, "O.K., leave Camilo out, he stays in his quarters until it's all over."

Camilo and another one, Ortega, were from the hills. At that time in Puerto Rico there was no electricity like now. In the country there was sugar cane, two or three little wooden houses, and they cooked with kerosene. Guys like these two used to work in the sugar cane. For the first time they had shoes and toothbrushes—they had to learn how to use a toothbrush in the Army. The captain used to tell me, "You're in charge of your platoon, you got to check the hygiene." They used to give us courses in hygiene. People didn't even know about toilet paper. I myself first learned how to use toilets when I came to the city.

About a year afterward—the war was on already—a new group came who were professionals. These were the guys that were drafted—engineers and teachers, guys that had jobs in civilian life even when times were bad. They were a little older than the original groups and more educated. They talked about Puerto Rico, they talked about de Hostos, Betances,[3] stuff like that. I remember I used to hear them talk. And ideas started coming up.

The captain used to tell us, "You gotta put on that rubber two times, because I don't want anybody here to get VD, because even if one person in the company gets VD, the whole company is going to get restricted to the area. So from now on you use that rubber. I think you better use two rubbers!" Goddamn! So one time I went to Cayey and walked up to a streetwalker. She said, "O.K, let's go," I had my pay with me. She said, "Give me ten dollars." So I said, "O.K." and off I went with her. I had never fucked before. And I went to the room and was shy to take my pants off. She was all naked, and I just stood there. She said, "Well, listen, get your pants off." I was all shy, I had never even seen a naked woman. So I took my pants off and then said, "Well, wait a minute," and went over behind the door. They didn't have toilets in those rooms. I took the rubbers that the company gave me and I put one on. I have that thing straight up, like a piece of wood, straight. I wasn't even close to her yet, and I was desperate, but I said, "Well, I'm going to put on two rubbers," and I put on the second one. Man, I was really following Army rules.

When the war first started, we used to go into the hills without rifles. We didn't have any. Whenever the Americans wanted to put us on alert, they would fire three shots, blanks, with a gun. Every time they shot three times, it meant that the enemy was coming. So there we were without weapons except for sticks of wood, that's what we used for rifles. The funny thing about it is that we used to go, "Boom! boom! the Germans are coming!" and we'd start running up the hills

---

3. Eugenio María de Hostos (1839-1903) and Ramón Emeterio Betances (1827-98), were eminent Puerto Rican political activists who advocated Puerto Rican independence from Spain and the creation of an Antillian confederation. De Hostos, who lived past the United States takeover of Puerto Rico, also hoped for independence of the island from the United States.

with a piece of stick, and simulate that a fuckin' plane was going by, and we were shooting at it ta-ta-ta-ta. I used to wonder, What kind of a thing is this? I hustled like a son of a bitch all the way out there, got out of that bed sometimes at seven o'clock, with a piece of stick to shoot at nothing in the air. I used to wonder because at that time I really didn't know what the Army actually was.

Later we started going to Salinas[4] where the Americans had their guns. We would use their guns and they would stand by. In artillery you have to fire indirect fire, you got to shoot over your infantry. You have to know a little bit about logarithms, and you have to make a survey of the terrain first, before you have all the data to get the guns to fire over the infantry. We finally learned all that, but the Americans didn't trust the Ricans.

In 1942 a new order came. They wanted to split up the Ricans, to separate the light Ricans from the dark Ricans. The way the colonel did that (nobody was told, but I figured it out) was just to line everybody up, the whole battalion, and walk with a stick. If he saw that a guy was too dark, he would hit him in the shoes and say, "Your shoes are dirty," and then another officer would take his name and number down. The 245th became the battalion of all the Ricans that were darker. Of course all Ricans have a trace of black. A full-blooded Puerto Rican does not exist, not even Muñoz Marín.[5] Anyway, they put the dark Puerto Ricans into the 245th Quartermaster, and they kept the lighter Ricans in the 162nd. The guys that had kinky hair, they put them away.

If you were one of the light ones, all the service records had written above your name the words "Puerto Rican" and then in parentheses, "white." That only meant "white Puerto Rican," not plain white. If you search in the Army records in Washington, you will find that for all the Puerto Rican soldiers it says "white Puerto Rican" or "black Puerto Rican."

---

4. A municipality on the southern coast of Puerto Rico.
5. Luis Muñoz Marín (1898-1980) was the first popularly elected governor of the island. The founder of the Popular Democratic party in 1938, he was governor from 1948 to 1964, and advocated a commonwealth status for Puerto Rico with the United States.

One day the captain ordered a platoon to St. Thomas to guard the submarine net in the harbor. We were it. They picked me to be in charge of those sixty men, with a lieutenant. That was the first time in my life that I had ever left Puerto Rico. It was only to St. Thomas, but we had to go there in a ship. When we got to St. Thomas, I worked all night to get all our gear off the boat. I got the guys whipped up, and I was strong. I even threatened them sometimes when they were tired, though I didn't hit them. We got done, and the captain was so happy. The next day we went over to the hills in St. Thomas close to the harbor, and the officers picked the place where the guns were to be kept, and I set them up. We put up our tents under the trees, camouflaged them, and everything.

I don't know why the Army always says that the enemy attacks at dawn. Anyway, we would have an alert all the time between five and eight in the morning. A full crew for a gun when we were on an alert would be six men. But the rest of the time I rotated the men, two guys to watch the gun each shift while the rest relaxed. It was quiet time. There was no drinking, no nothing.

I got a letter from a girl I had known before I went into the Army. She was never my girlfriend, but I think she liked me. Before I went into the National Guard I used to talk to her in the balcony of her house. She wrote me a letter, sent a picture, and asked me when I was going to come home. She wanted to see me. I never took her seriously. I wrote her a letter to send me some books. I wanted to read a lot now that I had so much time. I asked her for *Les Misérables*.[6] I remember, and also *The Three Musketeers*[7] and a couple of others. She sent the books, and I read them. It was at that time that I caught the thing of reading. I read all the classics I knew they were teaching in high school. Then I used to read a lot of magazines. Everything I could get my hands on, I read. I had missed school because I had no money. O.K., but I always kept it in mind that after the war was over, if I wasn't killed, I would go back to school.

---

6. The 1862 novel by French author Victor Hugo (1802-1885).
7. The 1844 novel by French writer Alexandre Dumas (1802-1870).

Then my life changed. No more quiet. They transferred me to the bigger guns. Not that I knew how to operate bigger guns—my guns before had been 37-millimeters. The purpose of these smaller guns in a field artillery battalion is to protect the headquarters. The 37-millimeters are antitank guns. I don't think they were appropriate guns to shoot at submarines and things under water. Maybe the Army didn't have such equipment at that time.

Anyway, they moved me to where they had 105-millimeter guns. The channel for submarines to enter the harbor here was much wider than the one at St. Thomas harbor where I had been with the 37s. The crew there was from Battery A. I was put in charge of the men, but this time I didn't have anything to do with the operation of the guns. I supervised the guys in charge of the guns, but I myself didn't know anything about them. They put me there because it was said that I did a good job as a sergeant.

These new guys were rough. To start with, they were very bad soldiers. Some of them had been in jail before the Army and some in the guardhouse. They were very undisciplined. So I said, "Goddamn! If I start tough, the job is going to crumble, and I don't want that." So I made friends with the toughest ones. There were about ten men to each gun, there were four guns, that's forty men. All together there were about sixty men under me. There was supposed to be a lieutenant with us, but the lieutenant was sent away, and I was left in charge of the whole place.

On my first day I could see that the guys were kicking. One afternoon after the watch I called them together and told them I had a plan. Now, from the main road to the gun position was about three miles. The captain who came to inspect would have to drive about three miles off the road to get to where the guns were. We had phone lines and phones and a lot of communications equipment, so I set up a system in which only two guys at a time had to stand watch and the rest could be free. We hooked up a telephone at the entrance to the gun position and instead of watching for the Germans we watched for the captain.

Every time the captain would come through from the road, the guy hidden in the trees watching the command car would ring us, "Cruz Diablo is coming." That was our name for the captain, *Cruz Diablo*— he was a character in Spanish comic books something like Batman. As soon as the captain passed the gate, we knew it. He had to drive three miles up a bad road to get to us; by that time everybody was ready and at the guns. Everything was so perfect. I would salute the captain and lead him around the guns, and the guy would be so pleased. He would say, "Goddamn! I don't know how this thing— Jesus—" When he left we would wait until the guy by the telephone rang us with the message, "Cruz Diablo is gone." Then everybody would get back to the sack. Out of sixty men, two worked at any given time, one to call up on the telephone and one to answer.

We had trucks, a command car, and a jeep. I could use my jeep freely, because there was nobody around. I said, "All right, the jeep will go over to get breakfast and bring it to the boys here." They practically used to have breakfast in bed, the sons of bitches. Everybody slept to seven, eight o'clock. Then the guys would come with the breakfast and wait until everybody got up. A guy could get his breakfast any time he wanted to—ten, ten-thirty. I had to drive the truck back with the dirty things from breakfast and bring the lunch. That's the way the whole operation worked. It was perfect.

I knew the Germans were in Europe, so I talked to the guys and said, "Listen, this is foolish, we're in St. Thomas, in the Caribbean. If they're going to come over, they're going to attack the United States, and that's far away. Hitler and Europe, they have too much troubles there to get all the way here in St. Thomas. Why we got to be awake all the time, standing around like a bunch of fools?"

But even if the Germans actually had come, my men were not too far away from the guns—the barracks were one hundred yards away—I could get them there in time. And in case of an attack, I would have rested men. And I would have happy men, willing to fight. Man, the way they were when I got there, they were bad. The place was all fucked up. They were continually putting guys in the guardhouse for being AWOL. Once I got there, these guys didn't go AWOL anymore. Why should they? They were free. Of course they had to be responsible, too, up to a certain degree. But nothing that would push them to go AWOL.

I used to get them passes in rotation, by order of Cruz Diablo. He used to give us seventy-two-hour passes, and I would extend them for seventy-two more hours. I was the one supposed to do the checking, the system worked perfectly. I said, "This place has to be immaculate, the guns have to be in perfect shape. The only thing, you do that once a week." That was it, the guys would go to fish, to sleep, to do whatever they wanted to do. There was never any trouble.

The other gun positions were always having trouble; mine was always nice and quiet. And I had the worst guys! The Army couldn't understand it. They said, "How come you have the worst guys, and everybody works so good?" I had already told my men what the score was. "If you want to be free, you only have to make a little effort—have your things clean and jump fast to your guns if the phone rings." They figured I was right. And they were fast. I was amazed myself.

At the beginning I used to get up most of the time. Then I started staying asleep. When I came to feel confidence in the guys, I slept nice too. I wasn't nervous anymore, because the guys were reliable, and they were reliable because they knew it was a good deal for them. My guys used to meet other GIs, but nobody ever told our secret. It was tested about ten or fifteen times during the four months I was there, and nobody outside ever knew. Imagine! The morale at that position had been the lowest, and then it became the most efficient in the whole St. Thomas. You know what the Army did? They wanted to give me a commendation. When we pulled out of St. Thomas, they called me over and told me, "Hey, you did a great job."

After we left St. Thomas, I was sent back to Cayey. Everything went back to the way it was before. I was a sergeant in charge of the antitank guns. The whole regiment was back, the colonel and everything. The war was really on, and Puerto Rico was getting about forty thousand soldiers ready. Just like in the United States, in Puerto Rico training camps were sprouting up all over. Tortuguero Camp, the main camp, was in Vega Baja.[8]

---

8. A municipality on the northern coast of Puerto Rico.

They had a problem because people were needed to organize all the thousands of new recruits coming into the Army every day. This is where a big bunch of guys who never had shoes on started coming in. There was no discrimination then in picking guys. "The guy don't know how to write, O.K." "The guy isn't physically fit, O.K." "The guy's flat foot, O.K." "The guy's young, O.K." "The guy doesn't know English, O.K." "The guy can't see, that's all right." And that's the way it went in Cayey. This was about July 1942, six months after the war started. They recommended me to be sent to the training center.

I went to Tortuguero. I was a drill sergeant, a DI.[9] There were three regiments, and each regiment had four battalions. The battalion had four companies. My company had four platoons, and I was in charge of one platoon, seventy-nine men. Colonel Jones, an American was in charge of the whole post, and it just so happened that my old captain from Cayey was with my platoon. He trusted me.

I started drilling my men. We would begin at eight in the morning and drill for two hours or so. Then we would have classes, different ones every day—half an hour of hygiene, half an hour of how to put the rifle together, half an hour of map reading, and so on. There was a big field, and the whole training center would be drilling at one time, thousands of men going back and forth, "one, two, three, four." After drill I used to take my platoon away from the others and go up a little hill. I would sit down under a tree and give them a class. For example, I remember I used to give them a class about the rifle and try to explain to them about stoppage. That means one of the bullets doesn't function right and the rifle gets stuck, and then you have to stop firing and clean the rifle and get the bullet out and get the thing going again so you can continue firing.

I used to read out loud from my Army GI manual. And some guys, these Ricans, guys from the hills—they never saw an American in their lives—they have to sit and listen to words like "stoppage." What is stoppage to them? They couldn't even pronounce it! So I would have to stop and explain. I used to do little comic things in

---

9. Drill instructor.

front of them sometimes, so they would laugh with me. But I kept them disciplined, so they would respect me.

I started thinking about my experience in St. Thomas, and I said to myself, If I do the same thing here, I'll get these people to cooperate more and be more efficient soldiers. So I started with the passes. Usually they would give you a pass from Friday afternoon at five until eleven Sunday night, before taps. I decided I was going to make an exception with my platoon. I would take the responsibility and report everybody present and let them have extra time. So I told them, "From now on you're going to have a longer pass than any guys on the post. You can stay away and report next Tuesday at reveille. But nobody can fuck up here. If somebody fucks up, the whole thing goes down the drain."

Everybody was crazy to have that extra time. I said, "I will report you present and accounted for, but there are other things you have to do for me. The things you have to do for me is have your mess kits clean, your tents clean, immaculate, and the surroundings of your tents have to be clean." A platoon has five tents in line. I slept in the first tent, close to the foot of the company street. "You keep the surroundings clean, the company street, you keep your shoes clean, you keep your rifles perfectly clean. They have inspection in the middle of the week here, the captain is going to come around, and sometimes the battalion commander will come around, and everything has to be perfect." And everybody agreed to the deal; it was like a code. The first time we tried it when the guys went off on passes, I remember I was so worried. On that Monday morning when I had to make my report, I stood in front of my platoon and said, "Platoon, complete! All present and accounted for." And the captain said, "O.K., fine," and went to breakfast.

The next day, Tuesday, was the day my boys were supposed to be back. So I got up at five and went to check. And everybody was there. You know what they did? They came to my tent first. "Sergeant, we're back, everything is fine, thank you for the long pass." "All right, O.K., everybody out there"—and we went out to drill. I had the best platoon drilling in the whole company because when I said, "O.K., let's go, hup, hup, hup," the guys, you know, chests out, they really did it good. They learned good, and they worked hard. The captain came around, the battalion commander, everybody and said, "Boy, that's a great platoon you have, Sergeant, that's a great platoon." What they didn't know was that these guys were having more and longer passes than anybody else on the whole post.

My tent was close to where my platoon would form. So I told them, "Let me sleep, that's my only break." I really couldn't take passes like them, because I had to be around. If I wasn't around, the whole system would go to pieces. They understood that. I said to them, "You guys can take extra time and I can't, so the only thing I get to do, I get to sleep a little longer. Instead of getting up at five, I'll get up ten minutes to six to make the report." Every time they took the report, I was out there. I'd jump off my bed, stand in front of the tent while it was still dark, the captain would take the report, and I would go back to sleep until seven o'clock. They would bring me my breakfast, the guys, a couple of eggs in the mess kit, with coffee, and everything. That was the only thing I really got out of my system of the passes. They would let me sleep, clean my shoes, and do all the other work for me. But I worked hard, too. I had to drill them, and I had to teach them. And they learned. We worked it perfectly.

Many times some guy in Tortuguero would blow his head off. He would take his rifle, find bullets, and kill himself. Some guys hung themselves. These were guys who had been treated like babies, *nenes mimados*,[10] at home, and Army life was too rough. They couldn't take it. But in my platoon, I didn't have that problem. I had the guys that could take it. Besides that, I had guys who were smart enough to understand the deal we had. They took the extra day with their wives or their girlfriends or their fathers and mothers. I think this went on for about seven months at Tortuguero. Then new cadres arrived, and I went back to Cayey, once more to the field artillery. And with another good commendation, just like after St. Thomas.

In Cayey there was a lot of fights between the Puerto Ricans and

---

10. Mama's boys.

the Americans. We used to hate the Americans. I was one of the ones that used to hate them like mad. I would say, "Goddamn the sons of a bitches, fuckin' blond guys, blue eyes." They were young guys, too, about the same age as us, twenty-one, twenty-two years old, nice-looking guys, tall guys with blond hair, walking around the town. They had most of the girls under control. We used to hope the Americans were needed overseas.

So when the 25th Infantry was going to be pulled out of Cayey, they put a few hand-picked Ricans in this 25th Infantry with the Americans. These Puerto Ricans were smart guys—more than fourth year high school—and spoke pretty good English. They were immediately promoted to corporals and sergeants. One of these guys was named Mariano. One night I was in town with Mariano. There was a fight with a big guy named Larry. This Larry was about six foot three, about two hundred twenty-five pounds. Big son of a bitch. He was having trouble with one of his girlfriends, and they started to have a fight. So Mariano and I and some others got together and said, "Let's beat up the son of a bitch." But the guy was so big, the first Rican he got, he blasted the shit out of him. We had to jump on him, about ten of us. We beat him to pieces.

Then came the MPs from the 25th Infantry. They grabbed the Ricans to haul them back to camp. And then what happened? There was like a riot. We started beating all the *yanquis*[11] we could find in the street. The colonel, I think his name was Colonel Jones, sent a battery with weapons into town. Like a martial law. The battery lined up in front of the *plaza de recreo,* the town plaza, with all those rifles and guns ready. One of the *yanquis* shot Mariano in the arm, and the rioting got worse. More troops were sent in. It was getting to be about ten, eleven o'clock, time to leave town. We returned to camp drunk and furious. "We don't have guns, we don't have bullets, we should have bullets and go and shoot those fuckin' *yanquis* tonight." But it was all talk.

The Americans, the 25th Infantry, pulled out. They left, and we

---

11. The Spanish translation of "yankee," usually used disparagingly.

stayed in Cayey. We moved from our tents to the new nicer quarters they had built for the 25th Infantry. We were feeling much better in them. They had inside toilets. And an inside mess hall. In other words, they were real barracks.

In the two or three years I had been in the Army so far, I never went to see my family. I would send them money. The government took twelve to fifteen dollars out of my pay and then added so-and-so much and sent it for my sisters. But I never went to see them. I don't know why. It's a mysterious thing about a person. I was a soldier, I had money, I could come and go. But I didn't want to see anybody from my past, especially not my father. I didn't even try to find out where he was!

Just once, when I was in Tortuguero, I got a message that he wanted to see me, and I went. He was living in Cataño.[12] It was payday. I was making close to a hundred dollars a month and didn't have any expenses. That's a lot of money. So I rented a car, a *público,* and looked around for the address and found it. I walked in and stayed about five minutes. I gave him thirty dollars. He kept saying "*¡Coño!* oh my son,*"* and stuff like that but something inside me kept telling me, "Get away, get away." I had told the car, "You wait for me," so when I gave him the thirty dollars and embraced him, I hurried out of there.

---

12. A municipality west of and across the bay from San Juan. Today it is considered part of metropolitan San Juan. In 1940 it had 10,000 inhabitants.

— 4 —

My New Way with the Army (1943–1945)

IN JULY OF 1943 we left Puerto Rico and went to Panama. I felt I didn't ever want to come back.

But I was beginning to have doubts about the Army. I used to listen to a lot of guys that came to Cayey and sat around the barracks talking about de Hostos, about Puerto Rico, against the *yanquis* and stuff like that. Sometimes I felt, Why was I in the United States Army? But at the time it didn't take root, I was just listening once in a while. I still wanted to go to New York, I didn't want to come back to Puerto Rico. But I began to have these other thoughts, too—to hate the United States. I started to get drunk a lot, and drunk and drunk.

We kept going to Río Hato[1] for maneuvers. Since I was a sergeant, I had the privilege of taking a jeep on Sunday and going wherever I wanted. One time I took the jeep and went to a small town called Antón[2]—the streets were not even paved. I got drinking with a couple of buddies of mine, and this guy shows up with a gun. He was the supply sergeant of our outfit. He had a Browning .45 with him. So we decided to steal a chicken. Like any Latin American town, Antón had a plaza in the center. We started running the chicken around the plaza and then we grabbed it and took it to some lady and told her we wanted to make *asopao de pollo*.[3] We gave her some money, as we always

---

1. A small town on the south coast of Panama, west of the canal.
2. Also on the south coast, west of the canal.
3. A thick chicken and rice soup, a Puerto Rican favorite.

did to people when we had it. We had taken the chicken more for kicks than for the idea of stealing it. We were drunk. I noticed that a cop was watching us without saying anything. Then my buddy started shooting his gun in the air. This supply sergeant had a jeep of his own and after a while he left. I stayed late.

When I was pulling out in my jeep with one of my friends, the cop came over and said, "Listen, you know, GI Joe, I want to go to the police station. I'm the lieutenant of the police, and the station is just on the way out of town. You're going to Río Hato, so give me a ride." I was such a fool I didn't think of what could happen. He got in the jeep, and we drove. He said, "Pull around here, in front of the station." He got out, and immediately five other cops with rifles came over and surrounded the jeep. I didn't have any weapon. Now, Ricans are small, but Panamanians are smaller. So I started pushing them away. I almost got rid of them, but more came along and waved their guns at us. So I decided not to fight, and they put us in jail. A lousy jail. It was dirty and stinky. I kept telling those Panamanian cops I didn't have anything against them, but they wouldn't listen.

In about half an hour two MPs, a sergeant and a captain, came to pick me up. In my broken English, I tried to say that the guys had put me in jail for nothing. The captain said, "All right, you get in the command car." They drove us to our headquarters. It was Sunday night, and it was late already, close to taps, and there was nobody there but the guard. I surrendered my papers to him, the MPs left me, and I went to my barracks. In the morning when I reported to the office, they took my stripes off. They degraded me to private. I didn't mind all that much. I said, "Fuck it, what the heck! Fuck this fuckin' army anyway!" This was the beginning of my new way with the Army.

I started hating it, and all I wanted was to get out. I told them I wanted to get out, I told my captain, I told everybody. "Discharge me, I don't give a goddamn, give me any goddamn kind of a discharge you want to give me, I only want to get out of this fuckin' shit." But you know, it doesn't work like that. I had to stay. Then they courtmartialed me. They gave me thirty days. For a summary court-martial they give you thirty days in jail or as the commander might direct.

For a special court-martial they give you six months. If you get a general court-martial, they can shoot you.

And then I really started fuckin' up. I wouldn't get up in the morning. They would have to drag me out of bed. Then my equipment was all fucked up all the time. I never cleaned the mess kits, I never cleaned anything. When inspection came, everything was all dirty. I remember the battery commander called me one day. He was a Puerto Rican named Marín. He was a first lieutenant, acting captain. He said to me, "Well, listen, Benjy, I can't understand you. You can't be the same man. I mean, something is wrong with you." I said, "Well, listen, that's the way it is." He sent me to Gorgas Hospital for psychiatric examination. The psychiatrist sat me down and started asking questions, here and there, there and here. I don't know what came out in the report, but when I came back to the battery, nothing happened.

I kept on doing things wrong. In Puerto Rican outfits they call the guy that is no good *una perla*.[4] I became one of the *perlas*. That was me then. There were about ten or fifteen guys like that. When the truck was waiting to pull out, I would be the last one to get there. At parades everybody would be at attention during the national anthem, but I would have my rifle on my belt, just resting, so I wouldn't have to present arms. And I spread my feet and relaxed. I would look at the other guys at strict attention and think, Hey, look at those guys, all fucked up while I'm relaxing here. When I started getting my passes in Panama City, that's when I really started getting drunk. They would send me to Quarry Heights, that's where they sent drunks. I slept whole nights there.

One night there was a big fight between the Puerto Ricans and the Panamanians in San Francisco.[5] I think there was a guy killed and a lot of guys wounded. The police had to fight with the Puerto Ricans. And I remember that night because when I came to camp I heard guys coming in and saying things like, "Let's get the guns and start blasting these goddamn Panamanians." Now, in San Francisco was a

---

4. A tough guy against whom one must constantly be on guard; literally, "a pearl"—that is, something very uncommon.

5. A small town in central Panama, west of the canal.

ballroom where the soldiers went to dance with girls. These Panamanian girls were mostly domestics, and they used to go there with the GIs. They had a Panamanian band, so the Puerto Ricans felt more at home and went there much more than the Americans, who went to clubs instead. They had shows and stuff like that. I would say that there used to be about one hundred and fifty Ricans at a time in the place, plus about two, three hundred women. They were not all professional whores—many of them just picked up GIs for a lay. That's how the big fight started. The Ricans killed a Panamanian over some woman. There was a big story in the Panamanian press, and in the camp that night the guys were really nervous. But nothing happened.

Another place there was called *Villa Amor*,[6] where the whores were Argentineans, Cubans, and Colombians. They used to charge six dollars for a quick job, as the Americans call it. I think a whole night cost about fifteen or sixteen dollars. The Cubans had some kind of organization for bringing these women into Panama. We used to go there a lot.

In 1944 they split our battalion into two in order to form a new battalion to go to the Pacific. Guys who had been together for two or three years got split up. They sent new guys from Puerto Rico to fill out the battalion that was left. We were sent to the States, on our way to Europe. We were the 162nd Field Artillery.

We left for the States at the end of July 1944. We sailed to Louisiana, Jackson Barracks. That was a port of embarkation, POE, near New Orleans. About five or ten miles before you get to the Louisiana coast you can already see the delta of the Mississippi. Five miles out to sea the water was dirty—that was muddy water from the Mississippi. That sight meant something special to me because I had always been in such small places—Puerto Rico, St. Thomas, and Panama—where the rivers are small. But when they explained to me that the muddy water I was looking at was the water of the Mississippi, I said, "This must be a monster, because miles and miles before

---

6. "House of Love," located in a section on the outskirts of Panama City called Río Abajo.

you get to shore the water is all dirty and swift." The power that the Mississippi had, to me it was a great thing.

Well, we got into Jackson Barracks. I remember this camp. That night I was walking around close to the barracks, and I saw a guy kissing another guy, two American soldiers. I called my buddy and said, "Look at that, two guys are kissing each other."

They didn't give us passes the first night, or the next day, or the next day. And what did I do? I went AWOL with two other guys. We took a taxicab and went into New Orleans. New Orleans was fantastic to me, too. There was a big street, it was called Canal Street. I went to the French Quarter. They had these people playing jazz, though I didn't know the word "jazz" then.

Then I went to Pontchartrain Beach. It was full of girls who were blonde and blue-eyed. I was very much impressed with that. And then I ran into this girl and discovered that in the States at that time the women were sympathetic to anyone wearing a United States Army uniform. This girl and I started talking, then we sat down on the beach, and I was kissing her and she was kissing me. So what happened? I spent the whole night with her, and when I came away it was about twelve-thirty, one o'clock.

Then I went back to the French Quarter, where those dark people were playing the jazz. I had a beer and started following another woman. Suddenly I see the MPs, and the MPs see me, because by then there were no soldiers left on the street. They started chasing me, and I started running and running. I was getting tired because I had had a few drinks, and my tongue was hanging out. I ran up some stairs and saw a door and went through it. When I got inside I saw a man in uniform, and a woman, a beautiful woman, too. The guy said, "What do you want?" "The MPs are chasing me." The woman said, "O.K., let him get underneath the bed." All this, with my broken English. So I got underneath the bed and—boom! boom!—the MPs started knocking on the door. The guy opened the door—he's an officer—and said, "There's nobody here." The lady said, "There's nobody here." But they started to look around. "He got in here! He got in here!" They started threatening the officer. I started thinking to myself underneath the bed, I'm going to get this officer in trouble. So I got out, "Here I am." They took me to where the MPs had their guardhouse for the night. The next day they sent me to Jackson Barracks, and they gave me another court-martial for that AWOL.

They gave me six months. It was a special court-martial. Every morning I went out to work. And for the first time I felt how hard it was to be a prisoner. I had a guard behind me, one of those white Americans. While I was still serving time, they moved the whole battalion to Camp Buckner, North Carolina. When we got there, they sent me to the guardhouse. Jackson Barracks had been an old army post; the guardhouse was small. Camp Buckner was different. It was built after the war started. The barracks were wooden, and the place was big, immense. And the guardhouse had all the facilities. It also had very many prisoners.

Being a Rican made me shy. And in this guardhouse I was the only Rican. The rest were all Americans. There were about five hundred prisoners. I was a guy that didn't know how to speak English well in the middle of all those guys, and it was very rough. There was a lieutenant that used to stand in front of the guardhouse in the morning for reveille, and every time you had to bring a paper or something to him, you had to run. Everything was running. Whatever. If you had to go anywhere, it was double time and double time back.

They had the blacks in one place and the whites in another. I was a Rican, so they left me with the whites. I remember in the barracks where I was there was a guy named Esposito. His eyes were blue, his hair white, and he was from Brooklyn. I hung around with him. My bed was two beds away from his in the guardhouse. He told me stories about New York, about zoot suits. On a sheet of paper he would draw a big hat, the pants tight on the bottom, and wide and long jackets. He liked me, and he kept telling me he was going to send me to New York. He was going to give me the address of a girlfriend. And he used to tell me such stories! That he was in show business, and stuff like that.

Then suddenly another Rican arrived in the guardhouse. He was from the battalion, his name was Díaz. He must have fucked up somewhere. I introduced him to Esposito. Another guy impressed me, another one with white hair and blue eyes. I had never seen people like that in my life. He was from Pennsylvania, his father had a funeral home, and he used to make a good living. All these guys used to sit around talking, and with my broken English I would sit like a dummy and watch them talk.

I became good friends with Esposito. I told him I had a sister in New York, that I always was crazy about New York, and that the first chance I got, I was going to go there. And I got the telephone number of his girlfriend in New York.

I also used to see a bunch of white guys marching, tall, blue eyes, nice-looking, most of them blond, very few black hairs there, three or four hundred in formation, and they would sing when they pass by. They used to march with something like goosesteps. "Who are these guys?" They told me these guys were Germans, taken in North Africa.

Finally they came and got me out of the guardhouse. The battalion was moving out to a port of embarkation. We were going to ship to Europe, and they were handing out equipment and everything. A week before we were supposed to embark they took us out to the firing range, and the battalion failed to make the grade. That was some battalion, man, that was something, a battalion that had been together since 1940. This was 1944, the war was almost over, and still the battalion was not ready to go into action! The Ricans don't seem to be very good soldiers. Anyway, the battalion didn't qualify. They decided to send us back for more training. And the more training was going to be in Fort Jackson, South Carolina, close to Columbia.

We traveled to South Carolina by train. On the way the train stopped in one of those small towns, and there were a lot of girls, American girls. During the war when trains with soldiers passed by, the girls would come around and wave goodbye and stuff like that. So they came close to the train, and they kept asking, "Are you the Italians?" I said, "We're not Italians, we're American soldiers, from Puerto Rico." But they couldn't understand what Puerto Rico was. The United States, it's great, it's so big and powerful, that the people don't know too much about a small island like Puerto Rico, and they don't need to. I think that a small country knows more about a big country. Any citizen that is just a little bit educated or maybe just with primary school knows more about a big country than a little one. They confused us with Italians because of the way we talked. We had American uniforms, but they couldn't understand how we had American uniforms with the blah-blah-blah-blah like the Italians.

When I got to South Carolina, I had to go to the guardhouse again, because I hadn't finished my six months yet. Then I went back to the battery. I still used to get up every morning protesting, it was tough to get me to get up for reveille. As a matter of fact, I worked out an arrangement with a friend of mine. A lot of the guys there in the battalion were guys that had been with me since 1940. I slept in their bellies, they slept in my belly. We had been driving, eating, drinking together for so many years. I made the sergeants feel sorry for me because most of them had only been privates when I was sergeant. So they had a little consideration for me, and I used to stay asleep. Everybody had to get up and report, but I'd be there sleeping. I said, "Listen, report me present," and the guy did it. He didn't take too big a risk because I actually was in the barracks and the report was close to the barracks, but nevertheless it was a violation. At breakfast time I would tell the guys, "I stay sleeping, you go for breakfast and bring me some." And they would bring me some breakfast in a mess kit. They felt sorry for me.

While we were in Fort Jackson, I made my first trip to New York. I had been out of the guardhouse two or three months, and I was entitled to a pass. I had thirty days. I was crazy to go to New York. I took the train to Pennsylvania Station. When I came outside and saw all the tall buildings, I was very much impressed. I got a cab to Amsterdam Avenue and 177th Street, that's where my sister lived. And I was so happy because I was seeing New York for the first time. At night I went down to Times Square, like everybody does when he goes to New York, walked all around, by the movies, the theaters. I said, "Well, when the war is over I'm going to come to New York."

My sister introduced me to this beautiful girl, Roberta. The first time I got up to her was when my sister went out of town for a few days or so. I took her to my sister's apartment.

The thirty days passed. And I went back to South Carolina. My sister gave me some money when I left New York, and I put it in my wallet, in my pocket. When I got to South Carolina, I was looking for my wallet and it was gone. I talked to some guy in the station, and he told me, "Well, man, you went to sleep, and if you went to sleep somebody came over and grabbed it. You had your wallet in a place that could be seen, so they did it nicely, you didn't even notice." All I could think was, This country is a lot of bandits.

They finally decided to move the battalion to Camp Shanks, New York, that was a port of embarkation for troops to go to Europe. I had some trouble because I was very much against going to Europe. Not because I was afraid, but I didn't want to go overseas because I figured I didn't have the need to go over there and fight for the United States. Those days I was much more inclined for Puerto Rico to be an independent republic. I thought it wasn't fair for me to go fight in Europe. I became quite anti-American. It's a paradox right there. I was both anti-Puerto Rican and anti-American. I didn't want to go back to Puerto Rico, but I didn't think I should go and fight.

About a year after I got in the Army, I met some professional guys, some of them teachers. I remember those guys talking about de Hostos and Betances and Albizu.[7] They blamed the Americans for almost everything, so I came around to thinking that I wanted Puerto Rico to be free. I thought it was the invasion of the Americans into Puerto Rico that had kept Puerto Ricans from developing themselves and having proper ties with the countries of Europe and South America. Maybe I was wrong. After all, at that time I didn't have too much schooling. Nevertheless, I believed that if the United States hadn't been in Puerto Rico, then Puerto Rico would have been better off. After I was busted and started becoming a fuckup and going to the guardhouse, I found excuses like that.

---

7. Pedro Albizu Campos (1891-1965) was a militant Puerto Rican nationalist and advocate of independence.

I was thinking about all this while we were lining up waiting to be issued our gas masks, and I said, "Well, look at this lousy gas mask. The Germans got a little gas mask that is more effective than this big American gas mask." The lieutenant jumped. "Now, what do you mean by that?" And he started arguing with me, and he got me so mad I said, "Well, I don't give a fuck. Fuck the president of the United States! Fuck President Roosevelt! Fuck the Army of the United States. Fuck the United States! I don't give a fuck! I just don't want to go overseas. I'm a Puerto Rican! I shouldn't be fighting this goddamn war!" Stuff like that, all in my broken English. So I left without the gas mask, and I went to the beer garden. There were a few more soldiers there from the battalion, and I started drinking with them. I was there about five or ten minutes, I had a beer or so, when two fellows from the battalion came in carrying weapons. They grabbed me and said I was under arrest. Again they put me in the guardhouse.

Remember, my battery was Headquarters Battery. Headquarters Battery was where you had all the fellows that worked in the headquarters of the battalion. Some guys from my battery were clerks and typists there. One of them came to me and said, "They're going to recommend that they make a general court-martial to you because of those words you said against the United States." I said to the guard with me, "Listen, I'd like to talk to the colonel" The guard said, "All right," and went to the colonel and said, "Listen, Lopez wants to talk to you." They arranged it, and they took me, under guard, in a jeep to the colonel's tent.

The colonel was packing his gear to go overseas because the battalion was supposed to leave the very next day. He said to me, "Well, listen, why you *metiste la pata otra vez?*[8] Why you fucked up again?" The colonel was a Puerto Rican and talked to me in Spanish. *"Esos Americanos,* those Americans, are going to put you in jail. If you retract what you said, then we can arrange to drop the charges." But

---

8. "You got into a mess again." Literally, "you put your leg in again," implying that you put it someplace from which you couldn't get it out.

I said, no, that I didn't want to retract what I said. I didn't want to because, one, I didn't feel it; and, two, I didn't want my friends to know that I was retracting. But I was very scared about getting a court-martial because I knew they could give me five to ten years.

The next day a lieutenant from the battalion came to investigate the charges. And he told me the same thing—to retract. I said I wouldn't retract. He said, "Well, listen, we're leaving tomorrow, and if you don't retract, you're going to stay over here in Camp Shanks, and you know what's going to happen? The Americans are going to take over your charges, and you'll have to face American officers here. Remember, you are a soldier of the United States." I started feeling bad because I figured everybody is going to leave and I'm going to stay here—but still I didn't want to retract.

What happened was the next day they took me to the battalion, and I was supposed to be in custody, but they gave me equipment and everything, and they took us in a ferry. And these ferries are the same ferries they use at Staten Island to cross the bay. They covered the ferry with canvas, so the soldiers inside couldn't see New York. I don't know why, but that's what they did. And they took us right where the ship was and loaded us onto it. Immediately we went below to the bottom of the ship, let's say about three levels down. That ship was loaded with soldiers. Mostly Americans—we were the only Puerto Ricans there. We were about four or five hundred men, the battalion was full strength. We pulled out of there, and they didn't let us see anything. We just knew the ship was moving. About eight hours later, when we were at sea, they let us come out on deck. Then I saw we were part of a big convoy. There must have been about fifty ships. And this ship was an army transport cargo. I found out later that this was the *SS America,* during the war converted into a transport. We were crossing the ocean, and I thought to myself, Maybe they forgot about my charges. But it wasn't so.

When we were about three or four days out, they called me and made a special court-martial right there aboard the ship. They had lowered the general court-martial to a special court-martial. The colonel would assign five officers from the battalion and then have a special court-martial. If you're free, you're free; if you're sentenced, you're sentenced. So I had my court-martial there on the ship, and they gave me six months. It wasn't long before that I had finished serving out my other court-martial, and now I was starting another six months again. Of course since we were at sea, they didn't have any guardhouse so I was just hanging around with the soldiers, but I was already serving time.

I think the trip across was eleven days. Around the eighth to the nineteenth of April. During this time Roosevelt died. Everybody was very sorry, but I said, "Fuck the president, that son of a bitch anyway." I wasn't giving a fuck, and I was very much against this thing of going overseas. I knew I wasn't the only one. When I was in the guardhouse in Camp Buckner, that fellow Esposito from Brooklyn used to talk against President Roosevelt. And there were a lot of soldiers there that didn't give a damn. "He's no good, he started the war, he doesn't know how to run the country." Stuff like that.

— 5 —

We Conquerors (1945)

WE GOT to Le Havre on 19 April. There were bombed-out houses, destroyed roads, ships and barges sunk on the beach very close to where the ship docked. For the first time I saw what the war was really like. Not the fighting, but the scars it left behind.

They sent us to Duclair where they were getting us ready for action. They were giving out carbines, and when it came time to give me the bullets for the carbine, the lieutenant said, "You can't get no bullets. You're a prisoner, you're not supposed to have any bullets."

The good thing about our Puerto Rican colonel was that I could go to see him at any time. The Puerto Ricans didn't have to talk to sergeants or anybody, we just went to his tent. So I went and said, "Listen, Colonel, they're giving out bullets, and they don't want to give me any. They say I'm a prisoner. But if we go to Germany and the Germans start shooting, they won't know that I'm a prisoner and have no bullets." The colonel said, "All right, tell them to give you bullets."

There was a lieutenant who used to hate my guts. His name was De Maria—an Italian. He was with us in Panama, he was with us in the States. And this guy was a son of a bitch, he always hated me.

So then I said to this De Maria, "I'll tell you one thing. Now that I'm getting the bullets, you better watch your ass." He was always one of the ones that recommended court-martials for me. I did bad things, I know. I had about seven court-martials. Some guys even nicknamed me "Court-martial," but not all of the officers went after me the way he did. There wasn't a lousy detail that I didn't get if De Maria was around. Now I told him to watch out. I had my carbine with the magazine, and I took two more magazines. De Maria was turning white, and the sergeant was laughing. After that he never bothered me again.

From France we went to Germany, to Mannheim, then a town called Rosenberg. By now the war was over. But I was still a prisoner and still having troubles. We stayed in Rosenberg only three days, and from there we moved to a place called Buchen. This was a small village with a big castle, a medieval castle, with big walls around and a gate.

The colonel went before us to the town and talked to the burgomaster, the town mayor, who made arrangements for the Germans to leave the castle, so we could sleep there. I was really surprised—not only me but most of the Ricans were surprised. We thought the United States Army wouldn't do a thing like that—kick somebody out of his house. But this was a conquered country, and the Germans started talking to us, "You conquerors. . . ." We conquerors!

The order came that all the prisoners were to go to the castle to clean it, so the battalion could move in. We were five prisoners plus two guards. We started walking around the place—it was huge—and came to the main bedroom, where we found some beautiful clothes. My friend Pelota[1] got dressed up in a tuxedo and high hat and a cane. At the same time other prisoners were down in the cellar finding cases and cases of schnapps and *vino de oporto*.[2] We went right down there and started drinking—the guard, too. We were there about two or three hours before the battalion came. And we were drunk. The guys were walking around with the cane, and Jesus Christ! It was funny.

Suddenly we see the dust of the battalion moving. There was a big yard in the castle, the jeeps started pulling in, and everybody began to get off the trucks and lineup. "Headquarters Battery, A Battery, B Battery, C Battery." Here we came all drunk with this guy in a tuxedo and high hat. The whole battalion was at attention, but they couldn't resist—everybody started laughing. The colonel got mad and started

---
1. *Pelota* is a nickname meaning "ball," usually given to someone who is chubby.
2. Port wine.

yelling, "Arrest those men!" We were so drunk that we didn't give a shit about the colonel, about anybody.

So they put us in the stable for a guardhouse with the guards, who were drunk, too. But by this time Pelota and the other fellows had hidden the bottles of *oporto*. They buried them beneath the straw. After chow we just got started drinking again.

The stable was at the very end of the castle. A young girl came around, a blonde about twenty years old. She passed by us and we whistled. She turned around and came back. We started to talk to her. In English. "Where do you come from? Why are you looking around?" She answered—in good English, better than what we spoke—that this was her house and that she was now living in the village. And then I spoke to Pelota in Spanish, and she switched to Spanish. She spoke beautiful Spanish, this girl. I was amazed. She spoke English, she spoke Spanish, and she spoke German; she was perfect in three languages. She told me her father had been the German ambassador to Mexico years ago under the Kaiser.

She was almost crying as she told us all this. She was living in one of the servants' houses and came to get some eggs and potatoes. There were hundreds of eggs in boxes and sacks of potatoes in the basement of the main building. She said her father was a general. I had seen the old man. When we came in to clean the castle, he was pulling out in a horse-drawn cart and had on a German uniform. He was a man about seventy years old or so.

We stayed a few days in that castle. Before we left they lined up the whole battalion and announced that a woman had been raped. There was the baroness standing there, the baroness's daughter—the girl we had talked to—and the burgomaster of the village. They were saying that she was raped by one of the soldiers in the battalion. So the colonel lined up the whole battalion to see if she could identify the fellow. The girl was standing there, and everybody was laughing and making fun in Spanish and saying, "Well, look at *la herida,* the wounded one. She's over there, with her face like something has happened to her." But what they meant was, "Well, after all, she got a blast, what's to be sorry about?"

They formed the batteries and went by her. First from Headquarters Battery, each man had to stand in front of the girl, at attention, and then let the next one step in. Then A Battery went by. She couldn't identify anybody there. B Battery went by, C Battery went by. Almost the whole battalion had gone by. "No! No! No!" Each time she stood in front of a soldier, the girl said, "No, this is not him." Then the captain called all the prisoners out and one by one he talked to us. There was one small guy he took out to the side, and then he said, "O.K., pass the prisoners in front of the girl, too." But the girl, *la herida,* couldn't identify anybody. Afterward when we were back in the guardhouse, I said to the little guy who had stayed to the side, "Well, listen, why didn't you go through the line?" That's how I found out he was the one who raped the girl.

Finally the battalion was getting out of the place, we didn't know where we were going. Everybody was already in the truck. The prisoners were ordered to take all the officers' luggage and put it in the truck. While we were carrying the luggage we discovered the officers had confiscated all the wine from the castle cellar and were taking it for themselves. The wine was being put in the same truck as the luggage. We found our fountain of youth. We said, "Well, we're the ones who are going to carry that." The truck was the last in the whole convoy of let's say about a hundred trucks. The battalion was moving out, and we started breaking the cases and drinking on the road. We passed the bottles to the guys that were driving the truck and to the guards, too. Everybody started getting drunk. We were driving through Germany like that, singing Puerto Rican songs. And as we were passing by we were throwing kisses to the German girls.

We got to a town, it was about ten o'clock at night. By the time we got there, they were starting the kitchen, and we were the last truck to get in. They were waiting for us. We got out of the truck drunk, the guard was drunk, everybody was drunk. We were trying to behave like we were sober, but it was obvious we weren't. Anyway, we had to sleep in tents, on the ground. So I told the guys, "Let's dig a hole first and put the bottles in there." We dug and dug, and then we buried about ten or fifteen bottles of schnapps and wine. Then we put up our tents right over the spot.

We were ordered to take the officers' gear to their quarters. All the officers were there waiting for their stuff, and that's when they found out we were drunk, because we couldn't keep our control any longer. They called the captain and started yelling, "These guys are drunk. We shouldn't have let them carry the schnapps. You guys are really going to get it this time." And we said, "O.K., whatever punishment we get, we're in jail already." They sent us to the tents and told new guards to patrol us carefully. They saw the old guards were drunk, too, so we had two more guards in jail with us. Now we were nine.

After chow—it was already about midnight or so—we started digging, pulling the bottles out, and drinking. We went straight to sleep. The next day, the same thing happened. About four o'clock we returned from work. And we started digging again. By the time we got to chow we were drunk. We had blankets, GI blankets, and I put the blankets down on top of where the schnapps was. The tent looked neat. Neat and clean. The mess sergeant, the captain, our new guard, they knew we were drunk but couldn't figure out where we could have gotten the schnapps. They kept looking but couldn't find anything. Then the captain came around, got us out of the tent, and lined us up. "Take up the tents." They lifted one tent, nothing, another tent, nothing, another tent, nothing. When they lifted mine, the captain saw that the dirt on the ground had been moved. So he got what he was looking for. But they only found a bottle or two, we had already finished off the rest.

The next day we moved to a new town. This time they didn't let us carry the schnapps! They put regular soldiers to do that. And with two sergeants in charge. The mess sergeant didn't want us around the kitchen either, because we used to grab the food and mess it up and laugh. The supply sergeant didn't want us, because he said we stole. The officers didn't want us to carry the officers' bags, because we drank. We were getting in such a state they couldn't use us anymore. They didn't want us to work. We were to do nothing.

Down the street from where the battalion was living was a big hole close to an open space. It must have been made by a bomb, an American bomb, about fifteen yards wide or maybe bigger. The prisoners had to pitch their tents there. All the way around the crater was wire, so they could patrol the whole thing. It was like a tiny concentration camp.

We were about eleven now. I think another guy came from another battery, that made twelve. The street ran right in front of us, and girls came by on bicycles. Right away the guys were taking these girls into corners. We used to throw the cigarettes out to them. They would pick up the cigarettes, and then they would come around, and they would laugh.

One day a girl came along that looked like a Puerto Rican. And I said, "Goddamn, look at that black hair." She was very light but she had black hair. Most of the people over there had blond hair or auburn.

The guards used to yell, "Don't talk." The order was no fraternization with the Germans. Of course I did start talking to all the people who went by—the girls, the boys, even the old people, and old ladies, let's say women about thirty-five years old.

First we gave the girls cigarettes, The next thing we gave them food. Sometimes when we finished eating we would get back in line again and say, "If something is left, give it to me because tonight we gonna be hungry." The guys in the galley were the same guys that were there when I was the sergeant. The whole thing was more like a family, because we had been together so many years and, besides, we were Puerto Ricans. It's not like being in an outfit where people are completely different. So they would give us extra food. We would tell them it was for us, but actually we gave it to the German girls. The black-haired one started coming and talking to me. I gave her Chiclets, I gave her cigarettes, I gave her pork chops. These people were really hungry. A kind of friendship started between the girl and me, and then I started rubbing her hands and things.

One Sunday everybody was out, so the girls came by, with another girlfriend for the guard. While he was talking to that girl, we brought the others inside the guardhouse, inside the tent, and we started kissing them. We were about a mile away from the battalion, and nobody knew that we were with the girls inside kissing and having a tremendous party. We kept on watching for the captain, and everything seemed all right.

I don't know what happened. One minute I looked at the sky and saw a plane up there but didn't think anything of it. Suddenly, about an hour later, the captain came around. He was mad. He said, "I saw you guys from up in the plane. You have women in there." But by the time he arrived, there weren't any women left. "You got women." "No, we don't have women." But he just said, "This is the end. We gave you a break. We tried to treat you right. We gave you every chance. No more."

The next day they drove us about a half-hour's distance to a place that really looked like a concentration camp. They put us in an old German jail, with rooms no bigger than three feet wide and three feet long. In other words, if you were more than five feet, you could never stretch out completely. The armed guards were Americans, no more Puerto Ricans. Chow was about a mile away, and we had to go there double time all the way. By the time we got there we were beat. They gave us food and then they ran us back after we ate, too. We couldn't go out and work or anything.

So I started kicking on the door. They didn't like that, so the next day a guy came over with one potato and a canteen of water. That's all they gave me for the whole day. There was only one little hole through which I could see light. I couldn't see outside, because the window or whatever was so high up. I started to worry then. Man, it was completely incommunicado, and I was going nuts.

I stayed there about a week, starving, my stomach had already gotten small. After a week they came around. "All right, you want to go back with the rest of the prisoners and have regular chow?" From then on I didn't make any more noise. I really started behaving. My buddies and I behaved, and they took us out to eat and then even sent us out to work. To go to work was a pleasure, because to go to work was to go out, to go in the truck and out in the street. We were cleaning the debris from the street and stuff like that.

One day we were picking up debris, and I saw the colonel coming by in the jeep. My colonel, the Puerto Rican colonel. When I saw him, I yelled, "Colonel!" The guard said, "Shut up!" and stuck the rifle in my back, but the colonel saw me. He came over and got out of the jeep. I told him in Spanish, "Listen, Colonel, please get me out of here. Please get me out of here, I'll be nice." "I told you, we tried—" "But, please, Colonel, get me out of here, I'll be all right." "All right, but are you willing to behave and do things the way you're supposed to?" "Yeah, I'm willing."

Of course I didn't want to give in too much, I had my pride, but that wasn't the time for it. I didn't really beg him, I just said I'd like to get out of there. But actually inside of me I was pleading. I didn't want to say that, but I wanted him to see. Anyway, he said, "All right," and he saluted the guard, and the guard saluted him, and he left in the jeep. About two days afterward Puerto Ricans came with papers to get us out, and they took us back to the battery. We went to the colonel's office. I saluted him very military, and he said, "O.K., are you ready to behave?" I said, "I will." "O.K., you can go back to your battery."

— 6 —

The System Is Upstairs (1945)

I GOT BACK to the Ricans. The first day, reveille, I got up and went out, they didn't name my name. So I stayed quiet. The next morning they didn't call my name, and they didn't look for me. The sergeant said hello, but he didn't bother with me. Nobody did. I started sleeping every day. I didn't report, I got up late, I hung around town, and nobody said anything.

Since they were not calling me for work or anything, I would get up about eight o'clock. Then I would go to town. I used to go to the USO, where they had free doughnuts and coffee for the soldiers.

One day I was walking around and I saw this girl. She was dark, with brownish hair. By dark I don't mean dark like a Puerto Rican, but darker than most of the other Germans. I started following her. I went into the USO and got a lot of doughnuts. She took them, and I walked her to her street. The next day I did the same and then walked her all the way home. She lived in a bombed-out building, it belonged to her family. Her last name was Möberg, two points on the ö, that's the way the German names are written. Her name was Elizabeth, I used to call her Lilybet. The next time I met her she took me upstairs and introduced me to her mother. She was an old lady, I would say about fifty or sixty years old. And her father must have been about fifty-five. I had a little wine and talked a bit. The father didn't say too much. I went with her and her brother to a room on the second floor with a wall half off. You could see outside, not the street, but outside. This was her room.

I sat down on the bed with her and her brother, and we talked. I told them I'm from Puerto Rico. She said, "But you're an American soldier?" "Yeah, I'm an American soldier but I'm from Puerto Rico." They were a little shocked by that. Though I talked to them in English, I had a tremendous accent. They could see I was not from the United States. They brought out a map of the world, and I could find Cuba and Santo Domingo, but Puerto Rico was such a tiny point I couldn't even find it. I stayed there about an hour and a half, talking, and I was very polite. Then I made a date with her for the next day and left.

It was late, but still light out. The German hours are very different from the Puerto Rican hours during the summertime. At nine o'clock at night it's dark in Puerto Rico, but it was light in Germany. Imagine how this hits a Puerto Rican who's never left the island.

Her brother, Klaus, was about fourteen. One day I was walking with him and asking questions about Germany. He said Germany was good, it just happened they had lost the war, but Germany would be rebuilt again. His sister was in the Hitler Youth, and he had a sign which said in German, "Fight to Victory." I wasn't really interested in what he was saying. I was much more interested in figuring out how I could get up to his sister. His shoes were beat up, and I told him I could get him a new pair. "Oh boy! That would help a lot," and he told me he wore size eight.

He spoke very good English, good grammar, the only thing was he had a rough accent. He spoke better English than I did. So did Lilybet. They used the word "fetch" a lot. I didn't even know what "fetch" was.

Anyway, I went to the supply sergeant, he was a friend of mine. He told me he didn't have any size eight shoes. "You wanna sell them or something?" "No, I just want them for my girlfriend's brother." He said, "All right, Benjy, you've always been a nice guy with me. I'm gonna get them for you. It so happens that we're going to get more equipment tomorrow." So the next day I got the shoes.

They started leaving me and Lilybet alone up there in the room more often, so I started cuddling myself a little closer to her on the bed. And then I began to be romantic with this girl. I was a little timid, I had the feeling inside me not to force myself on her. Because

I knew I could if I wanted to, it would have been very easy for me to. But I was brought up—in spite of everything—to respect human beings. If I wanted a girl, I wanted her to do it willingly more or less. I had my weapon with me at that time, full of bullets, hanging on my back, but I didn't want the power of being the conquering soldier. Some guys would do that, they were doing it—Americans, Ricans, everybody. But I didn't want to, so anyway that's why it took me so long to get up to her. It was like a love story, and I liked it that way.

My friend the supply sergeant had a deal with a German woman who was supposed to be from one of the best families in the area. She lived in a section that was once very rich. I told him about my girl, that I was crazy about her, that she was beautiful, and cute—I mean actually nice. I felt that way about her, and I could see she had a feeling for me, too.

The supply sergeant had an arrangement with these people in the good neighborhood. I went with him one time to their house. It hadn't been bombed. The place was no castle, but it was a pretty nice house. The people had been in the government during the Kaiser's time and then during Hitler's time. They were from the ruling class—no, they were from a class higher than the ruling class, the aristocracy. They have that in Europe—counts and stuff like that. We don't have that kind of thing.

When the supply sergeant went there, everybody came out to receive him. Now he parked his jeep inside, in the patio, and we walked in. His girlfriend came in with her mother and introduced us. We sat down, and they gave me schnapps and then brought some little crackers. Very, very well-mannered people. My friend left the room with his girl, and I stayed with the old lady and the old man and other people. There were only old people in Germany. There were young girls, old women, and old men. Men about twenty-five to forty-five you didn't see in all of Germany. The war was only two months over; the prisoners hadn't begun to return yet. That night I realized the reason these people were living so good was the supply sergeant was supplying our food to them.

He arranged it with his girlfriend that I could bring Lilybet to her room. I hadn't yet blasted the woman, I didn't want to do it in the house, where the kid could walk in or anything. The next day I told Lilybet I wanted to take a ride with her. All the way from Mannheim, where she lived, to Neckerstadt—or some name like that—where the sergeant's girlfriend lived. I knocked on the door, the aristocrat opened it for me. I walked through the patio and went into her room with Lilybet. I got into the sack and start blasting her, I was feeling great. But I stayed longer than I was supposed to stay. The sergeant came over, he had to knock on my door. I was blasting away. Because, remember, I haven't blasted for a long time. I was in jail, and this was my first connection.

I went out with her the next day. I wanted to blast again. But since I had already broken through the sound barrier, I didn't need the sergeant's help. I was walking with her, and it was getting late, about eleven already, it was a little dark. Close to her house I looked around in a bombed building and pushed her in there. And I started kissing and blasting and kissing and blasting and kissing. I got hot with the blasting, because once you start, you blast more and more. So I took her back the next day. Sometimes she didn't want to, "I might get caught in there."

Some soldiers told me about the other side of the Rhine River. It was called Ludwigshafen. That was where the French were, and it was a VD area where Americans were not supposed to go. Off limits. And my buddies told me there were a lot of bars and women blasting away there—not like the American side, where we had the nonfraternization order of General Eisenhower. If the MPs patrolling the streets saw you with a German, they would pick you up. Most of the time they would just take you off in the jeep somewhere and give you a talking-to, "Get away from the Germans, you know you can't do that." But on the other side the Frenchmen weren't going with that shit. They had bars, and the German girls were there, and everybody was drinking and dancing and blasting and everything. So we said, "Listen, we gotta cross this river some place."

The Neckar River had a pontoon bridge. It was a dead river, quiet, like a lake. If you fell into it, you could swim. But the Rhine has a powerful current, you couldn't put a pontoon over it. Now, there had been a bridge once, but it was blown away. So some Americans had strung a steel line across the river, with the cooperation of some Frenchman on the other side. They were charging fifty and one hundred marks to get us across. We would go over and pay the guy. Then on the cable, it had like a little wheel. We hung onto the pulley, and they pulled us across. It was a small distance.

Coming back, the Frenchmen collected from the other side. To get back was rough, because we would be drunk. I don't know how we did it, but we would somehow hang on.

Anyway, we did get across and went to the bars. And there were German whores, and Frenchmen were drinking and dancing and *"Barrelito di-da-di-ti-ta"* and all the German songs.

I heard that many soldiers fell in that goddamn river and were half drowned, and had to be taken to the hospital. The authorities broke off the racket later on, but it took time to find it. Then those guys that were making money on it no longer had that good deal. And were they making money! It just shows you that the system is upstairs, and everybody downstairs is trying to fuck it. The Germans do it their way; the Frenchmen do it their way; the Ricans do it their way; everybody tries to fuck that thing up there.

A racket got organized in the ration dumps, where they had acres and acres of food. The dump was big. My battalion was ordered to guard duty for one section, another battalion was ordered to do another section, and so on. On the Puerto Rican side that we were guarding, the sergeant would come with trucks at night and take food out. I remember the bacon cans. He used to sell cans of bacon—about fifty pounds—for twenty-five dollars.

So I got into the racket. I got myself a weapon carrier, filled it, and brought it to the black market in Mannheim. In one bombed building there would be a few guys, Germans and some Americans. The Americans handed over food, and the Germans paid off. I found that I had taken two thousand dollars worth of stuff. Each time I would get my money, and then I would try to buy something. One day, for instance, I bought shoes for Lilybet. The Germans would give me money for the food and then take it all back for the stuff you bought! "This nice pair of shoes will cost you five hundred American dollars."

One day I heard in the company that we were pulling out to Marseilles. The war with Japan was not over yet, and they were moving us to Marseilles to be reoutfitted and sent to the Philippines. Nobody figured the war in Japan was gonna finish so fast. Nobody knew about the atom bomb—it came like a blow, a surprise, to everybody.

I went to say goodbye to Lilybet. Oh, man! I felt miserable, my heart was broken to pieces. I had a big pain inside of me. I remember coming down the stairs of her house and crying and seeing her cry. We left in a big convoy. All the German girls came out and threw flowers to us. We went over the pontoon bridge that was close by Lilybet's house. And from the river I could see where the bombed place was. I looked over there and she was standing—saying goodbye, I guess.

We pulled through France and got into Marseilles. Now, there was an enormous port of embarkation. Since we were supposed to go to Japan, they gave us new equipment, new uniforms, new underwear, boots, and everything. And gas masks. They always kept on checking the gas masks, giving out new ones. The United States during the war kept on coming with more improvements in the equipment. And every three or four months they got a better gas mask than the one they had before, so the other one was obsolete. This was the fourth time I got a new gas mask I never used!

Then suddenly—boom—they bomb Japan. Soon the war in Japan is gonna be over, in August. So what happened? Instead of going to Japan, we were left standing by there in Marseilles.

And then came orders we were to go to Puerto Rico, the war was over, everybody's happy, and they're gonna send us to Puerto Rico. They had a point system for sending people back. The longer you were in the service, the more points you had. And if you were overseas, you had even more points. The Puerto Ricans had lots of points because they were almost always overseas—even in Puerto Rico they were overseas! And we had points for being in combat areas even though we were never in combat!

But I didn't want to go to Puerto Rico. I don't know whether I was right or wrong, but the dark picture of Puerto Rico came to my mind—not to mine alone, to many guys. Some of the guys had no choice—they had wives, they had kids, they had everything in Puerto Rico. But darkness came over me. See, I was twenty-two, twenty-three years old, I didn't know too much about the world yet. . . .

Anyway, I found out that guys who had venereal disease were not getting shipped to Puerto Rico but had to stay in France. They were getting three ships ready—"*las tres caravelas de Colón,*"[1] everybody called them. The *Santa María,* the *Pinta* and the *Niña* were coming to pick up the Ricans and sail them straight to Puerto Rico, like Columbus did. No more stops—the discovery of America! I said, "I don't want to go." So, O.K., right away I thought, I'll go to town immediately to look for the VD women so I can get myself VD.

They used to give soldiers prophylactic stuff to use when they went to town. I threw all of that stuff out, I was looking for the germ. I went to this whorehouse, to the other whorehouse, looking and looking. I went to five different whorehouses; five different women. Then I waited two days to see if I was dripping. Nothing. So then I tried it a different way. I went over and started talking with a woman and said, "I wanna woman that is sick." "Oh, no!" "I'm not saying you are the one, but if you are, you're the one I'm with." I couldn't get it that way either. So instead of going to the whorehouses, I went to the edges of the town where they had the really dirty people, the people living in little shacks. There were a lot of women there, too, blasting for money. Well, I finally got sick. In three days I was dripping.

And then the order came. The guys were leaving Monday. I went to get a checkup. "You're sick, you can't go to Puerto Rico. Stay over here." They sent me to the hospital. In the hospital they had different uniforms for the guys with VD. If you had on red pajamas, that meant you had venereal disease. The other guys got blue.

The Puerto Ricans left in their three ships, and I stayed in Marseilles like I wanted. I stayed in the hospital for a while, and then

---

1. Columbus's three sailing ships.

they sent me to an American outfit. That was the 353rd Ordinance Outfit.

There was a guy in the outfit with black hair like me. I looked at that guy, he looked like a Puerto Rican. He was Italian. It's amazing how the minds of human beings react. You see how people classify themselves? I guess like the animals and the ants. If you drop a little animal in a forest, and there's another animal that looks like it (let's say a cat and a tiger), it will try to go close. There I was with all those blue-eyed blonds and the Italian, and because he looked like a Puerto Rican, I tried to make friends with him. I didn't go to a blond guy and say, "Listen, you're from New York, I'm scared, a Rican, imagine this." No, I went to an Italian. I was afraid to go up to a blond. And I'm way ahead of a lot of Ricans. Imagine, say, a mentally retarded Rican from the country. He would have gone crazy. He wouldn't even have approached the Italian!

So I went to this dark Italian and talked to him. And the guy was nice. He told me, "I'm from Bah-ston. Where you from?" I said, "I'm Puerto Rican. I just came in." "O.K., take that bunk." Every time I didn't understand something he said, I'd say, "Tell me slower." The days passed, and I got to be more relaxed, like I could feel the floor beneath me. I didn't talk much to anybody, just to the Italian. Little by little I started talking to the others. Everybody saw that I was a quiet guy, so I didn't have any trouble.

One day it was already December, we got into the ship and sailed back to the States. They had Bing Crosby singing "I'll Be Home for Christmas" over the loudspeaker. And then we landed, I think in the Boston area. It was impressive the way they fixed it. There was a map of the United States on the ground. So when I jumped off the ship the first thing I saw when my feet landed was that map of the United States.

Then we got straight onto a train. There were signs—"Job Well Done," "Welcome Home"—all along the tracks. We went to Fort Dix, New Jersey. On the way we pulled into a long tunnel, and the train stopped. I didn't know where I was, it was all dark. The trains were underground. A guy walked through selling something—coffee maybe. One of the soldiers bought something from him, and after the train began moving again, he came over and said. "Hey, where is that guy? I gave him five dollars for the cigarettes and he walked off and didn't give me my change!" Somebody in the back yelled, "Hey listen, man, now you know you're in New York!"

New York. We were underground in Penn Station. I was lonesome about not being in San Juan, about being with all these *yanquis*, but I was also worried about being sent to Puerto Rico. I thought maybe I should just step out of the train right there. But I didn't do that. I went to Fort Dix, New Jersey, still afraid that when they processed me they'd say, "Well, listen, you gotta go to Puerto Rico." But when it came time to get discharged, they gave me my mustering-out pay, three hundred dollars, and I got myself on the way to New York.

I got into the bus with all the other guys that were going to New York. Everybody was happy. I tried to behave like I was not too scared, but I was. I said to the bus driver, "Tell me when we get to New York." He said, "Relax, buddy, this is only the tunnel." So we pulled into New York, I think on 34th Street, the Greyhound Station there. Then I got myself into a cab and said to the guy, "O.K., Amsterdam Avenue, way up by 170th Street." I paid him, walked across the street, and found the stoop where my sister lived. She wasn't there, but Mrs. Murphy, that's the Irish woman that used to live upstairs of my sister, said, "Well, your sister will be back any minute now." My sister came about five o'clock or so. She let me in, and I stayed in New York.

— 7 —

Marine Tiger, or "500,000 Came for Dinner" (1946–1951)

TO GET TO NEW YORK in the 1930s you had to go by ship, and it took five days. And you had to have at least three hundred dollars. The only people who went to New York in those days were the ones whose families had jobs, the ones who were a little better off—let's say, the tiny middle class, very tiny. My sister, for example, married a fellow whose father had a good business, a store, and I remember taking them to the ship, *El Borinquen*,[1] in 1937 or 1938. And once they got to New York, those people worked as elevator men—even high school graduates or people with one or two years of college who couldn't get jobs in Puerto Rico. They couldn't speak English, so they couldn't do any better.

The Ricans really started going to New York after World War II. There was a ship that sailed from San Juan to New York called the *Marine Tiger,* and that's why a Rican was often called a Marine Tiger then. Passage was very cheap. The *Tiger* used to make two or three trips a month, and on each trip she carried one thousand Ricans. Once the *Daily News* carried an article about us with a big headline: "500,000 CAME FOR DINNER." In other words, in New York in those years after the war a Rican was nothing, shit. Those were the years of my trouble.

I know that things are different with the Ricans now in New York.

---

1. *Borinquen* is the Spanish rendition of the name given the island of Puerto Rico by its original Indian inhabitants.

Now you have Badillo,[2] the big politician. I know Badillo personally; he's married to a Jewish woman, and she helps him a lot. So now it's different. But at that time the government hadn't known that the Ricans would be coming in such force. The society hadn't foreseen that all these thousands and thousands of people, American citizens, would be sailing in. Or flying in. Right from the start, guys who were ex-World War II pilots with two-engine planes started taking Ricans from San Juan and dropping them off in Miami, from where they would hustle their way up to New York. New York, New York, was the Promised Land. In New York were the jobs.

With all the trouble I had getting jobs—and with all the fear that kind of trouble breeds—I understood right off that being a Rican made me inferior. I used to say to myself, It's not that I'm less than other people, I'm a human being like everybody else. But that didn't help the fact that since I was in New York I was less because they wanted to make me less. I admitted that to myself. They had that power, that I understood.

In New York I was branded. When the Americans look at the Puerto Ricans, they don't see the difference between a guy like me whose father made twenty-five dollars a week or the guy whose father made sixty cents a day. Even more, I knew Puerto Ricans in New York whose fathers were really rich, they owned farms that cost twenty-five thousand dollars in those days and would cost a million today, and in New York nobody knew the difference between them and the guys that never had shoes. We were all in a bunch together. "You're a Rican and that's it, you're no different from the other."

But we were different. With us there was a difference in culture and behavior and upbringing. My father wouldn't go to the sack with my mother if I was around, while some people—not that they wanted to do it, they had to, they only had one room—they shacked with the mother with the daughter right inside the room. Maybe their minds got so, I don't say corrupted, but broken down by the economic situation.

---

2. Herman Badillo (b. 1929), the first Puerto Rican to be a borough president in N.Y. (Bronx), was a U.S. congressman as well as a candidate for mayor of New York City.

Some of these Ricans made their living in *bodegas*[3] and in businesses like that. They were people from *el fanguito*.[4] They knew how to fight and how to work. They could go to the dishwashing, save money, go to the *bodega* and work for fifteen hours a day. They were already trained, they had cut sugar cane. With that type of upbringing they could make it in a business where you have to be a slave. They were used to taking beatings, it didn't bother them. They didn't make it big, but they had a *bodega,* ten, twelve thousand dollars a year.

But I was struggling on the streets. I didn't want to be beat, beat down to the dirt all the way, even though I sometimes played with the dirt.

Now, the Jews they did it right. I got to admire the Jews. To begin with, I didn't understand about them. The only idea I had about the Jews when I was a kid was they killed Christ. I mean, I used to go to see *La Muerte* y *Pasión de Nuestro Sr. Jesús Cristo,* "The Death and Passion of Our Lord Jesus Christ"—they even made a silent movie of it when I was about ten. I used to see it every year and cry my heart out. So the only thing I understood about the Jews was that they killed Christ.

In New York I began to understand not only about Jews but this whole thing with different races, different groups—the Wops, the This, the That. But it was the Jews who were always the lawyers, the *bravos*[5] in school. I took a look at NYU—they had about thirty thousand students at that time—and about eighty per cent of the student body were Jewish.

I was getting into trouble in those days. Once I got arrested. I was taken to a judge—the judge was a Jew. I had to go see a lawyer—the lawyer was a Jew. It made an impression on me and on all the Ricans.

We all started thinking and talking about groups, looking for someone to look down on. We were trying to find somebody to blame for our troubles. We couldn't talk against the Englishmen,[6] they

---

3. Grocery stores.
4. A large slum alongside the Martín Peña canal that separates the Santurce and Hato Rey sections of San Juan; literally, "the muddy place."
5. The cool ones.
6. The WASPs.

owned the country. So we decided that the Irish were the stupid ones, because they were even more ignorant than we were. We started calling them "donkeys." Anytime one of us had an argument with an Irishman, we would say, "You're a fucking donkey, you're no brain."

We also used to kick a lot about the Italians. But speaking Spanish, we felt a kind of special relation to the Italians. We could understand them much better, even if we did have fights with them. Something always broke through with them. We used to fuck their women, and guys used to marry Italian girls. And we used to love spaghetti.

The people we really couldn't get through to was the Irish. They were completely different from us. They were blond, blue-eyed, fair-skinned, nice-looking, and to us they seemed behind the Italians in many ways.

In school you discover there are a lot of prominent Irish people, and a lot of intelligent ones, but the average Rican doesn't understand that. The experience of the average Rican was that he was moving into an Irish neighborhood, and the Irish thought the Ricans were trying to take the neighborhood for themselves, and they didn't like that. Not that anyone planned it this way, but that's why there was a special kind of antagonism between the Irish and the Ricans. And of course an Irishman would go into a bar and fight. A Rican would come and say, "I just had a fight with an Irishman, and I had to pull a knife and cut him up because the guy was beating the hell out of me."

With the Jews we didn't have that kind of trouble, because a Jewish guy would say, "I don't fight." Jews would go to the law as their way of settling matters. The Irish would use fists, and Italians, too.

One guy alone can always blend into a society of people who are different or even speak a different language. One guy alone could easily be taken for Italian or Greek. But put ten together—put ten Ricans together and immediately you notice a distinction!

Everybody used to go after us because of the things that were said, like the articles in the *Daily News*. Every two or three weeks there would be something against us in the papers —from New York, or they would even go to Puerto Rico and take pictures of *el fanguito*, the slums, and make a five- or six-page spread of them. I could feel the way New Yorkers were against us in the subway, in my building, on the job, wherever I went. It was like a nervous tension. There were fights starting up all the time all over New York City.

Once when I was out of work and doing nothing, I was hanging around with a bunch of Cubans. We used to play *la charada*,[7] a Cuban game you can play where the cops can be looking right at you and still not be able to know you're gambling. The way it's played is, I put a number from one to fifteen on a piece of paper—let's say twelve. And I hide the number somewhere, underneath the bench. Then you start betting on what number I have there. I give you a hint, I say, "The most wonderful women, the greatest of all. A woman that is beautiful." So you start betting the number. See, each number has an identity. One is death; ten is president; twelve is *puta,* the whore; thirteen is *chulo,* the pimp; five is a bird; and so on. So one night we were playing, and the cops came over and grabbed us. They checked us out and couldn't find anything. One of the cops said, "O.K., you goddamn Ricans get in the corner," and one of the Cubans said, "Hey listen, man I'm not a Rican, I'm a Cuban." And the cop said, "It's the same goddamn shit!"

I remember the time a bunch of Irish kids beat me down at St. Ann's in the Bronx. It was 1948, I'd been in New York a few years. They beat the hell out of me, there must have been ten of them. I was on the ground in the yard of St. Ann's, they were kicking me, and I was trying to pull my arms around my head to protect my face. I bent my head close to my chest, and then they got on my back. I can still remember the kicking. What saved me was a few guys who saw what was happening and called the cops. When the cops came, the Irish guys ran. So the cops grabbed me. But what could they do? They just put me on the trolley, and the trolley brought me to 145th Street, and there I took the subway back to where I was living. After that I had a pain in my back, I needed a disc operation.

And just one year later, after I had the operation, I almost got

---

7. Charades.

killed again. One night—I had been out of the hospital three or four days—I was going downtown on the subway. Two sailors came over to me and started looking for trouble, insulting me. "You lousy Puerto Rican," and stuff like that. I didn't know what to do. I had a suit and topcoat on, they couldn't have known I was an invalid. One of them was getting rough, the other one seemed as if he didn't want to. If the guy had hit me, that might have been the end of me, because if I had fallen off the seat and he had kicked me on the floor. . . . So I was praying to God, hoping that I could get out of this. I started backing away, and then the other guy said, "Aw, leave him alone, he's just a dumb spic!" I think I was more scared then than at just about any time of my life. I was scared because if he had hit me and hit me, I might have been crippled for life, and I was scared because I was helpless to stop him. I just gave him a face of innocence, a face of pleading. I got up to his eyes to let him know that, I kept that face and I got him to relax.

Not just for me, but for all the Ricans, things had gotten very bad.

— 8 —

A *Jíbaro* in a Goddamn Place Like That (1946)

BUT THAT WAS LATER. When I first got to New York, I went to live with my sister and became very friendly with her husband's brother. I used to call him "Uncle." He wasn't my uncle, I just called him that. He was about twenty-five years older than I and lived alone. He was a cab driver. He had always been a cab driver, he died a cab driver. He lived in an apartment with the bathroom outside. You know, in one of those houses that were built in New York in the 1800s—if you had a sink inside the room, you really had it made.

One night I went to visit him. When I walked in, this girl was in the bed, and Uncle was sitting on top of the sink washing his balls. And his face was very, very happy. That was the first time I saw Beth. She was looking out from under the sheet. I will never forget that scene, especially his face. He was old, don't forget, with white hair and wrinkles.

Cab drivers often run into whores. That's how he met Beth. He picked her up on 50th Street and Eighth Avenue in the Greyhound Station. He took her to his house and shacked up with her. Beth was from St. Louis, Missouri. She was once married to an Italian but actually she was an Irish woman. She was very tall, about six feet, with blue eyes and she was a hustler. Her husband had started her in the business. She was no chick, she must have been about thirty-two, thirty-three, already over the hill in that kind of business. In New York an Irish girl twenty-two, twenty-three years old in the whore business is a chick, but once you get over thirty years old you're no more one of the nice call girls, you gotta go out and hustle on Eighth Avenue.

I went to see Uncle a couple of times, he used to give me a couple of bucks now and then. When he went out to hack at night, I started shacking up with her. Since I was young, she got hooked on me, so we kept on shacking up. Uncle was trying to keep her—"I have a woman," that was his idea. He didn't even want her to go out and hustle. But she left him and moved to the Endicott Hotel on 81st Street. I went to stay with her there, and we went on and on for three days, blasting.

She used to take some pills, so I started taking these pills, too. I didn't know what I was doing. These pills would really put us to sleep, deep sleep. Then we would take other pills, Benzedrine, to control the sleeping. She used to go to a drugstore near Central Park to get these pills from the pharmacist. I would meet her in the park, and we would sit underneath a tree, on the grass, taking the pills. It was like a lost weekend for me. I slept and slept and slept. We kept on this way for a while. She used to go out at night and come back with money and give me some. Goddamn, that was strange! Man, in New York you meet all kinds of people! How did this *jibaro*[1] get to a goddamn place like that?

Uncle got a little mad at me for taking her away. You know a piece of pussy like that is hard to get; he didn't want to lose it. Anyway, one day she, too, got mad at me and kicked me out. Years later Uncle told me that she died of an overdose.

He was a character, that Uncle. He used to read the *Daily News* all the time—you know, most cab drivers read the *Daily News*. He used to wait in line with his cab, say, on 59th Street or Central Park West, wait for a passenger and read the paper. I would walk around nights, and if I was around Sixth Avenue or so and saw a line of cabs, I would look for him. He liked to line up in front of the St. Moritz. Sometimes

---

1. A Puerto Rican term for "peasant"; it connotes a person of rural virtues unspoiled by urban vices, a hillbilly, but it also refers to a person of hidden capacities for astuteness. The term is used here somewhat facetiously.

he told me to lie down in the back of his hack so he didn't have to start the meter, he would lock the doors and drive me home to 181st Street. He was a very nice guy.

He died of a heart attack in 1959. Because of the wear and tear of driving that cab, I swear. If he would have had the right kind of job, he wouldn't have died. Most cab drivers in New York die of heart attacks, nerves.

All those years since 1938 I had been longing to go back to school. I heard about the GI Bill and decided to finish high school and take advantage of it. So I registered in George Washington High School. That was where I met Johnny, who became my best buddy. As soon as classes started, there was a conflict. A lot of GIs were there, doing what I was doing. And most of them were twenty-three or twenty-four years old. Now the girls and boys in that school were most around sixteen to eighteen. The GIs all smoked and drank, and were hotter for a piece of ass and knew their way around better than the young kids. Put them into a regular high school—guys who had already been all over the world, fighting a war—and you have trouble. The principal announced that they were going to give the veterans a room where they could go and smoke. We used to go to the bar across the street for lunch and come back to class high. In the same class with kids of sixteen or seventeen, such a thing makes a difference that's hard to bridge.

I ran into a young girl at school, a Jewish girl, very beautiful with blue eyes. I forgot her name. I made a date with her on Amsterdam Avenue close to the school, it was about seven o'clock or so. That place gets quiet at that time of the night because it's after school, it's like a park. I took her over there and I start kissing her and giving her a hand, I tried to make her, and I tried to give her my tongue, and she told me not to do that. It surprised me, and she says, "It means too much to me, I like you, but it means too much to me." I still remember the words. I didn't dare, that was the truth. I didn't dare! She was so young, that was it.

I didn't wreck her because once a girl had it the first time, that's a wreck. It could be for the positive or it could be for the negative. She might find the right guy to whom that doesn't mean anything, or she might find the right guy to whom that means everything. So when she said those words, "It means too much to me," I accepted it. I only have my *goce,* my fun playing, and I forget about putting it in. I had a big hot arm[2] because I was twenty-four years old and that thing was breaking, but I didn't do anything.

My friend Johnny and I and some other guys from school became a crowd. There was a guy we called "the Rich Greek," because compared to the rest of us, he was like a millionaire. He and his brother had a new car. In 1946! He had a sister. The Rich Greek was very light-skinned, but his sister was dark, dark like a Rican. They lived in a pretty big apartment. It was only on Amsterdam Avenue but compared with everybody else on Amsterdam, they were in good shape. His father worked in Frank's, a big restaurant on 125th Street where Negroes who had money would go. Whites would go there, too. Joe Louis once opened a big restaurant in Harlem, but Joe Louis's restaurant flopped. Frank's never flopped, it's there to this day. The Greek, I think, was the boss or the owner—anyway, he was some kind of a big man.

There was another guy in our crowd, Matt David. He was a Navy veteran who lived in the neighborhood. He went to Cornell. We were all twenty-three, twenty-four, twenty-five, all war guys. We used to do things together. One day they took me over to Jersey, I didn't want to go. I couldn't understand where I was, and I knew if they were to drop me off there, I would have gotten lost.

We used to meet on Saturday night and go out drinking. Sometimes the Greek would pay. Maybe Johnny had a couple of bucks, or if I had a buck that I got from my sister or Uncle, I would pay. We drank beer. At that time beer was cheap, about ten or fifteen cents a glass, on tap. One day we went to this place on Audubon Avenue. I must have been one of the first few Ricans who started going to bars like this—in those days the Negroes wouldn't go to these places. And

---

2. "Hot arm" is apparently a reference to the slang expression "hard on" for an erection of the penis.

some guy at the bar made some nasty remarks. I couldn't even understand exactly what he was saying, but Johnny protested. I kept asking, "Well, listen, what's up?" But the others just kept on talking to the guy, telling him I am a veteran, a friend of theirs, that I went to school there. Finally I just got mad and decked the guy—wham—with one blow. The guy was flat, flat on the deck. After that the guys said, "We're gonna call you Big Blow Benjy, man." I was the only Rican, and I took the only action. But I was feeling pretty good that I wasn't alone, that I had my crowd with me.

They always took me to neighborhood bars, and the conversation between Matt David, the Greek, and Johnny was always about shacking up. You know, young kids, hustling in bars, got a hot arm, gotta get a piece of pussy. I didn't even think about getting anything. One day they started saying, "We gotta get Benjy a break." They fixed me up with a girl who had blasted with everybody, Johnny, the Greek, David— she was one of those crazy kids they have in every neighborhood. I was the new guy, so they arranged it for me. So I got my hot arm, and that was one of my first blasts in the neighborhood. I remember walking down to my house after, twelve or one in the morning, feeling like a great guy. *Pepito* had had something to eat!

There was another guy in our group, Ralph Cruz. He was a Rican who had come to the States early, before the war. Ralph spoke English pretty good. When you first heard him he sounded like an ordinary New Yorker, but if you paid close attention you could tell that something was slightly off. Ralph lived in the Bronx. He was a little ahead of Johnny, out of high school already, going to college. The thing about him was, he always had lunch money. With us, by lunchtime on Saturday we were usually all broke. If there was nobody at home in my house, for example, I would take them into the house and raid the icebox, everybody would eat. This Cruz though, he used to disappear at lunchtime. He went to eat alone. He didn't want to pay for anybody. Whenever I got a couple of bucks from Uncle, I put it right into the kitty. Anyway, they always carried Ralph, too, as a friend. Of course he had more conversation with them than I did because he could really speak English.

We went one time to the Greek's house and got into his car, a real big Buick, for a trip to Poughkeepsie. I didn't know where Poughkeepsie was. I went because they looked for me. They wanted me to be with them. Otherwise I wouldn't have gone. When we were driving they were talking about getting pussy, stuff like that, what kids talk about. I didn't talk too much because I couldn't understand half the conversation. They would have to repeat themselves two or three times so that I could get it. We got to the town at night. I remember seeing kids marching in a parade all wearing blue jeans. It struck me funny seeing all these blond kids in dungarees. In Puerto Rico dungarees are for the workers, not the middle class. How come these people were walking with dungarees? Everybody was in dungarees here. How naive I was.

My big problem in school was my English. I couldn't understand the teachers because they would speak too fast. I don't remember any other person in my classes who didn't speak English. Still, I always managed to get something.

I used to go to school about eight and come out at three. One day about two months after school started, I was coming home from school and I met this Cuban. I saw this guy all sharped up. He called to me in Spanish and said he was having trouble. He wanted to buy something, and he needed me to interpret. My English was bad, but I could speak something.

Well, afterward I went with this Cuban to his room. His name was José. He had some pot and offered me a smoke, my first. Every day when I came out of school at three o'clock, I used to meet him on the corner. I used to hang around with him, go to restaurants and everything, and be like his interpreter. I became very close to the Cubans.

This José told me he was working in a restaurant downtown as a dishwasher. He had been working there for a while, and then he met this woman. She started to give him money. One night I went with the guy on the subway to 103rd Street. Right there on 103rd Street he walked over to a woman standing around. I stayed behind while he talked to her for about ten, fifteen minutes, and then he came back and said, "O.K., Benjy, let's go." When we got into the subway, he showed me ten dollars. He said, "She gave me ten dollars for nothing, just for coming over and talking to her. She's going to be my woman, she's going to give me ten dollars every day." I said, "Man, what a racket this is!" He said, "Well, I'm quitting the dishwashing business. I'm going professional like I was in Cuba."

The next day at three o'clock I saw the guy again, and we went to Columbus Avenue to collect the ten dollars, and three or four more days I went with him. In the meantime I was going to school every day. Things were starting to get fouled up because by now I was smoking with these Cubans regularly. I started goofing up in school. One day I had an argument with my sister. I don't remember exactly what it was about, but I got so mad I said to myself, I'm going to get the hell out of here. I had been out of the Army only five or six months, and I quit school. I was disgusted with my English. I was hanging out with this Cuban. I said the hell with it. Moreover, I was broke, and all the money I had saved from the Army was gone.

So I moved in with Uncle, planning to get a job as a seaman. At that time Uncle had an apartment in the Bronx. He was hacking like I said. I lived with him, and I was drawing twenty dollars a week. A World War II veteran out of work got twenty dollars a week for fifty-two weeks—it was like unemployment insurance. We had only two rooms besides the kitchen and dining room. One was small—that's where I lived—and one was bigger, where Uncle lived. He would always give me a few bucks. That's when I started meeting Ricans who were born in New York, Neoricans. I met this guy Jorge, the son of a Puerto Rican. He spoke English good. In Jorge's crowd there were some chicks, Rican chicks born in New York. They were sixteen, seventeen years old. I was the elder of the crowd because I was about twenty-four.

I went to a party with them one night, in a place at 134th Street and Broadway called *La Democracia Española*. It was a nice party, people were dancing. One guy came over and said something to me about a girl, so I took a swing at him. Suddenly there was a big crowd of guys all jumping on me. Jorge was standing there, he didn't move—and there was another guy, another Rican I knew from uptown, too—he didn't move either. They knew these people. I didn't, I was just a new guy coming to the area for the first time. They were beating the shit out of me.

The trouble was the door was so far away. In New York you have these places for dancing on the second floor, and there is only one entrance. You have to jump through the window in order to get out. I was in the corner and would have had to go all through the dance hall to get to the door. There was a guard in this place, and he was trying to protect me, but they were like animals swarming on top of me. By the time I broke for the door, the cops were coming up the stairs. I said to myself, Well, if I tell the cops it's me, they're going to grab me and take me to the police station, so I said to the cops, "They've got a big fight up there. Hurry up!" I got on the trolley and went home.

Those were the days in New York when all the gangs started up. I found out later that the guys who beat me up were the Puerto Rican Diplomats. This fight in the dance hall happened before my disc went bad—that, as I told you, the Irish were to do for me, but later—and I was still strong. I had it in mind to get those guys one by one. One day I got on a bus that was traveling uptown. And one of the guys from that fight got on, too. And he came up to me and started apologizing, saying he had to take part because he was afraid of the Diplomats, and so on. He was a Neorican and spoke pretty bad Spanish.

The bus turned up 125th Street. The Diplomats worked 137th Street, so I figured once the bus turned off 125th Street and got up to 137th Street, I'd get this guy. When he got off the bus, I got off the bus. And I beat him up. I was stronger, a veteran, and twenty-four years old. He was just a kid. I didn't really damage him, just gave him a couple of blows, that's it. I did it to satisfy myself. What a place is New York!

— 9 —

What the United States Was All About (1946)

IN MAY THAT YEAR, 1946, I got a job as an ordinary seaman on the *SS Alexander Baranoff.* Ordinary seaman is the man that paints around the ships and hangs the lines and lays down the booms.

That ship was a strange experience for me. I was the only Rican. There were two Negroes. One they called Red because he was white in color with bad hair,[1] red hair, and a big nose, one of those mulattoes—how do they call it in the States?—high yellow. The other one was the cook and used to wash the dishes, and the high yellow was the messman, the server. He was also a drunkard. He was a funny guy. All the time he used to say, "Yeah, man, I'm Judge O'Leary's son." He pushed that O'Leary line so hard that sometimes we just called him O'Leary.

Beside the kitchen crew, of course, there were the seamen on deck. One was a Canadian, and the rest were mostly from the South, tall guys, blue eyes, blond hair. They were from North Carolina, a little group that all came together to work in that ship. I was the only dark guy on the deck. This was practically my first job as a civilian. Sailing south to Galveston. Everyone had to do guard duty at night. All you had to do was touch the *campana,* the bell, if you saw lights. I had a good time because I had the four-to-eight watch. It would be daylight, and I would sit and look at the sea. The sea was quiet, beautiful. Then it would be my time at the wheel, and another guy would stand guard.

When you're at the wheel, you just run the wheel. You're supposed

---

1. He is referring to kinky hair.

to keep the ship on the course, and you have a mate with you always, standing on the bridge. Every time I came up to the wheel the guy on the bridge would say, "The crazy Puerto Rican is up there," because the ship would be moving around like a *culebra,* a snake. It was my first trip, so I didn't know how to keep the ship in a straight line.

We got to Galveston. We were staying on the hook[2] for six or seven days, so we used to put on our suits and throw ourselves into the water and swim around the ship after hours, after four or so in the afternoon. I was going to be daring, and instead of jumping from the level deck, I went up to the boat deck, which is quite high, and I dove from there into the ocean. When I hit the water, my back felt like it cracked a little bit. It hurt and then I forgot about it. Only later I found out that's a very dangerous thing to do.

It was here, when I went ashore, that I really started to find out what the United States was all about. Practically the first thing I saw was two signs: "White" and "Colored." I began to debate with myself about which door I should use. Everybody was going ashore that time. There was one guy who had really become a good friend to me. He, too, was a redhead—they also used to call him Red—and he was an Irishman from California. Red and I had got together to go ashore. Red walked through the fuckin' "White" door, and I was left thinking about which way I'm going to go. I didn't know what to do, but I said, "All right, shit, I'm going to follow Red." Nothing happened. I said to myself, "It's O.K., I won't have trouble here.

We went to have a drink in a bar. The steward, who was a Southerner, was there. As Red and I were having our drink, the steward kept looking at me funny. Finally he said, "Listen, man, what are you? You're a Puerto Rican? What's that? You Spanish, French, or what?" So I drank my drink, and Red said to me, "O.K., let's go," and then we went to a Mexican place. The next day the same deal, no trouble. Not even going through the white line to get into the movies.

Then one day while the ship was in the hook, I twisted my foot and couldn't walk, so they took me to the Marine Hospital. I looked at

---

2. Lying at anchor.

the forms they filled out for me, and saw that I was listed as a Mexican on the papers. I kept saying to the woman, "Listen, man, I'm not a Mexican, I'm a Puerto Rican!" and she said, "I don't know, you're a Mexican." I tried to tell her that Puerto Rico is one place and Mexico is a different place, but she didn't seem to understand. In the end I just gave in and said, "O.K., I'm a fuckin' Mex."

But it bothered me, it hurt my feelings. Why couldn't they find out about Puerto Rico? After all, I was a GI, even though I wasn't a very good GI. I served the country. I was supposed to be a hero. You know, they made me feel like that when they discharged me in Fort Dix and gave me that "Welcome Home." And riding in the train in New Jersey before I got into New York, they had big signs for a mile, "Welcome Boys, Well Done." So I'm a Rican, and I didn't understand this American country. Maybe, I told myself, if I would have been born here and raised here, I wouldn't have all these goddamn troubles, but it just so happens I wasn't.

Next the boat traveled to Houston to pick up coal. In Houston I said the hell with it. I don't want to be where the whites are. I also don't want to go to the Negro side. From now on I'm going to the Mex side. They call me Mex, so I'll just go to the Mex side.

I went into Houston and asked for a drink in a Mexican bar. Then I tried to talk with a whore who seemed to me to like me a little bit. I tried to buy her a drink, and some guy came over and said to me, "Listen, you son of a bitch, what you doing here?" I said, "Listen I'm having a drink, what do you mean—" Wham! He blasted me right in my face. When I tried to fight back, two or three other Mexicans got up and started in on me—ping! bang! ping! bang! Then I saw a guy pull a knife. I was terrified but I didn't want to show it. I began to yell at them, "Goddamn it! Why are you doing this to me? I'm a Puerto Rican. I always loved Mexico, to me Mexico was the greatest, I used to see it in the movies, I only thought about Mexico, it's the greatest place on earth, I always love the Mexican, and this is what I get from the Mexicans." So the tide turned, and everybody quieted down. Even the bartender and the whore told them to leave me alone.

The woman helped me get out, so I went with her, and she took me to a shack. She told me, "Listen, man, you just lucky you aren't dead. It isn't the first time these guys they do that, they would have cut you three or four times." I kissed that woman, I loved her all over the place, blasted my ass off, and in the morning I left.

When I got back to the ship, I said to myself, I don't want to be a Mex anymore. So what the fuck I am? I'm not a Mex, I'm not a white, I'm not a Negro. What am I? The truth is that in the crazy United States the same goddamn thing happened to me two or three or four times. I guess it happened to a lot of others. That's why after all those years when I came to settle in Puerto Rico, I decided I would never again leave unless I were a rich man.

When we sailed out of Houston, I was sleeping in my bunk, Red in the bunk below me, and this cracker from the engine room walked in with a young Irish kid from Brooklyn—I guess it was his first trip, too. They grabbed Red and started hitting him, one from one side and one from the other. They kept looking at me. I couldn't understand what was going on, why they were beating Red. I had just had my own beating from the Mexican, and I had this feeling that I should do something, that—¡coño!—Red was my buddy and maybe I should get in, but I didn't have the guts because the odds were so bad.

Just then somebody walked in the door and broke it up. But I kept thinking, Did they go after Red because he's my friend, because he walked with me? My psychological situation was very different in those days. If the guy that I am now were taken back then into 1946 to a situation like that, the goddamn thing would have been handled different: "Listen, you guys wanna beat me because I'm a fuckin' Negro, I'm a fuckin' Rican, I'm shit. O.K. But leave the guy alone. I'll stop walking with him"—you know, stuff like that. I would have used my Jewish savvy that I got so much of now. But I didn't have it then. The only thing I had at that time was the Rican desire to fight, and nothing else. And that was not enough, because with the beating the Mexicans gave me I wasn't up to fighting.

Well, we kept sailing. By now the trip was not so nice, because we were moving into the North Atlantic, and once you get into the North

Atlantic—no more of the Florida waters—that ocean is a bitch. By eight o'clock at night I was freezing my ass off.

Finally we got to Rotterdam to unload the coal we picked up in Houston. In those days unloading the ship would take about five, six days—not like today when—bam! bam! bam!—they empty and get out. We had a long time in Rotterdam. I went around town with Red. We started talking to some girls, and one of them starts telling me in pretty good English she's a businesswoman. But I was still such a fool I thought she meant she was in business! This was a beautiful woman, my blonde businesswoman. She took me on a trolley to her house, and finally I understood what business she was in and paid up.

Now, many of my generation and the generation before me in Puerto Rico were really ignorant. I don't know if it was that we didn't have enough education, or if it was just how primitive things were in Puerto Rico before '38. We were the guys who were just practically out of the sugar-cane fields. I didn't know the score, like with that "businesswoman." It was as if I had just left San Juan, because the Army years don't teach you all that much. The Army is your family, and the head of the family is the captain. And above him the colonel, the general, and the whole government of the United States. It was on this trip that I first came into the world.

We got back from Rotterdam and put in at Baltimore where we got paid, and Red and I went ashore. We were having a hamburger when suddenly some guy comes over, a white guy, sits down and calls me "Boogie." I didn't know what "Boogie" meant, but I could see on peoples' faces that if someone called you it, that was no good. So I knocked the guy down and jumped on top of him. The police came and wanted to take me in. But Red made a big speech to the cops, telling them that I just came out of the Army, and this guy was abusing me, that I had a lot of medals and bullshit like that. He turned the tide with that speech. Instead of going to jail, I went off with Red. But my heart was crying out, I was that kind of a fellow.

— 10 —

Forced to End Innocence (1946–1947)

SO NOW that I was back from the ship I was going to New York. Red was uncertain about what he was going to do, so I was uncertain, too. We got a room in a hotel on Eighth Avenue near the Post Office. We went to the union halls to look around for ships, but nothing was available. The weeks kept going by and the money running out, and then I began to think I better go to my sister where I can get a room without paying rent. Red decided he wanted to go to San Francisco and said I should go with him. You know, I almost did make that trip. I had enough for the ticket, but I wouldn't have had anything left. But anyway there was a thought in the back of my mind, What am I going to do in San Francisco that I can't do in New York? New York is New York, and that was that. I don't know what would have happened if I'd have gone with Red. But I really felt sorry to see him go. He took the train, he went West, and that was the end of Red.

I was looking for jobs. I would go downtown, way downtown, below 14th Street, where they had a lot of agencies for jobs: "Dishwasher here." The one thing I could always be was a dishwasher. A guy didn't speak English well. A guy didn't know anything. But he could always be a dishwasher—forty bucks a week was the pay, and then you had to give the agency guy twenty-five bucks just to get the goddamn job. If you didn't have the money, the guy would say, "All right, you don't have the money. Sign here." That meant that the first week you worked you paid the twenty-five and had about fifteen left. I didn't want that. I didn't want to be like most of the others.

They would come and first thing get jobs washing dishes. I didn't want to go into the dishwashing business because I thought if I did I'd be a dishwasher all my life. In fact guys I knew who had started washing dishes when they arrived in '46 and were still washing them in '50.

I went around looking for jobs, and I ran into this Puerto Rican who had been with me in the Army. García Marín. He was living in a little room by himself on Columbus Avenue. That was a lousy neighborhood. The houses were old, and the toilets were outside. He had a little bed and a record player, that was all. And records, too, of course. We went to his place and listened to records and drank. He told me that he smoked pot, and I told him I did, too, but he didn't have any. I told him about the *chulos* I met, those guys with the women. He was an oldtimer in New York. He had once been a *chulo,* too, but now he was in drafting school, he said, and told me I should go there.

You had to go to the Veterans' Administration and get some paper, and you could go to the drafting school free. For GIs it was easy to go to school; even the dentists were free for us. Actually, all my teeth were under the GI. I said, "Well, I'll go to drafting school and see what it is." I figured drafting was a nice job. If I learned it, I wouldn't have to be a dishwasher. So I went, and they put through the papers immediately. They gave me a drafting table, and the teacher would come and show me how to draw lines. But I couldn't get my mind on the lines, it didn't appeal to me.

On 181st and Broadway there were three theaters. I would go there once in a while. I saw The *House I Live In* about five times because I wanted to hear Frank Sinatra sing. He sang "The House I Live In" and "If You Were but a Dream." I went not to see the meaning of the movie but to listen to him. I liked to listen to his voice, and I liked his pronunciation. That way I tried to improve my English a little bit. I even took the pronunciation he had, and the guy had good diction. Not like other singers.

One day I had a date with a Neorican girl, and we went to Morningside Drive. It was early evening, and we were sitting on a bench necking, nothing too dirty, just talking and necking. Then we slid down onto the grass for about fifteen, twenty minutes, and she left her bag on the bench. When we got up, the bag was gone. I was so ignorant I thought the bag was just misplaced. So we started looking for it. It was dark by then, so in order to see I lit a fire in one of the wire trash baskets that they have in New York with all the newspapers.

Suddenly the cops were on us. We had been thinking only about the bag. She was worried about her keys and papers mostly because she didn't have much money. When the cops grabbed me, I explained about the bag, and they understood. They told us to forget about the bag, it had been stolen. I didn't have to fight with the cop because the girl could speak beautiful English and fast, so I didn't have too much trouble getting myself understood. Otherwise it would have taken me longer, and—who knows?—the cop could have beat me in the face or pushed me or something. That's one of the difficulties of people who don't speak English good and fast. Sometimes maybe the cop doesn't mean to fuck you up, but if you can't explain, he right away thinks you must be a criminal. Anyway the cops explained to my friend that these thieves dress in dark clothes, they even put on gloves and come around at night. There was a crowd like that, it was their profession.

I don't really know how New York is nowadays, but even in Puerto Rico you can't neck any more, anywhere. I mean, you just can't park. You park on Sunday, you get killed. The thing has gotten to a point where you can't go anyplace with a girl. I'm afraid, she's afraid, you're afraid. The end of innocence, that's what it is, the end of innocence. You gotta lock yourself in the room. In other words, necking and lovers' lanes are gone—people have to shack up. Before in the romantic days it used to take a guy maybe a week to get up to that pussy, but now you get there faster on account of the crime and violence and the drunks that are around town. The end of innocence used to come naturally. Now you're forced to end innocence, by our society and the new crimes. What a crazy world!

Anyway, one day when I was looking for a job I ran into Eugenio. Eugenio was one of my men when I was the sergeant in charge of the guns at St. Thomas. He was a great guitarist. Eugenio always used to say, "I'm an artist. I can't touch those guns, they're too heavy. That hurts my hands." Or, "I can't pull the grass, my hands." And I used to say, "O.K., you don't have to do nothing, just play the guitar." The guy couldn't even drive on account of his hands.

I hadn't seen Eugenio since 1942 and then there I was on 14th Street and in front of me was this short guy, about four foot nine, his coat reaching to his feet. Suddenly this guy turned his face, and I saw it was him. He was like a little midget. That's how short he was. But you know, he was such a great guy. So we said, "Let's have a drink," and we went down on Eighth Avenue to one of those Spanish restaurants near 14th Street.

Eugenio said, "I have a business now. Let me show you." I said, "Hey, man, that's great!" We got in the subway and didn't have time to talk about the business because we kept on talking about the Army and stuff. We got to the East Bronx, where the Ricans were and, of all things, he had a grocery store. I wanted to laugh my head off. Eugenio said, "This is my business, and I got a wife and kids," and what did I see but Eugenio cutting a piece of ham! That's what happened to Eugenio's magic hands—cutting a piece of ham! *¡Coño!* I had once forced sixty men under my command to believe Eugenio's idea that he was great! So I said, "Listen, you can't play guitar no more, look at your hands." He said to me, "Well, once in a while I hit it, but you know, that's the way life is."

Sometime later I ran into Johnny Newman, my friend from George Washington High School. Johnny was already finishing. He said, "Well, I'm almost done and I'm going to Aaron Prep School." This prep school was one of those schools they started after the war with all the money from the GI bill. This one was in Union Square. Johnny told me he was going there because he could make high school in one more year. I had been on the ship for those three months while Johnny was in school, but by that time the course in George Washington was over anyway. They gave me credits, because when I left it was almost at the end of the course.

So Johnny kept insisting, "Listen, Benjy, don't be a fool, come with me. I'll finish in a year, but you can stay there two years and make your high school and then we can go to NYU." I did it. They gave me credit for my one year of high school from Puerto Rico because I was a GI. Johnny finished in December, by Christmas, and then he was going to NYU in February. And I stayed on in prep school. With Johnny gone, I was by myself, helpless again.

I was helpless because of the country. I started feeling all the tremendous pressure and the antagonism many Ricans feel in New York. The thing is that at the time Johnny left I was supposed to start my other year, and if I would have hustled, I could have been through in June and had my diploma. But I was left to myself, and the Cuban, José, was just around the corner, tempting me.

José was living with the woman who gave him money. He supplied the pot, and the bunch of Cubans and I used to get high. All these guys had women who gave them eighty, a hundred on the weekend, and two hundred, three hundred dollars every week. And I was broke. Then José started giving me money. "Here, Benjy, don't worry about it, here's ten bucks."

Johnny met José and he said to me, "The Cuban is O.K., Benjy, but that stuff is no good for you." So what happened? Johnny went to NYU, and I stayed with the Cuban.

— 11 —

B-29s (1947)

"I'M GONNA GO TO CUBA," José said to me. "You wanna go with me?" And I said, "All right, I'll go to Cuba with you." José had his problems, because he was a B-29. A B-29 was a Cuban that left Cuba on a twenty-nine-day visa,[1] to Miami, and would then go somewhere else in the States (like New York, for example) because the economic situation was so bad in Cuba. He was one of the lucky ones who could raise the money you needed in order to get a twenty-nine-day visa. So if José went back to Cuba, he wouldn't be able to return to the States. That was his problem.

He asked me to help him. "Do you have a brother who has a birth certificate?" I said, "I have a brother, but he's in Puerto Rico." And then, "Well, I have a brother who's dead." And he said, "That's it! Send a letter to your sister in Puerto Rico, and tell her to send you his birth certificate. Then we can work this thing out." In New York with Puerto Rican papers you can get a birth certificate in English. So I wrote to Puerto Rico, and my sister sent me a birth certificate of a kid who died about twenty-two years before. I took the certificate and went with José to the Puerto Rican office in New York. He got himself a Puerto Rican certificate in English, so he could be assigned identification in the States.

For additional papers we went to Boston. José and I found out about a guy that was in this racket, selling seaman's papers for one hundred dollars. Now the Coast Guard issued these papers for free if

---

1. Apparently the visa was officially identified as a "V-29"; however, Cuban pronunciation of V as B turned its popular identification into "B-29," after the World War II bomber.

you had a birth certificate proving you were an American citizen. But this guy was selling them. I don't know what kind of a connection he had with the Coast Guard, but the guy was a Portuguese. You know, there are a lot of Portuguese in Boston!

We went by train to Miami. And in Miami we got onto a ship and went to Havana. When we got to Havana we went to José's house. His mother was a nice lady. I don't think she knew the kind of life her son was living. I myself at that time couldn't evaluate his life as I do now. I went all around Havana with José.

One day we were in downtown Havana, in a district called El Barrio Colón, about a block off the main drag, not too far away from the Capitol. This section of the city was about ten square blocks, and the whole place was whores. I would say there were about one hundred and fifty or two hundred whorehouses all concentrated in that section. I had never lived through anything like it. I had been in Europe, I had been in whorehouses in Marseilles and other places in France, but nothing was like Havana.

José says, "Let's go in." And I went in, and what happens? Immediately this woman puts out her hand and grabs my thing right there and tries to feel it. I got so surprised I was shaking. Imagine a woman grabbing your thing. Anyway, I pushed her away, and then everything calmed down. You walk in there and immediately, *"Ven conmigo,* come with me, come with me." I didn't know which way to go. I asked José how much the whores charged, and he told me fifty cents. Imagine the economic situation if you can have a whore for fifty cents. No wonder there was a B-29 to New York! People had to do better than that.

We went to a bar to have a few drinks. Suddenly a guy came in and laid a piece of paper on the table. And in the middle he threw a lot of white powder. Cocaine. Everybody grabbed a piece of cardboard and sniffed the stuff. I didn't want to look like a fool, so I did the same.

After I did the cocaine, I stepped out on the street. I saw a cop coming, and I ran back and yelled, "Watch out! A cop is coming!" They all laughed, and then I saw the cop walk in and go over to the table. I was scared, pushing myself close to the door. But the cop just came over, took a sniff, shook hands with everybody, stepped out to look at the street, came back in again, and sniffed a little bit more. Then they introduced me to him. "This is our friend from New York, a Puerto Rican. *Un Americano,* this is a good boy, a buddy of José." I was completely shocked. The point is that Cuba was really a corrupt society.

When they would introduce me to someone, they would say, "This is Frankie." They always called me Frankie because I used to sing all the time. I loved to and at that time I used to sing like Frank Sinatra. I used to learn his songs, I knew them by heart, and every time I had a few drinks I would sing Sinatra songs. "Close to you/I will always stay/Close to you/ Though you're far away."

I stayed in Havana thirty days. José's mother, as I said before, was a very nice lady, and his father was a very nice man, too. He was a real *guajiro*,[2] *un campesino,* what you call a peasant. This man didn't know how to write. He was quite old, he must have been over sixty. Looking back, I can see that he was a good man. He loved the land, but he couldn't work anymore, so he came to live in the city with his family. All José's brothers were in business. One seemed to be smarter. He was the president of some business organization. He was a good man, too. Another brother was a nice man, too, but like José, he just couldn't learn to write.

José didn't have too much education, maybe second grade, third grade, something like that. He couldn't write his name clear. I showed him how to write it. He was intelligent, he wasn't a bad guy, but the only thing was, he was a pimp. I don't blame him for being a pimp, he didn't have the means to develop his intelligence. He didn't know what he was doing. It's like my father used to say, many years ago when I was a kid, *"Dime con quién andas y te digo quién eres,"* tell me who you walk with, that's who you are.

I know. I did it myself, pimping. I never put my heart and soul in

---

2. A Cuban term denoting "peasant"; like the Puerto Rican term *jíbaro*, it connotes both "country bumpkin" as well as a person of rural virtue. As in the case of *jíbaro*, *guajiro* has a connotation of astuteness: *"un guajiro lepero,"* for example, refers to a crafty peasant.

it, I guess I never got my license like they told me, because I was always a failure at it. I think I tried three times. Three times they actually got the women for me. Put them in my hands, and I couldn't hold them. They did know how to make a business out of it, my Cuban friends, and they did make money out of it. On this trip to Havana, José spent about two thousand dollars. I wasn't paying anything, he was paying everything for me.

I met this girl who lived about three or four blocks from where José stayed in Havana. In the beginning I started looking at her, she started looking at me. Her name was Marta. I started going out with her and talking with her. One day I got up to her house. She introduced me to her mother, and her mother was divorced. I was like infatuated with her. She was only about seventeen years old, very nice-looking. I took her address and she took mine, and then I left for New York with José.

On the way back into the United States, José's certificate worked without any problem. We stayed in Miami for a while, lying around on the beach. And then we took a train to New York. When we got to New York, José went home to his old lady. Her name was Yolanda. She was in her forties, close to fifty years old. And that was the woman who gave him the ten bucks every day before he started living with her. That's the way she *levantó a*[3] José, as they say in Puerto Rico. She was quite happy to see him, and she had a lot of money for him. I think she had a thousand or two thousand dollars saved, from her working those thirty days.

This Yolanda, she had two houses in New York, one on 77th around Central Park West or Columbus Avenue, in a basement, and another on the Upper East Side. I never went to these houses, and José never did either, because that's the way these pimps worked. They didn't see their women, except at night when they would come around with the money. She had three or four women every day inside these houses of hers. She collected from the women, I think, and then she

---

3. To have picked someone up and made him yours.

would give the money to José. She was quite happy because José was a nice-looking guy, young, and she was an old lady. Of course this is one reason why women do these things.

With my experience of being around those people, I could see three reasons why a woman would work like that and give the money to a man. First, because she is alone, she doesn't have anybody to look after her. A whore is worth nothing in society, she can't go anywhere, she's nothing, and she gets chased by the cops. I would call pimping and prostitution the lower depth, the lower depth. You can go down as deep as you can, but once you get into that, you're really in the lower depth. No matter how much money can be made down there.

The second reason she gives her money to a pimp is because this man, she thinks, belongs to her, she controls him, even though he seems to be controlling her. "I give him so much money," she says, "He's got to be nice to me." No matter how rough the guy is, there's always a tender moment in this relation. He has to surrender to her, one way or the other. That's the way it is between a man and a woman.

And number three, the economics. I guess in a society like ours nowadays, if there is money in it. . . . For example, there are women who charge a hundred dollars for one night in New York. Beautiful women, and talented women, too—but a hundred dollars a night!

Anyway, this is my opinion of the business, I think it is the lowest any man can get into.

All this time I was still living with my sister. One day I ran into Johnny. "What've you been doing, Benjy?" I didn't give him too much of an answer.

— 12 —

Marriage by Proxy (1948–1950)

ONE DAY I got a letter, from that girl Marta in Havana. She said she wants to come to New York and get married. I told José about it, and he said, "Listen, Benjy, why you don't write her to come to New York so she can go to work for you." I didn't want to do that. In Havana we had had a real romance. Still in her letter she said she had had some kind of trouble and wasn't a virgin any more. You see how cruel life can be when I found out she wasn't a virgin, José's idea didn't seem so bad. So with his help I sent Marta my proposal.

A few days later I got a letter from her. "I'm willing to come to New York any way I can. Whatever you say, I'll do." She wanted me to come back to Havana, marry her, and bring her back. But I didn't have any money for the trip. José said, "Well, listen, I know what we can do. You sign a power to a lawyer in Havana. My brother will find you one."

So we wrote to his brother and made all the arrangements. We had to go to the Cuban consulate and fill out papers, then a lawyer in Havana could marry her by proxy, and she could get a visa. José gave me the money for all this and also for Marta's trip. Finally I got a letter that she was coming over as my wife.

I didn't want her to get to my sister's house, because I didn't want my sister to know what my plans for her were. So I decided that she should fly to Miami and take the bus from there to New York, and I would meet her in the Greyhound Station and take her to a room somewhere. That was the plan, but at the Greyhound Station buses were coming and going, and I didn't see her. What happened, she went to 33rd Street, and the girl was not dumb, she had some money and took a cab to my sister's house.

By the time I got home she was already sitting in the living room and talking to my sister. I was very upset because I didn't want the girl to be in my sister's house. And right away my sister started putting ideas into her head. "You go to work. I'll get you a job." And that's what happened. I took a rented room, I think it was on 180th Street, and I stayed with her there. My sister got her a job in a factory. When José found out, he was mad at me. I saw him three or four times, and he wouldn't even speak to me.

And then I ran into Johnny. He came and visited us. We went out together, downtown, to the movies, and soon we were hanging out with Johnny's crowd.

She was working, and I went back to school. I got back into Aaron Prep School as a veteran drawing $105 from the government again. I think she was making about 35 bucks a week or something like that. We used to go out on Sundays like an ordinary couple, and I felt we were normal people.

Sometimes Marta would go to school with me. One of the teachers there kept saying to me, "Listen, that's a beautiful wife you have. I understand she's working in a factory. She could come work in my house and make a lot more money." But now I was falling in love with Marta, and talk like that made me jealous. You see, prejudice ends with the blast. The blast can even turn around the virginity problem. Once you fall in love, you forget and you forgive, and it's gone. Once you get hooked you don't care if the woman was blasting before. The blast can do that, pussy can do that. It's what José used to say. "A pussy has more power than two ox."[1] He related that to when he was a kid where an ox was the most powerful thing in the field. The pussy was more powerful than two ox!

Marta had a sister in Cuba. She was really desperate to get to New York, too—things in Cuba were so bad, and she was out of work. She figured with a sister in the States married to a Rican—after all a

---

1. "*Un bollo jala más que dos bueyes.*"

Rican is a citizen—it would be easier for her to come to New York. We got her a room somewhere near us, I don't remember exactly where, because Marta was the one who used to go there. And she got a job in the factory, too.

One day Marta told me her sister had a boyfriend and was going to get married. I remember the name of the boyfriend, and I can't remember the name of the sister! Isn't that something funny? Ronzoni was his name—Italian fellow. Once I went to her room and found a priest there. A young priest, Father Ahearn, the guy must have been thirty years old, blue eyes, very tall, very fair, very nice-looking guy. With the dirty mind I had in those days, I said to myself, This priest might be trying to make it with the girl.

In any case, instead of getting violent, I held myself in check while he was trying to explain to me that I was living in sin. Right away I told him that Marta and I were married, that we had papers. And he said, "No, in front of God you are not married." He wanted us to get married in church, like this Italian *beato*—how do you say it in English? This believer, this fanatic.

I was going to be the godfather[2] at the sister's wedding, so I had to go to the rectory and sign a lot of papers. There was a picture of Pius XII on the wall, and I spit at it. My wife said, "Why are you doing that! He's gonna go crazy, the Italian." The Italians, and the Spaniards too, believe that the Pope is a big thing, but to me the Pope was nothing. The Cubans are more like the Ricans. The women go to church even when they don't believe in it. The Italians are more like the Irish. So the wedding took place, I stood godfather, and Marta was the bridesmaid.

And afterward Father Ahearn kept after me to get married in church, too. We were starting to have trouble anyway, because the marriage was illegal in the United States, even though Marta got married by proxy in Cuba. The Immigration Department didn't approve of that kind of marriage. So I gave in to Father Ahearn, and he did the ceremony. It was not like the sister's, which was a wedding with a

---

2. Lopez mistranslated *padrino* here; he meant "best man."

lot of people. There were just the two of us, and two witnesses, in front of the altar.

So Marta was not hustling. I was mad at José, and José was mad at me. One night I went with her to a Puerto Rican dance on 180th Street. After one dance I went in the kitchen and started drinking. Suddenly I saw a crowd of guys coming over. "Listen, can I dance with your wife?" I was drinking and didn't know what was going on. I said, "All right." One after another—"Can I have a dance with your wife?" This crowd was young, Rican high school kids. So I began to wonder what was going on. Finally I understood that she was so good-looking, she was the queen of the goddamn place, and everyone wanted to get it on with her. I got crazy mad with jealousy, grabbed her by the hand like some kind of savage, and dragged her out of there.

By this time we moved to 189th. We were living with an old lady from Vienna. And this lady was very crazy about us. We used to pay about eight or ten dollars a week for the room. She used to take us into the rooms and look at us like we were something and said that we looked beautiful, like two little things, words like that. "I like to see young people that are so nice." She had a piano there and she would play for us sometimes. You know, "Listen to this," and I would stay quiet and listen to it, and it was beautiful. She used to listen to the operas on Sundays. She would open the door so that the music would get into our room. Sometimes she would want us to take coffee with her. She was beautiful but she was old, a very nice lady. She loved me and Marta.

Then I started up with José again. His brother came from Cuba and was living in a house where a friend of mine, Joe, was the super. I ran into him when I went to see my friend and he was visiting his brother. He started coming to my house. One day he came when Marta was away at work and caught me trying to press a pair of my pants. He said to me, "Look what you're doing. See how fucked up you are! You don't have to do those things. You're a fool, you're a fool. You have a woman and she's doing nothing. And you don't have any money. You could have all the money you want." I told him that

Marta was O.K. the way she was. One day I had a fight with her and yelled at her that I couldn't help it, she had to keep on working till I finished school. I went and got drunk with José. He said to me, "You go over there, man, and tell that woman she should go out and do what she promised to do." I went back to the house, half drunk, and told her, "Why don't you go work with José's woman." And she answered, "Yeah, man, I'd rather do that than work in this factory and get my hands all blistered and cut up!"

The next day I took her in the subway to 110th Street. And standing there were José's brother and his brother's woman, and José's woman, and a whole lot of other Cuban women. Pretty soon they were all laughing together, and Marta said everything was O.K. Everybody was happy, and we had a few drinks, José and me and his brother. The women didn't drink—José and his brother wouldn't let them.

José gave me ten dollars and said, "Listen, Benjy, you bring Marta around tomorrow." So the next day she went to work. When she came back that first night, I remember, I was feeling very bad. José told me, "When you pick her up and bring her to the room, you don't take the money. You let her put the money in the drawer. Then you come by later on and take the money, and the next day you give her ten dollars for a cab." I don't know if the other women instructed her, but she put the money in the top drawer. I think she must have had about sixty dollars or so. I grabbed the money like José told me, and I gave her ten dollars.

Then José said to me, "Listen, now you got money, you can start playing the numbers." So I started hanging around like that. We used to play a lot of pool in a few poolrooms where guys hung out and sold reefers and things like that. I never liked pool, but the Cubans came straight to these pool halls in New York, along with the little tough boys from the neighborhood. They would smoke reefers right out in the open, not just in the bathrooms! Have a drag, pass it around fast, keep an eye out for the cops. You get to the point when you hang around a place like that for long enough you can feel the cops even when they're in plainclothes. José was keen on pool. I couldn't play very well, and I never felt too happy in that poolroom. Still, with José I had security—I mean I had a safe meal ticket.

But as time went by I started feeling violent toward Marta. I knew I was wrong, because she was doing it for me, and before I had made her a hustler I was in love with her. I was all torn up because she was sleeping with other men, and I couldn't stand it.

And finally one night I beat her up over some argument—I can't remember, it was twenty-five years ago. I broke her nose. She was bleeding, and I had to take her in a cab to Columbia Medical Center. When we got there, she wouldn't tell them anything. "How did it happen?" "I fell." That only made me feel worse. In fact, she didn't seem to mind or get mad at me. I was the one who was suffering from this life. You see this is a transition for me between the naive guy of the island and the shit of José.

At this time, I was still going to school, but I started to goof off. This thing broke down my schooling completely. I stopped reading my books. I couldn't study anymore. So I started missing school. And then I had worse trouble when I went back. At the beginning I had good marks, but in the end I had to leave Aaron Prep for a while.

The first time I went to see Joe I had met his daughter Barbara. Now I started to go for her. She must have been about seventeen years old when I met her, she was only in high school. And she kept chasing me. One day when I was coming out with Marta, I found her on my sister's stoop. I said, "Hello, where's Joe?" "Well, Daddy wants to see you," she told me. Marta was smarter than I, she told me right away that Barbara was after me. I wouldn't touch her then on account of Joe.

Then there was this time after Marta had started whoring. I was visiting José's brother upstairs of Joe, and Barbara was alone downstairs. She called me through the window, "Benjy, come over, I want to ask you something," and I couldn't resist. I went, and I grabbed her and started kissing her, and right then and there I had her. I blasted her with rubber bands.[3] I wasn't too worried because I didn't give a

---

3. Lopez means "rubbers" or "condoms."

damn about Marta anymore. She was a whore. Barbara was not a whore, and I got myself tied up with her. Joe didn't say anything, nobody said anything—Barbara and I were now blasting away, and everything was terrific.

Then one night Marta and I were waiting at the subway on our way downtown to Times Square, and Barbara came up to us. These two goddamn women started a big fight, one in Spanish and one in English. This one is telling the other in Spanish that I'm her husband, and the other one is saying that I love only her. Barbara called Marta a whore, they almost got into a fistfight. I tried to get between them, while people started gathering around us. Finally Barbara left, and Marta and I went on our way.

Another time Marta came to me and said she didn't want to whore anymore. "I want to be with you, Frankie. I don't want to be with all those other guys." I said, "Man, that's it!" See, I was already a son of a bitch. I still might have had some feeling for her, but I got like stone. "Fuck you, you're a fuckin' whore, that's it." José had always told me you have to treat women bad. In Cuba he had a reputation for being a *perchero,* someone who would hit a whore with a clothes hanger. I wasn't that bad, but I was a son of a bitch.

Then she missed her period. I was afraid she was pregnant. I said to myself, I can't let this woman have a baby, because I don't know whose baby it is. I took her to the doctor, and she was pregnant—and the whole thing was on my shoulders. I talked it over with José, and he said, "Don't worry, man, I got a woman who will take her over, put in a little *goma,* a little rubber thing, and pull it out like nothing." But I was scared. Then Marta said to me, "If you don't wanna do it here in New York, I can go to Havana and in no time everything will be fixed." I bought her clothes and a ticket and sent her off to Havana to get rid of the kid.

I felt lonely. You get used to living with a woman steady. When you live alone and shack up once in a while—you get a woman to stay with you a few days and then get another one, let's say, for two or three weeks or for a day—when the woman leaves, you don't miss it.

But when you live steady with one, let's say for six months or so, you just feel lonely At first I thought she'd be back.

Anyway, she wrote me that she met the doctor in Havana who was going to do the abortion. Soon she said it was all over and wrote, "Benjy, come and get me." Now I was still lonely for the woman, but I didn't have enough push to go to Havana and bring her back. About two weeks later I got a letter from her mother saying that I was no good, that I had done bad to her daughter. She must have told her mother what she had been doing in New York. So that was the end of that. She stayed in Havana and I stayed in New York.

I was sorry to lose Marta, but at the same time I was glad she didn't come. I missed her, but if she had come back to me, she would have had to go out and hustle—there was no other way. And I couldn't have stood that. Whatever happened, I sure didn't want a woman that was hustling to have a kid of mine. It was bad enough that I had let them make me get married in church.

After that I was a mess. I didn't shave, I didn't comb my hair. One day I was smoking pot with José and his brother, I wasn't shaved, and José told me, *"Coño, este* . . . you made a big mistake. You didn't have to send that woman to Havana. That could have been done over here." They started saying, "Frankie doesn't sing anymore, Sinatra is sleeping."

— 13 —

Every University Has a Dubinsky (1950–1951)

MEANWHILE somehow I finally got enough credits from Aaron Prep to graduate. My old friend Johnny, who was now studying at NYU, came to me and said, "O.K., Benjy, you're going to NYU."

The day I went to register I met Johnny, Dubinsky, and a few of the fellows. Every university has a Dubinsky. I already knew about Dubinsky. Everybody used to talk about him. He was the brain, he got all *A's*. They called him "the Commissar" because he was so bright.[1] All the students, the professors, everybody respected Hyman Dubinsky tremendously. He was a short guy, blue eyes and black hair. He liked me immediately, and I liked him, too. I liked the way he handled himself. He would sit on the stoop of the student building looking over Washington Square, and everybody would come around him.

When I was registering he sat down on the stoop, grabbed my program, and said, "Let's see what we're gonna give Benjy." We registered in the gym, in the basketball court, and thanks to Dubinsky I was in and out in a jiffy, and I came away with a terrific program. I didn't even know what the heck I was taking, but it was a terrific program!

The classes started. I had a course in psychology and a course in philosophy. I had history with Dr. Henry. I got Rogers for language and Mann, the son of a bitch, for education. My first grades showed that I was doing O.K. When I had trouble doing a term paper, Johnny would take me to Dubinsky's house in the Village. I have never seen as many books as he had—he had more books than a library, that son

---

1. A more understandable reason for Dubinsky's title is revealed at the end of this chapter.

of a gun. He could knock off two books a day. He was a phenomenon. Johnny would say, "We've got a problem. Benjy needs a term paper for this or a term paper for that." And Dubinsky would say, "All right, we'll give him a term paper immediately." Once a teacher gave me an *A* for Dubinsky's term paper. He would just sit down at the typewriter and rattle it off. He even put in English mistakes so it would look right. Johnny used to say sometimes, "Goddamn, my English is getting broken working with this Benjamín around all the time. I can't even speak the language anymore!"

Each professor has his own way in class. I remember Dr. Henry's pattern of history course. He would go to the board and draw a big line with hills and valleys and, according to him, that was the pattern of history. I got a *C* in that class. In philosophy I had a woman professor. I had a paper to do, and I did it myself. She called me over and said, "Benjamín, you think hard. And that's good." She gave me a *B*. I loved that time, it was terrific.

The psychology teacher was strange. I don't know why, but sometimes he used to come and put his finger on the answers for me. It was something amazing. I would be struggling away with my exam paper, and he would walk around the room, and when he got to me he would put his finger, ta-ta-ta, on the true/false answers in the exam. I had a good grade, I think a *C*, in that psychology class.

The history of education I studied with a Dr. Mann. He wrote a book on education, and he was a prick. He gave me a *D*. I just couldn't get through to that guy. He used to think he was a great teacher. The textbook for the course was his book—I guess that's why he was so proud. "That's my book ... in my book . . . you're getting my book. On page so and so. . . ." Anyway, he didn't like me, that guy. I think I submitted one term paper, and he knew it wasn't mine He gave me a *D*. If there is ever a revolution in the States, that guy should be shot. He taught us about John Dewey[2] and William James[3]—easy stuff. I

---

2. John Dewey (1859-1952), an American philosopher, was one of the founders of "pragmatism."

3. William James (1842-1910), an American psychologist and philosopher, another of the founders of "pragmatism," was well-known for his work on the psychology of religious experience.

could have had an *A* on that stuff if I had only read the book. Dubinsky, of course, knew it by heart, but he gave Dubinsky a *D* on my paper. Dubinsky—who had never even had a *B*!

But one thing about that class, there was a girl from Boston in it, a red-headed Irish girl, and she used to like me. Wherever I went, there she was, talking to me. So I said to myself, O.K, I'm gonna give her a blast. She was a major in psychology. She came from Massachusetts to NYU to get her master's. I said to her, "How come you go to school in New York if you're from Massachusetts? Why didn't you go to school up there where they have so many schools?" One day the idea came to me, Today's the day I'm gonna blast her. I think our class got out about four in the afternoon, and I grabbed her and said I wanted to talk to her. I took her up to a little hotel on 59th Street that I knew. I got a room and a bottle and started giving the psychology woman drinks. So we were drinking, and she was talking about psychology, and I was putting my hands up her legs. She was getting hot, too, it's human. I wasn't doing nothing that's not human, you know. And then I blasted her. It was her first. She cried and everything, and we went again and again. Good thing I was a young guy.

When I saw her in school the next day, I didn't want to blast her any more. I went to Johnny and said, "You have to help me do something with that Massachusetts business there. She won't leave me alone." Johnny and the guys didn't like her too much. I don't know why, she wasn't a bad-looking woman, but Dubinsky didn't like her, Johnny didn't like her, nobody liked her. I think she got the idea because she stopped coming around.

All this time I was still mixed up with my Cuban friends. One of them introduced me to a woman, thirty, thirty-five years old, an average-looking woman. She was Puerto Rican, I found out she was a hustler. She didn't have a steady man with her, she worked just for money to get by on. I never thought about getting into the pimping business again, but I talked to my friend the Cuban, and he told me, "This time you gonna get your license. This time I'm gonna supervise the operation."

I used to come out of school around three o'clock. Then I would go and pick her up and hang around with her for a while. I moved into her apartment and brought my books and clothes in. Every morning I went to school, and she would go to work. Soon she was giving me money. She was hustling then at 110th Street, 111th Street and Fifth Avenue. That's the lower deck, as we used to say in New York, the worst place in the world.

I would come out of the school, take the subway up there to see her, and she would be standing on the corner. She told the other whores, "This is my man here, he goes to the university," and then they would all look at me like I was something strange. Whenever she came in, she would put the money on top of the drawer. Then in the morning I would take it, put it in my pocket, and give her fifteen bucks or whatever she told me she needed. She used to make, I would say, an average of seventy-five bucks a day. So I would take almost sixty for myself. She was keeping me, as the New York pimps say.

Let's face it, with sixty bucks a day I could be a sharp dresser and always have money in my pocket. I had five topcoats, $150 topcoats. Every day I put on a new topcoat. The regular students didn't dress like that. I used to go to the student building. I had a girlfriend I would meet there. Her name was Ruth. She was a Jewish girl from Jersey. And she was great. She was beautiful and nice, that girl, and she was so intelligent and sympathetic. She wasn't really wealthy, but her family lived very good. Ruthy was always on my side, and wherever we went she was one of the crowd.

We used to go to Rocco's on 4th Street. It was a student hangout. And I used to put my feet up on the table and say, "O.K., let's have a drink." Johnny would drink, Dubinsky would drink, everybody would drink, because I was paying, man. Because I had the money, you know! Johnny used to tell the guys, "Benjy has an oil field in Venezuela." Ruthy and another girl used to go with us, and we used to have a lot of fun. Sometimes we would drive around. I got myself a Buick, and now and then I would drive Ruthy to Jersey. Aye-yi-yi, what days those were.

I went to Phil Kronfeld's and bought myself a big fedora like Truman had, and I walked into the student building with a big cigar.

Ruthy and everybody started teasing, "Look at Benjy, a big Havana cigar and that crazy hat." I was pissed off at what they said about that hat. I was holding a book I was supposed to read, *Brave New World* by Aldous Huxley,[4] brand new. I threw the book on the floor in a temper. It was as if I had committed a crime. Those guys didn't just read books, they loved them. "What the hell are you doing?" said the Commissar.

This was the time when North Korea invaded South Korea, and Truman decided to send the American troops in. Johnny was mad at Truman for sending the GIs. "The sonofabitch is crazy!" The students were all clear in their mind, they were against going to that war. One day, it was November 1950, some Puerto Ricans tried to shoot Truman in Blair House. When the news of that came out, I happened to be in the subway. And I thought, goddamn, everybody's looking at me because I'm a Rican and some Puerto Ricans tried to shoot the president. I got out at 4th Street and bumped into Ruthy and Johnny. I said, "Goddamnit, those headlines, everybody's going to blame all the Puerto Ricans." Ruthy started laughing and said, "Well, the only thing wrong is they failed, Benjy." I can still see her face, her beautiful face, Jesus Christ, so nice, that was class. Here I was worrying all the way down on the subway with all those peasants looking at me like they'd like to get me, and when I got to school, my friends, Ruthy, Johnny, the Commissar were saying, "The only thing wrong is they failed." Goddamn! I said to myself.

Some of the girls I knew in the university used to have sorority dances. They had them, I remember, in the Broadway Central Hotel, that's on Broadway close to Washington Square. One Saturday I went to one of those dances. When I got there, the lights were out, and the guys with the girls were lying around all over the place. At first I was a little bit thrown by this because Ricans don't do that, though it's very common with the Americans, especially in the universities. Anyway, so that night I didn't get home until about two or three

---

4. Aldous Huxley (1894-1963), an English writer, was best known for *Brave New World* which warned that science and technology could triumph at the expense of creativity and the human spirit.

o'clock. And my woman was mad because I was coming home so late. I said, "Listen, I can't be here waiting for you all the time." But I went to sleep, and in the morning when I woke up, she was still mad, shouting, "There's lipstick on your suit." I must have got lipstick on my suit when I was dancing with the girls. That was on a Sunday. I went downtown to a movie, and she went out to work, like she always did. When I came home that night, she was still mad.

The next day I came from school in the afternoon, and all my clothes were missing. I had about ten suits, a couple of heavy coats, and she took everything. She left me my shoes. So I went to Fifth Avenue and 110th Street to see if I could find her, but I couldn't. The next day I went to see the Cuban who introduced me to her, and he got in touch with her through his woman. Finally she returned my clothes to the Cuban, and he said to me, "You lost your license again! You have to take care of your woman, you can't screw around with another woman." So I said, "Maybe I'm not a good pimp." I was with her something like six months. After that I went to live with my sister again.

One day at my sister's house I met this *cura,* this priest, his name was Father Illich.[5] The guy was very suave. He spoke Spanish perfectly. I was going downtown, and he offered to give me a lift. See, this priest used to come uptown to Incarnation Church. I think he was then working in Cardinal Spellman's headquarters at 51st Street and Madison Avenue.

In those days I was reading a book called *The Power* of *Positive Thinking* by Norman Vincent Peale.[6] And I was getting very interested in this thing, partly through Johnny who used to talk with me a lot about religion. Johnny had grown up a Protestant, then he became a Unitarian. So anyway I was reading this book, and I thought it was

---

5. The reference is to Ivan Illich (1926-2002), the author and social commentator. Illich at this time was assistant pastor in an Irish Puerto Rican parish in New York City. Subsequently he served as vice-rector of the Catholic University of Puerto Rico, before he founded the Center for Intercultural Documentation in Mexico.

6. Norman Vincent Peale (1898-1993) was a Protestant preacher and author promoting what he called "positive thinking."

hot stuff. This Peale guy said, "Suppose, for example, you're driving, and the street is full of snow and dangerous. You say, God is with me and nothing bad is going to happen, and that gives you confidence. And you can control your car better. And then you get more optimistic about whatever you're going to do."

Father Illich had a big Cadillac with a uniformed chauffeur and everything, and all the way downtown we argued about the book.[7] "Forget about it," he kept saying. "Forget about that *Power of Positive Thinking.* Read the book of Father Sheen." Illich understood all my crazy ideas. At that time I was very leftist in my thinking. I was for independence for Puerto Rico, and I used to go around writing on the blackboard in my classes, "Down with the free enterprise system!" Father Illich understood all this, but he kept on pushing me to read that book by Father Sheen.[8]

That was a great time at NYU. Johnny worked hard. His father was dead, and his mother, an Irishwoman, was desperately poor. He used to tell me how in the 1930s he walked around practically barefooted. He had been in the Navy, and when he came back he was in a big hurry to make something of himself. He and Dubinsky, those guys were intelligent and at the same time very good students.

Dubinsky worked out some kind of system for getting thousands and thousands of dollars' worth of books on the GI bill and reselling them. You know, we were supplying all the students with books that were being paid for by the Veterans Administration. At the end the VA came to the school to investigate. They called Johnny, they called Dubinsky and a few others. They called me, too, but they didn't press too much on me. They must have figured this dumb Puerto Rican didn't know what was going on anyway.

They charged Dubinsky. We had a farewell party for him before

---

7. I checked this out with Illich who told me he often brought people with him to discuss one matter or another on his way to funerals. Lopez subsequently suggested that this conversation must have taken place after some such event when the big car owned by the archdiocese was being returned.

8. Fulton John Sheen (1895-1979), a Catholic archbishop, was one of the first religious television broadcasters and author of over 70 books.

they took him off to Riker's Island. I think he only went to jail for seven or eight months, and the last I heard of him he was a professor at the New School.

The university, it's a nice life, man. I think I had about a year and a half or two there, and it was great. But first Dubinsky got taken away, and then Johnny left to go get his master's, and I was by myself. Ruthy was gone, even the redhead was gone. And I just couldn't work out in another crew. My guys were already graduate students, and everybody knew them! I even had my connections in the bursar's office because of them. I mean, they had a kingdom.

Anybody can get a degree in any university in the United States without too much effort. "I came out of Yale, I came out of Harvard." That's bullshit. To get a degree from Harvard all you have to know is how to work your way around. You have to get in good with the crowd—if not, you're fucked. Dubinsky wouldn't have done a term paper for just anybody. But for me he would do it because he had a soul, and he liked me.

If I had entered school with Dubinsky and that crowd from the beginning, I could have pulled together with them. But now I was all by myself. I just couldn't get to the new crowd of guys coming up. So I decided I couldn't go back to school, I had to get a job. The thing was, I didn't want to go washing dishes, so I started going out on the ships more steadily.

— 14 —

How Eisenhower Ruined the Neighborhood (1947–1952)

DURING ALL THIS TIME the Cubans were dealing marihuana and cocaine and other drugs. I was in a kind of whirlpool just moving around with the current, and I was able to pull through without really getting hurt bad. But a lot of friends of mine really got fucked up with the law.

The Cubans I hung around with always were smoking reefers. They would get up at nine o'clock and light one up; they smoked an average of eight or ten a day, every day. A reefer is something that you can take or leave alone. You can go without for months, and it won't bother you. It's all a matter of economics. If you don't have the money to buy it, you get along without it.

Now cocaine, that's a little different. Cocaine is much more expensive. You had to pay fifteen dollars, sometimes twelve for a little bit, for a *pomito*[1] the size of the tip of a pen. I tried cocaine ten or fifteen times, maybe more, but with me it wasn't a steady deal. Cocaine doesn't hook you like that other goddamn thing, that *tecata,* that heroin. We used to blow cocaine in the nose. Or we would put it in our mouths and feel like our tongues were so big. Sometimes we even put it on our pricks when we were going to shack up. Then we would start blasting and blasting and blasting. Sometimes you put your hand on a woman's pussy with that stuff and then blast. She will feel like she's got a tree trunk inside her, one of those goddamn Canadian pines!

That *tecata,* though, is another thing altogether. I had it one time,

---

1. A small bottle.

and I almost died. It was that time when I was still living with Uncle. He was out hacking one night, and some Cubans and Ricans were with me in the apartment and started shooting up. I was chicken and didn't want to take it, but finally I said, "Fuck it, I'll try this goddamn thing, too." I took a shot and went to my room. Instantly it got bad, I felt like vomiting, like the world was going out from under me.

I said to myself, That's it, never in my life again. Because in addition to feeling sick, I had lost all my powers, and that is one thing I have always been very careful about. I never get drunk to the point of losing my head, my mental capacity. I drink scotch with everybody, but while all the rest get drunk, I decide how far I'm going to go and stick right there. I've been like that ever since one time in the Army when I was drunk and almost threw myself under an oncoming truck.

Anyway, I swore I would never lose that goddamn mind again, and that night with the *tecata* was the very last.

I knew this guy Paco who got into heroin. I liked the guy, but he used to sit in the streets with his face gone—a young guy who couldn't even shave himself. I would say, "Hello, Paco," and he wouldn't even know me. I don't know why, but the Ricans got hooked on heroin easier than did the Cubans. In general—you have your exceptions—Cubans prefer cocaine and Ricans prefer heroin. Maybe it was the price, heroin was cheaper than cocaine.

The president of Columbia University lived on Morningside Drive, Ike Eisenhower. On that street guys used to sell reefers, *bolita*,[2] all the rackets. It was quiet on that street—no guards, no police, no nothing. But once Ike got nominated to run for president of the United States, suddenly there were a lot of cops all over the place. The guys got scared. Not that these cops were actually paying attention to them; the cops had other things on their mind than whether a guy was having a reefer. They were looking out for the security of the candidate. But the whole system of rackets moved away from that street because the guys they served didn't like the cops and wouldn't come around. And when the rackets moved, the merchants started protesting,

---

2. The numbers racket.

"There's no business here anymore." You know, the guy that ran the numbers in the morning used to have a cup of coffee or a breakfast. Now the *chulo* wasn't going to the restaurant any more. And the restaurant owner really started kicking and yelling, "Goddamn, that Eisenhower really ruined the neighborhood!"

Somewhere around 110th Street there was a Cuban restaurant, Martín's Place. That's where all the whores used to hang out, and it was a meeting place in general. One day at Martín's I met this guy I had never seen before. He just showed up. His name was Pete Rodriguez,[3] and he was like an electrifying force. As soon as he came in, people would gather around him. He was big and looked more like an American than a Puerto Rican—light skin, light hair, very light brownish eyes, and he also spoke like the Americans.

He used to walk down to Manhattan Avenue. Right on the corner in those days there was a Spanish-speaking movie theater showing Mexican movies. Pete Rodriguez took control of that place.

There were fights there sometimes, and I remember one—even in Puerto Rico I never saw a fight like that. Two guys with knives, Ricans, started fighting right there in the middle of 109th Street, cutting each other, with blood pouring out all over. This Pete Rodriguez just came over and stopped them. It was as if he had iron hands, he got right into the middle of the knives. The two guys separated, their friends moved in, and the whole thing was over, just like that. I looked at the guy and said, "Jesus Christ! This guy is tremendous." So then I started walking around with Pete Rodriguez.

He had a Puerto Rican woman who lived near 105th Street. We used to go to her place and fix ourselves food. Pete was a big eater. He told me he was a seaman. I never met him in the union hall, but I guess he was a member of the S.I.U.[4] and I was a member of the N.M.U.[5] Anyway, he was an able-bodied seaman, and I think he was ashore then because he was waiting for his card or something like that before he could ship out. So he established himself in the neighborhood.

---

3. Spoken in a deliberate American accent.
4. Seafarers International Union.
5. National Maritime Union.

He also had an American girlfriend, a beautiful girl who must have been about sixteen or seventeen years old. She had a friend for me, and Pete and I used to shack up with these girls. We would take them up to the house of Pete's Rican woman when she went to work. We would hang around there all day, cook, eat, smoke reefers, listen to records, and then about three, four o'clock clean up the place and leave.

Pete always seemed to me like a man that wouldn't do anything really bad—maybe fight a little, but that's all. But then one day I saw in the *New York Post* that Pete Rodriguez was in jail. He had beaten hell out of that young girl. I couldn't believe it. He was a powerful guy, but I never saw anything like this in him. I don't know what happened. Maybe he wanted her to hustle or something. He was used to getting money from his women, but he was not like José, who would just grab the money out of a woman's bag right on the street. Anyway, there in the *Post* was a picture of his young girl—he had beat her with a chain.

For a long time I used to notice the name of this big star, José Ferrer.[6] It was on posters in the subways, because he was in a hit play, *The Silver Whistle,* and in a lot of other big plays. He was always top drawer. Now his name was Spanish, but I never thought he was a Puerto Rican. I was having my troubles in my own mind about being a Rican, and it just didn't occur to me that this guy all the critics were raving about could be a Rican. When the news started getting around that José Ferrer was a Puerto Rican, all the Ricans like me said, "Goddamn" and really started paying attention to him.

Once he won the Oscar for the movie, *Cyrano* de *Bergerac,* and that was when he made the big mistake of his life: He came to Puerto Rico and gave the Oscar to the University of Puerto Rico and identified himself as a Puerto Rican. The Ricans started to think he was great, but the critics went the other way, and the guy never made it from there on. I remember, because that was when I started following his career in the papers.

---

6. José Ferrer (1909-1992), stage and film actor and director, was the first Puerto Rican to win an Academy Award.

He had left Broadway when he was on top and had gone to Hollywood. He married Rosemary Clooney and forgot about New York for a while. When he came back to Broadway in the late fifties, it was with a play called *Edwin Booth,* about the guy that killed Lincoln.[7] The critics slammed him, and suddenly he was a flop.

So he started fighting back. I used to listen to this Jewish fellow that had a nighttime radio talk show, Barry Gray.[8] Barry was a guy that was always picking on something important. He had Ferrer on one night, and Ferrer was crying his heart out, "You know, I don't want to brag, but I have always had good ratings in this town, I have always been a top star, and now I have this show *Edwin Booth,* and I think the critics aren't fair." Barry was giving him the line, "Well, listen, how come before you believed in the critics, and now you don't believe in the critics?" Because that Barry Gray was a bitch. Anyway, then Ferrer said he had already put up more than a hundred thousand dollars of his own money to keep the show going. Eventually the show closed. And that was the end of Ferrer, anyway for the time I was living in New York.

---

7. Edwin and John Wilkes Booth were brothers and well-known actors in the mid-1800s. John Wilkes Booth killed Lincoln.

8. Barry Gray (1916-1996) is considered to be the father of talk radio.

— 15 —

These Cubans, They Were All My Friends (1952)

MARTA WROTE TO ME and enclosed papers for our divorce: "If you don't present yourself in court. . . ." I'm not sure how the law worked over there in Cuba, but I didn't show up, so the divorce went through automatically. About our marriage in the eyes of the church, though, I don't even want to think. I don't know what the score is with that. I may still be married to that woman as far as the church is concerned. All I know is I once wrote and asked for my birth certificate and got it back with a note underneath: "You're married to so-and-so." I curse the church a thousand times, they don't understand human beings.

I took another trip to Havana. This time I had a car, and I took it on the ferry from Miami. I went with José's brother, Rogelio.

We rented a little house in Lawton Street, in front of Parque Dolores, and I started hanging around with all the guys down there I had known before.

My car was a 1951 Buick. It was brand new. Rogelio didn't know how to drive, because he was a country boy. Now, José was a sharp-looking guy, he knew how to dress, and you would think he really knew his way around. But José didn't even know how to read. And if José didn't have any education, you can't even imagine Rogelio. Rogelio was at least six or seven years older than José at the time, about thirty-seven. I think he was probably intelligent, but he didn't have good reflexes, maybe because all he had ever learned to do was dig holes to plant sugar cane. My big project for that visit to Cuba was trying to teach him to drive the car. I had to be very tactful so as not to make the guy nervous. I kept on with him, and eventually he learned to drive. It took about a month. Then I let him go alone, and sure enough, one day he cracked up the car.

Rogelio was the oldest of José's brothers. They used to call him el *buey de oro,* the golden ox.[1] When Batista[2] came to power in the forties, Rogelio was a soldier, a sergeant. He didn't know how to write, but then Batista himself didn't know too much either. In that army you weren't promoted for being good but for your loyalty to the boss. So Rogelio made it to sergeant. That must have been when he learned the pimping business and introduced José to it.

This trip to Havana was different from the first. By now I had some education—from Aaron Prep School, from NYU, from reading books, from talking to Dubinsky and Ruthy. So this time Cuba looked very different to me. To begin with, I didn't want any part of living off whores any more. When my money started running out, one of my friends offered to go to the country and bring in a young woman to work for me. That's what they used to do for themselves. They would take my car and drive into the countryside, where people were living in huts made of palm leaves with the earth for a floor. When they saw a shiny car and guys all dressed in suits, they would come running out to look. One of the guys would go in and talk to the father of one of the young girls, give him a present, and take his daughter away to Havana. Some of these girls ended up in New York.

The women were desperate, they would go crazy with you. Maybe they were not whores in their hearts, but they were hungry. Hungry does a lot of things to a human being. Hungry drives you to degradation in a hurry. You can crumble, man. If you're hungry you crawl. And that's what those girls did, they crawled. They crawled up to the man talking to their father, got into the car to go to Havana, and went straight to the whore district.

---

1. The term is used to refer to someone who is illiterate but not necessarily dumb, unschooled but moneyed.
2. Fulgencio Batista (1901-73), Cuban strongman (1933-58); he was chief of staff of the army (1934-40); president by election (1940-44); president by coup d'etat (1952-54); president by election (1954-58).

So they brought me a girl. I was supposed to be her whoremaster. But I couldn't. Blasting to me was all right, but I just couldn't make it as a *chulo*. The Cubans were always taking my license away. As far as they were concerned, I was a failure. But I had never been trained to live that way, and it was not my way. I've lived plenty bad but not that bad.

There was a tremendous difference between a Puerto Rican and a Cuban. They speak the same language, and they have the same culture. Nevertheless, they're as different as night and day! I know Cubans, for example, who could accept the fact that his wife is sleeping with another man; to a Rican that would be death.

Spanish-language movies made in Cuba always had women in bad trouble who had to go whoring—"I have to give my body to save my kid!" That was the routine in Cuban movies, also Mexican movies.

The mind of Cuba at that time was like that. The ones that want to have good things, they realize that by working they can't make it, because by working you only make a few bucks a week. A few bucks a week doesn't solve anything. So some women figured it's better to give their body and get a hundred bucks a day! It's not the rich rich or the poor poor or the upper middle class that have to make it doing this kind of thing. No, it's the lower middle class that had to make it this way. In Puerto Rico every time the cops grab some whores, you read in the paper that most of them are from Colombia or Santo Domingo or Cuba. In Puerto Rico people may have to live in the *fanguito,* and the women will sleep with a guy for free, but in Cuba it was strictly for business.

For example, the Cubans accepted a guy like *el gran Yarini*.[3] Yarini lived in Havana at the beginning of the century, and he was a *chulo*. Magazine articles talked about Yarini as if he were a great man. He had fifty women working for him!

In many Cuban families I met there was a sister who was a whore

---

3. The big Yarini became the archetype of *el chulo*, the pimp. Ballads were written about him, and he represented the macho lover. He was a household word in such phrases as "*Ese come mierda se cree que es un Yarini*," meaning "That shit thinks he's a Yarini, that he's irresistible to women."

and a nephew or a cousin or a brother that was a pimp. These people had a stronger taste for the good things in life than the Ricans did. Young girls used to tell me they wanted to be whores when they grew up. I knew families where it was the mother who was the whoremaster working her daughters. In Puerto Rico you wouldn't find anything like that. Jesus Christ! In Puerto Rico a girl who became a whore disappears—has to disappear—from her family forever. And a man would rather starve than give his wife to another man.

Havana looked like a sharp city, better than San Juan, especially at that time. But people were starving there, right in the middle of the city. Also every four blocks you found somebody selling drugs. You could get anything you wanted. And the Cubans were illiterate, worse off than Puerto Rico a thousand times. Seventy percent of the population didn't know how to read or write![4]

Compared to Puerto Rico, Cuba is a big country—thirteen times the size. They have seven million people,[5] and there was nothing around except the sugar cane. What were they going to do for jobs? At that time Cuba produced five or six million tons of sugar a year, most of it controlled by the United States sugar companies.[6] So were the shipping lines. So were the telephones. So was everything—completely controlled by U.S. companies. That's why they were starving, and that's why they finally had a revolution.

Another difference between Cuba and Puerto Rico was that there were a lot of Spaniards in Cuba. Since 1898 if you could get a visa into Puerto Rico, that was a visa into the United States, and people preferred to go to the United States. So we don't have any Spaniards any more. It has been many years since Spaniards came to Puerto Rico. We have some older ones, but their sons are Ricans. And Ricans get married with more Ricans. Cuba has lots of Spaniards, the influx has been continuous. The kids my age in Cuba had straight noses and

---

4. The 1950 U.S. Census found 24.7 percent of the Puerto Rican population over ten years old was illiterate; the 1953 Cuban National Census found 23.6 percent of the population illiterate—41.7 percent in the countryside.
5. 5,829,029, according to the 1953 Cuban National Census.
6. United States companies produced a little under 40 percent of Cuba's raw sugar.

good hair. They were intelligent guys, too, but they didn't have any jobs, they were in the streets.

It isn't that I want to knock the Cubans, just to tell the facts as I saw them. I haven't got anything against Cubans—as a matter of fact, these Cubans, they were all my friends.

And when they're given the chance, the Cubans are more competent than the Puerto Ricans. Puerto Rico has been a colony all its life; Cuba has been independent for a very long time. When the Cubans got into Miami after the revolution, it took them a lot less time to establish themselves than it took the Puerto Ricans in New York. I call them the Jews of the Caribbean. They are the unusual ones in the Caribbean. Right now in Puerto Rico who runs the shows, who runs the television, who runs the sophisticated businesses like advertising—who are the miracle millionaires? Cubans. You never find them in the bad neighborhoods here, only in the better places in Puerto Rico.

On 10 March very early in the morning, Rogelio came in to where I was sleeping. "Get up, Benjy, get up, there's a coup d'état going on. Batista is in Columbia."[7] So I got up and dressed, and he was outside waiting for me in my car. I got in the car with him, and we drove around Havana. Everything was quiet, very quiet. We could see a few tanks and half-tracks[8] with guns and soldiers positioned in various places around the city, but nobody was moving around, only us. Nobody bothered us because they would see the American plates on the car and it was like us having special permission to do what we wanted. By morning, people were starting to come down the street but not like normally. Stores still were closed, everybody hadn't opened up.

We went to a place that was open and had a cup of coffee with bread and butter. The guys were talking, "Well, now the general's in

---

7. On 10 March 1952, General Fulgencio Batista and a group of his followers entered Columbia, the main military encampment in Havana, and harangued the troops to join in a military coup against the constitutional government of President Carlos Prío Socarrás. He was successful.

8. An armored vehicle with rear driving wheels on special treads.

there. Now he's gonna do it constitutionally." I heard that thing and laughed to myself. I start thinking about our system, in Puerto Rico and in the United States, that if you wreck the Constitution once, then it no longer is worth anything. I thought, Suppose in the United States there'd be a coup d'état and they changed the president and then the guy comes and makes a new constitution, then the whole fuckin' thing would go to pieces. That's what I was thinking. I was drinking my coffee and didn't talk to anybody. I laughed to myself that the people kept saying, "Now he's gonna make it legal, now he's gonna be a constitutional president, and everything will be O.K."

Rogelio finished, we got in the car, and I said, "O.K., let's go to the presidential palace and see what the score is." So we drove right to the *Malecón*;[9] the presidential palace was not far from there. We saw a car driving into the palace grounds. I didn't look at the plates but knew right away it was an American embassy car from the American flag flying from it. We drove in right behind the embassy car, and there was the president[10] outside with some men. He was getting into a car flying a Mexican flag. He was going into exile to Mexico.

Rogelio, as I said before, was a Batista man in the forties and had an ID showing him as a sergeant in Batista's army, so we were protected all the way. Batista was not in the palace. He was in Columbia. Columbia was the military post, the strongest post near the city. We drove there. Rogelio showed his ID and we were allowed in. Batista was there in his headquarters with his staff. There were also a lot of troops lined up, and Batista came out to them and made a speech about the unity of the Cuban people. That speech had three main points: one, the American interest would not be disturbed; two, the police were to have raises in pay; and three, the soldiers were to have raises in pay. That was the key to the coup d'état—the police, the army, and the Americans. The greatest period of American supremacy was from 1945 to 1960, because in those fifteen years the U.S. was

---

9. The roadway and promenade by the sea encircling most of the perimeter of Havana.
10. Carlos Prío Socarrás was the last constitutional president of Cuba. Elected in 1948, he was deposed by Batista in March 1952, three months before his term would have expired.

the whole world. No matter what the U.S. did, it was right. So if you had a coup d'état, the first thing you had to do was make it O.K. with the Americans. Then you did the same with the police and the army. Most of these Latin American dictators worked by that system.

After Batista's coup we really began to have a ball. On account of Rogelio's license, that ID, we would go to the whorehouses, and Rogelio would show that goddamn thing, and everybody else would go down on the deck, we would get the best women. Whoever was the madam of the house was immediately very nice to Rogelio. In those days all you had to do was show the document proving you were a soldier. The soldiers walked around the streets of Havana carrying guns. In the United States Army you can't do that.

Batista put Cuba twenty years behind, because before him the country already had had two constitutional governments in a row. It was easier to use special influence with Batista's people than with Prío's—not that there wasn't influence before, too, but then things were at least a little bit more legal.

— 16 —

Don't Use That Goddamn Word "Crime"! (1953)

ONE DAY I WAS WALKING up Columbus Avenue, from 103rd Street to where José and all those pimps used to hang around. José was dressed in his Phil Kronfeld suit. He looked like a fuckin' businessman. José used to buy three or four suits, never less than a hundred dollars each. He had rings—I never liked rings—he had one that cost two thousand dollars. For the Cubans, jewelry, *los hierros,* was very important. You gotta have a ring, a nice bracelet, a nice necklace with the *Virgen del Cobre,*[1] eighteen-carat deal. That's the *virgencita* that saves everybody in Cuba. She's so important that even Fidel bows to her. They make big parties for her.

All of a sudden three guys showed up and stopped us. "Line up!" They flashed some kind of badge, so I figured, The FBI! Jesus Christ! But I said to myself, I've got no trouble. No one even had any pot at that particular moment.

They were from the Department of Immigration and Naturalization. They checked me, and I had my seaman's paper, and they said O.K. José had seaman papers, too, and again they said, "This is O.K." We started going, but when we had gone about half a block, they stopped us again and grabbed José. "This is the guy we're looking for. You come too." They took us to an office on 69th Street and Columbus Avenue. "No, I'm Puerto Rican," I said. "That's my younger brother." I got a little belligerent, and one of the men took me by the arm

---

1. The *Virgen de la Caridad del Cobre* is the patron saint of Cuba. She reportedly appeared to three Cuban fishermen in Havana harbor.

and shut me into a little room. The man, he was an Italian, came to me and said, "Listen, you better talk, we got all the papers." One of José's goddamn Cuban friends had squealed on him. Still, it was his fault in a way. If he had kept quiet, instead of going on and on about it and flashing the papers we had got for him that time, he could just have gone to Cuba and come back with nobody knowing anything about it. The Cuban who squealed on him must have been inside the car, and when the Feds let us go, he must have told them José was the guy.

The Italian said, "You're committing a crime." I told him, "Listen, don't use that goddamn word 'crime'." I meant it, too. Even though I had gone to school, I couldn't understand what "crime" meant. I thought that crime was when you killed somebody. When I was a kid and people talked about *un crimen,* they meant a murder.

Anyway, the guy kept on using the word "crime," and I kept on protesting. He kept giving me a strange look. Then he asked me, "You wouldn't mind if instead of 'crime' I said 'committed a violation' or 'violated the law'?" And I said, "O.K., that's O.K., that's great!" He looked at me very funny and said, "All right, we won't use the word 'crime' anymore."

Finally I realized that when these men were taking down my statement, I had admitted that José was in possession of my brother's papers. The Italian had told me that was a violation of the law of the United States, because I was giving citizenship to somebody who was not entitled to it. And every time he slipped into the words "committed the crime," I would jump, and the whole thing would stop, and it would take about five or ten minutes of discussion about the word "crime" before he was able to go on again. Now I have to laugh, but then I wouldn't let him say that about me—he had to say "violated the law." They took José to Ellis Island, and they let me go.

After Ellis Island, José was sent back to Cuba. But after a while he popped up in New York again, this time with a student visa. I had given him the idea of claiming to be a student, but now he had to go to school. So there I was, having to do for him what Johnny had done for me! There was some kind of school on Broadway, and José paid a lot of money to go there. He was learning how to write.

I used to go looking for him at school. His classes were from two in the afternoon to three or four. He used to sit there with one hand on his left cheek and the other holding the pencil. Sometimes he would say he wanted to quit school, and I would tell him, "You quit school and you're gonna get kicked out of New York." His whore, his only whore, told him the same. Anyway, he even learned something, how to write his name.

José and his woman had moved into a big room with a kitchen. One evening José and I were sitting there and smoking reefers, and Yolanda, his woman, came home and started fixing us dinner. Then there was a loud noise like a crash from the kitchen. We rushed in to see, and there was the woman staggering and falling all over the place. She was foaming at the mouth. I ran and got the car and we rushed her to the nearest hospital, to St. Luke's. They put her to bed, and the doctors came in and checked her. I waited with José while he paced back and forth very worried. Finally the doctor came and said, "I can do nothing for her here."

That was a private hospital. José had a lot of money. But I guess we goofed, because they told us to take her over to a city hospital, and without thinking for a minute, we grabbed her, threw her in the car, and raced to the municipal hospital further downtown. Man! José was so scared. He didn't want to leave the hospital and go home, but after a little while someone came to him and said, "She's doing O.K., she looks all right." So we went home. When we came back the next day, they told us she was dead.

We had to take her to the funeral parlor and then from the funeral parlor to the cemetery in New Jersey. A lot of people that died in New York got put into the hole in New Jersey. The guy that I called Uncle, the cab driver, he wound up under the ground in Jersey, too. I remember when I took him there. I said to myself, This is a cold place for a Puerto Rican to get buried.

You don't know about cemeteries until you have to go there for someone close to you. You just live and forget. It's like hospitals, you don't know about them either until somebody you care about gets sick and you have to go there and see the suffering. To get to the cemetery in New Jersey the cars go at a tremendous speed on the parkway; in Puerto Rico you go walking. When my mother died in the thirties, I had to walk with her to Río Piedras.

The men that bury people have tough faces. When they lowered the casket, those guys just started shoveling dirt on it. It was the first time I'd ever seen that; when my mother died I didn't watch them put her down. So now I got mad and said to the guys, "Stop!" Because it hurt me to see the dirt hitting the casket. They didn't stop, they just held their shovels in their hands and looked at me like that—tough. Then I realized, The woman's dead, they have to throw dirt on her, they have to cover her. I walked back to the car, and we left.

When Yolanda died, José lost his income. Everything finally gets down to economics. You could say that the vital interests of José got all loused up. He had suddenly lost his source of income at the same time as he had had to spend a lot of money. Two or three days after Yolanda died, he had to go out on the streets and look for some woman to work for him. He had a lot of advantages in this business, but still it wasn't all that easy. He couldn't find what he was looking for right away. So he just upped and went off to Cuba to get hold of some women. I think that was the last time I ever saw José.

— 17 —

Trip Guy (1951–1953)

FOR A COUPLE of years now I had been shipping out whenever I could get myself a place on a ship, and driving a cab when I couldn't. Sometimes I would disappear onto a ship for months. Whenever I came back I would have a wad of four or five hundred dollars, and with that and what I could pick up in hacking, I was able to keep an apartment and everything was fine.

It was hard to get a ship because I wasn't what you call a book member of the union, even though I paid dues like a member. I think that was illegal, their collecting money from me so I could get onto a union ship. There was a whole group of guys like me called "trip guys." If there was some ship around and the union members didn't want the jobs, they would say, "O.K., get the trip guys." But at the same time we had to pay dues.

I got onto the *Santa Paula,* a ship that used to sail to northern South America. I was really looking forward to this trip because I was broke and had the chance to make some money. I was working as a steward, sort of like a porter. At night after everything was shut down, I was supposed to clean the mess room. I would put the chairs on the tables and sweep and mop it out. There were two of us, an American and me. When we got to Venezuela, we went ashore together.

I went with this guy to La Guaira, the port for Caracas. We went into a bar, and I noticed the bartender was looking at me bad. I asked him what was wrong, and he said in Spanish, "What are you doing with this gringo[1] here?" He called me a lousy Puerto Rican because I

---
1. Among many Spanish speakers, *gringo* was an offensive term for an English-speaking foreigner; in Puerto Rico, it typically referred to U.S. citizens without that judgment.

hung out with the gringos. He didn't want to serve us. I threw him a ten-dollar bill. He didn't want to take it. He said, "That kind of money I don't want, you have to pay in bolivars." "Listen," I said, "we only got American dollars." "That's no good here," he told me. So I had to tell him that I was for independence, that I hated gringos. Meanwhile the gringo was watching all this but he couldn't understand what was going on.

I happened to know a lot about Venezuela, about Bolívar.[2] I once read a book by Thomas Rourke called *Man of Glory, Simón Bolívar* —I think it was written sometime in the thirties. Anyway, I knew a lot about Bolívar, his campaign, his ideas, his love life. He was my hero. When I started talking to the bartender about Bolívar, his attitude began to change. But the other villagers in the bar were against the gringo, and the poor gringo didn't know what a problem it was that he was a gringo. He was just some poor guy from New York, with not much education, no Spanish, a porter.

The rest of us talked about everything, about Albizu Campos, about Puerto Rican politics, about the attachment of Puerto Rico to the United States. I told the bartender that I'd rather see Puerto Rico belong to Venezuela, not as a colony but as a province in the north. By now the guy was very happy with me and started giving me free drinks. So the gringo cheered up, too, and started taking the free drinks as well. We all got drunk. We went into the bar at about three in the afternoon, and we came out about two-thirty in the morning. Every Venezuelan that came in the bartender had to introduce me to, and every time he looked at the gringo, I would say, "He's a good one." I got back to the ship loaded, and I couldn't work, man! The only thing I could do was go to sleep.

When I was in Aaron Prep there was a guy Schwartz, who was from Colombia. He was blond, blue-eyed, but he was a Jew. There were three guys in that school who spoke Spanish perfectly, and he was one of them. We got friendly, and when he told me he was Jewish,

---

2. Simón Bolívar (1783-1830) was a Venezuelan leader in South America's struggle for independence from Spain. He was called "the Liberator."

I couldn't believe it. How could a Jewish guy speak Spanish so good? If he had spoken with difficulty, I would have understood that was a Jew trying to speak Spanish. But this one could speak Spanish even better than I.

When I got to Cartagena[3] I went to look for Schwartz. His family was from Europe, I forget what country. Some of the family went to the States, and some went to Colombia. The part of the family that was in Colombia owned stores. When I started looking for my old friend, people told me he was from a rich family. He lived in a nice house, and when I went up to the house, they told me Schwartz was in the States going to the University of Delaware.

So I got into a taxicab and asked the driver to take me around. There's a lot of pot in Colombia, and he drove me to a section where the shacks are made out of palm leaves, and some guy next to a pile of wood sold me some *pasto*—that's what they called reefers. I was smoking and getting high with this guy when suddenly the wood in the woodpile began to move. "Goddamn! I'm too high." What happened was, a woman was lying there and I hadn't seen her until she got up. The woman was so dirty—her clothes were so dirty and she was shoeless—she was almost the same color as the logs. Then I really began to look around. I said, "I've had rough times in my life, but never was Puerto Rico this bad."

For one thing, those Colombians had lost their hope. They didn't hope for anything better. And they talked about their life as if it was just great. A man would say he had a wife and family and a house in one place, and now he made some other woman pregnant and was going to marry her, too, and have another house. Somewhere in Santayana's *Persons and Places*,[4] he talks about the conformity of man. That time in Cartagena I saw that the people, despite their terrible dirty poverty, were satisfied. They must have seen better because the slum they lived in was on the outskirts, and they could easily have

---

3. On the north coast of Colombia.
4. George Santayana (1863-1952), a Spanish philosopher and novelist, wrote in English. *Persons and Places* is his autobiography.

gone to the center of town where there were nice houses. But they accepted their condition, and if they kept on accepting it, there would be no chance for a revolution, no chance even for a little improvement. I got out of there and went back to the ship. And all the way in the cab I was thinking about how the human race can adapt itself to just about anything and even claim that what is bad is good.

My next trip after the *Santa Paula* was on the *Francis Lewis*. We sailed to North Africa and into the Mediterranean. We shipped out from Baltimore, and before we sailed I went into a bookstore and bought myself three books—*The Age of Reason* by Sartre,[5] *The Culture of Cities* by Mumford,[6] and, I think, *Dominations and Powers* by Santayana.[7] (Santayana was the easiest for me to understand because he used a Latinized English: "facility," "conformity," etc.) Every time I got into port I used to go to a bookstore. I was always buying books. On that ship I used to work only at chow time. I would feed the officers and then not have anything to do, so I'd go to my room and read.

It was wintertime in the North Atlantic, and it was very rough. Also the ship was small. I used to think it was going to sink. One night I went into the mess hall for coffee. The captain came down for coffee, too. I left a book on the table. "Who the heck is reading this kind of book?" the captain, who was Jewish, asked. He came over to me. "Are you reading this kind of stuff?" "Yes, I'm reading that kind of stuff." After that, that Jewish captain and I were big buddies.

We got to North Africa, Spanish Morocco. It didn't belong to Spain any more, and Arabic was the language. But Spanish was still being spoken a lot. It was early in the morning—like five o'clock—when we put in at Ceuta. I said I wanted to go to shore.

I put on my cashmere suit and tie and everything, I looked like a

---

5. Jean-Paul Sartre (1905-1980), a French existentialist philosopher was one of the more important figures in 20th century French philosophy. Sartre's novel is about freedom and reason.
6. Lewis Mumford (1895-1990), an American historian, was known for his critical studies of urban life.
7. The subtitle describes what the book was about: *Reflections on Liberty, Society, and Government*.

businessman. I grabbed a cab, and the driver took me to this place where there were about fifteen beautiful women, all speaking Spanish. And young. I would say they were about sixteen to forty, none older. Little by little they started coming around. It was an odd time to be there, six in the morning. I had the women all to myself. And they were competing for my attention. When the time came to choose, I didn't know what I wanted to do. So I took two of them.

The captain said the ship was leaving about one in the afternoon but, "Don't worry, stay on shore until the last minute if you want." When I got back, the captain was on the bridge. He was great to me— I don't know why. I guess he liked me. The steward liked me, too— everything I did was right. And I didn't do anything! On my first trip I was a messman. On the second trip I was a utility man—you know, I made beds and cleaned. But actually I didn't clean anybody's room but the captain's. So being a utility man was a better job; I didn't have to be on hand at chow time. And cleaning and making beds was not that important to anyone anyway.

Late in '52 I shipped out on the *Santa Barbara,* a ship belonging to the Grace Lines. It sailed from New York to the west coast of South America, through the Panama Canal and down to Chile. On a trip like that you hit all the ports. The shipping companies work that way—they take all the cargo they can get. In Lima I went over to the plaza and met a guy named Lucio. Guys like him in these South American countries always hung around the ports waiting for American ships because the American seamen always had more money. An American seaman came ashore and didn't know anybody— —say, it was his first time in the place—and someone would come around and tell him, "Listen, I'll show you anything you wanna see." So he would give the guy five bucks, five bucks was a big deal. Lucio came to me this way, and when I told him, "O.K.," he took me to the Bolívar Hotel, that's one of the best hotels in Lima, near the presidential palace. I love that town, Lima, it looks like San Juan in certain places.

Anyway, I was drinking with Lucio, and it got to be night. He said to me, "Listen, what about getting cocaine?" But he couldn't make a connection. So we went to the *plaza del mercado* where they were selling these leaves. To me they just looked like leaves, but Lucio told me they were coca leaves. You chew them, and your mouth starts getting numb. I bought a bunch of the goddamn stuff and started chewing. My mouth got numb, but it didn't give me the kind of high I was used to with cocaine. I must have chewed for hours, but I didn't get anything out of it. So Lucio took me over to the women, and I got myself one. If I haven't gone with two hundred, three hundred women in my life, I haven't had one. That's a fact.

On the trip back from Chile I got sick. My back was out again, and I couldn't get off the bed. I couldn't work or do anything, just lay there helpless. I thought I'd never get up again. So when I got to New York, I went to the hospital. They gave me heat treatments, and my back started coming back. When you have a disc operation, like I had, you are always in danger of back trouble. Your spine is so delicate. I guess my job as a messman in the kitchen, peeling the potatoes and carrying the garbage out, was bad for my back. I had to stay off the ships for a while. Later I had a couple more jobs—I went to England—but I got to hacking more and more steadily.

— 18 —

The Hacking Deal (1952–1956)

TO GET INTO the hacking business, you first have to get a license. You get it from the Police Department. I had a lot of trouble because I had a misdemeanor on my record from something that had happened to me one day sometime before when I was with Rogelio in the Bronx Zoo.

Rogelio liked to get high and go somewhere to feel the asses of women. That was something these Cubans were very expert on; they called it *rascabuchear*.[1] *Rascabuchear* is when a lot of women are gathered together—looking at a store window at Christmastime, for instance—and a man, in this case Rogelio, opens his coat, gets behind some women, and feels her up. To Rogelio that was always a great thrill. I never really understood it myself, but a lot of Cubans used to go for it. Another thing that the Cubans would do, too, was to get their prick out and show it to the women. In Cuba that was practically routine. Marta used to tell me stories that guys would come over and show her, when she was a little kid, and their friends would be looking on and laughing. In New York some of the Cubans would get up early in the morning and go into the subway especially to do that. In Puerto Rico that kind of thing didn't go, but in Cuba it was practically rice and beans.

So there I was with Rogelio in the Bronx Zoo, and he was out to feel up women. Since I was walking around with him, I got involved with it, too. And I have to admit sometimes—¡*coño!*—it was nice. I guess they had cops in New York looking out for stuff like that.

---

1. Voyeurism. More specifically, it can denote "to cop a feel," usually on the buttocks.

Anyway, I got caught. The cop grabbed me and said, "All right, get in the wagon over there, you're going to jail." They took me before a judge in night court, and the judge set a date for the trial. That night I thought I would go crazy by myself in jail. In the morning they took me in a truck to the judge in the Bronx. Rogelio was there, too. It wasn't only me and Rogelio either; there were a lot of old men hauled in for the same thing, and not only Cubans, Americans too.

Rogelio still had his ID with the picture of Batista. He showed that to the cops, and they dropped the charges against him. The guy got out of the goddamn thing! But I didn't. The judge called me to the bench, and the cops told me, "Listen, you wanna get out of here fast, right? O.K., you go over and tell the judge that you did it, and he'll give you a suspended sentence, and you're out of here." I was so goddamn scared I didn't argue. I went to the judge and pleaded guilty. The judge said, "All right. Fifteen dollars fine, fifteen days, suspended sentence."

That's a real piece of discrimination against people who don't understand the big town. They have no understanding of the goddamn laws, so they have no civil rights. Now, I think New York is the greatest. The system of law is pretty fair if you know how to manipulate it. To that extent there is really no discrimination. But the ignorance and fear of the people who don't know how to manipulate it make it unfair. If I had had a lawyer in that court, he would have told the judge, "Wait a minute, they say this guy was doing so-and-so but actually they can't prove it. He was just a bystander." And that would have been that.

But, as it was, that trouble haunted me. I became even more scared. I was afraid of trying to get a license to drive a hack, because they checked into your record before they gave you one. If you had a bad morals record, you wouldn't get a goddamn license. I don't remember exactly how I managed it, but I had to pay one of the cops downtown. You pay the cops in New York a lot. I paid fifty or one hundred dollars to one of the cops there in the hack bureau, and he said, "All right."

So I started hacking steady. Steady means I was getting a hundred bucks a week and wasn't mixed up in any bad business. I felt secure then. I wasn't afraid of the cops because I knew that if they stopped me, they would see that I was a real workingman. Also, the other drivers taught me what to do if I ever got stopped for going through a light. When asked to show your license, you fold up in it a five-dollar bill or two or three ones.

I got my job through a nice guy named Grossberg. He was about sixty years old and had once been a hackman himself. The company I worked for was called The System. The garage was on Eleventh Avenue and 45th Street, and it was a big outfit; they had about four thousand cabs. In the whole city in those days there were about eighteen thousand cabs.

In the beginning I had a few accidents. After one of them Grossberg started yelling, "Goddamn! You got here only two months ago and you already got four accidents. I ain't gonna give you any more jobs." One of the guys came over to me and said, "Don't worry, you can always quiet Grossberg down. Give him ten, and you'll get a cab." It was cold and I was wearing a coat and hat. I called Grossberg to come outside and handed him my hat with a ten-dollar bill in it. He took the hat, kept on walking, and called out to me, "Here, you got a cab." I learned that if I gave Grossberg ten bucks every two weeks, I was safe. Even if I didn't feel like going to work now and then, I didn't lose my job. There were a lot of guys giving him money like that.

I drove for The System for a while, and then I drove for another company. All the owners were Jewish, and I always got along with them fine. They always knew me, and they always gave me a break. I just knew how to handle myself with the Jewish bosses no matter where I worked. Not even the Jews could do it. I was the only cab driver who could goof off for two or three days. They would call me into the office, but whenever they came out, they would come out laughing, "All right, Benjy, you got a cab." I don't know why they were always like that, but every time I wanted a cab I could get a cab.

One of the things I liked about hacking was the flexibility. I could do things I couldn't in a lousy dishwashing job, for instance. I was my own boss. While I was working, I didn't have nobody telling me, "Go this way, go that way." Since I knew I couldn't get any other job in New York unless I went into the rackets, it was the only way for me to do what I wanted and make some money, without being a crook. I could have gone into selling drugs, I could have run numbers, I could have got tied up one way or another with the Italians and the Mafia. And knowing myself and knowing how much I liked money—and how far I might go if I saw a real chance, I was afraid of getting started. I said to myself, Once I start making money illegally, I would never be able to stop, and I would surely end up in Riker's Island or Sing Sing.

One day I'm driving and I only got fifty cents on me when I pass a stop sign. An Irish cop stopped me, "Come over here, you passed a stop sign. Come over here and give me your fuckin' license. Goddamn, you Puerto Rican?" "Yeah." "Get over here, give me your license." "Listen, I'm a cab driver and I'm trying to get uptown to get some gas from my buddy so I can go hack." "No, no, man, I gotta give you a ticket." I said, "Don't give me a ticket," So he said, "Well then, give me something, you got something?"

I was afraid of telling the guy I only had fifty cents. I'd give him five bucks, but I didn't have five bucks! So I said, "Well, listen, I don't want to." The guy said, "No, no, you gotta give me something. If you ain't got five, you still gotta have something." If I had two bucks, I would have said, "Gee, I got two bucks, here take it." But I tried not to reduce myself so low and to reduce him so low as to offer him a lousy fifty cents! So I said, 'No, man," "But you gotta have something!" I said, "Listen, man, I just have fifty cents." "Goddamnit, Jesus Christ, goddamnit, give me the fuckin' fifty cents!" How low can a cop get! That Irish cop. That's a bitch, that New York is a bitch. Isn't that something, the guy got to degrade himself so low, an officer of the law. "Give me the fuckin' fifty cents!"

I used to meet all kinds of people. One day I was going down Broadway, and at 42nd Street a guy hailed me and got in the car. "Hey, get me to the St. Moritz." I look back and recognized the guy as someone I had seen on television. It was Walter Winchell.[2] He was

---

2. Walter Winchell (1897-1972), newspaper columnist and radio commentator, is credited for having invented the gossip column where the private lives of public figures would be exposed. His columns were frequently nasty and salacious.

short and a little bit husky. He gave me a buck. I didn't like the way he acted, he was too . . . conceited. Like he was trying to show that he was a big man in New York.

I also drove Ed Sullivan.[3] He was more of a quiet man. When Sullivan got in the cab, I knew right away he was Sullivan. I had seen that face so much, and it's a face not to be forgotten. He tipped me good, too. I don't remember how much, but I remember I was very happy.

Another time I was working on a Sunday. Now, Sunday is a dead day for hacking, so I drove to Penn Station and got in the line to find a customer from an incoming train. I guess the train that came in must have been from Miami because the man I picked up was none other than the old president of Cuba, Prío Socarrás. He got in with his wife, and I just couldn't keep from saying something to him. "Listen, I was in Cuba when they knocked you off." He laughed, gave me a buck, and then fifty cents extra.

One day about one or two in the morning, down in Cathedral Park, I run into a guy. He got inside the cab and said, "All right, man, take me to the Polo Grounds." I was driving, and he continued, "You know what, man? Life is a piece of pussy. You are made through a pussy, they bring you out through a pussy, you work for a pussy, and whatever you think about, it's a fuckin' pussy! Shit, man! Life is a piece of pussy!" I started laughing. I had about ten lights, and I was listening to that guy, "Life is a piece of pussy." I look back and there's a Negro there, not too old, maybe about thirty-five years old. I guess he must have come from a nice piece because he was relaxed and he was talking about pussy. He was laughing, and all I could see was his white teeth when he laughed. He was speaking so eloquently. He paid me and I said, "O.K., so long, philosopher!"

One night I got one of these American women in the cab, a New Yorker. She was going a long way, out to Long Island, a four- or five-dollar ride. We had a lot of time to talk, and she started asking me

---

3. Ed Sullivan (1901-1974) was a columnist and host of a popular television show. Many careers in America were launched on his show, including those of Elvis Presley and the Beatles.

about who I was. "You're a Greek?" That's New York all right! She wouldn't have thought I was a Negro right away because I don't look that black. So she figured, he's a Italian or a Greek. Many times people thought that.

I said to her, "No, I'm not a Greek, I'm a Puerto Rican and I'm an American citizen." "Oh, you're a naturalized American citizen." "No, I'm an American by birth, I didn't ask for it, they just threw it on me." Then the bullshit started to fly. "Oh, that's interesting. Where is Puerto Rico?" "In the Caribbean." "Oh, around Cuba?" I start bullshitting a little myself. "The Caribbean is the place that is called the Spanish Main. You know the Spanish Main?" She says, "Oh, you sure are very well educated." "No, I'm not very well educated, but that's the way it is and Puerto Rico is right there."

Then she said, "Well, listen, you seem to be a guy who reads a lot. What kind of books do you read?" "I try to read those big books, the classics. I try to read, like Shakespeare,[4] though I don't understand him very well. I read *Don Quixote*,[5] Dante's[6] *Inferno, The Divine Comedy,* stuff like that. I tried to get into Goethe. I don't know if I pronounced it right, but that's the German *bravo."* Then she started laughing and said, "Goddamn! I'm gonna tell you one thing, you read too many of those big books." I said, "I don't read other books because I haven't been able to cover what I want to cover of the classics." She said, "Well, don't underestimate fiction!"

She was right in a sense, because fiction has a lot in it. The truth is, you have to read fiction if you want to know what's going on in this world. But some of the classics are fiction, too! Anyway, she convinced me I had missed the boat. She took me out near La Guardia airport and directed me to a nice house, where I dropped her. She gave me a ten-dollar bill and said goodbye. All this time she had her legs open. Every time I turned around I had a look. The average

---

4. The reference is to William Shakespeare (1564-1616), regarded as the greatest writer in English.
5. *El ingenioso hidalgo don Quijote de la Mancha* by Miguel de Cervantes (1547-1616), is thought to be the greatest literary work in Spanish.
6. Dante Alighieri (1265-1321) was a Florentine poet. *Divina Commedia,* as the work came to be known, is considered to be the greatest literary work in Italian.

American woman is a nice-looking woman, let's face it. For every ten under the age of thirty-five that a taxi driver drives around, eight are going to be nice!

I met this guy Herbie, a shylock. Whenever you needed money, you could get whatever you want. You have to pay every week, it was twenty percent at that time. But you gotta keep on the wall with that guy, you couldn't fuck around with him. Herbie was a great guy, a good friend of Uncle, they knew each other for years, I guess in the hacking business. There's a diner (one of these places that they have in New York but not in Puerto Rico) on Eleventh Avenue and 43rd or 44th Street. That's where Herbie used to hang out. After the night the cab drivers would sit down and have a cup of coffee before they go to sleep, and do cab driver talk. One night I needed a hundred dollars for a date. So I went to see the shylock down in the diner. I have a cup of coffee there and bullshit with Herbie Kramer. "I need some money." "All right, I know that you work steady. There's no trouble with you, besides I know your uncle." He started pulling out the money when another guy walked in. The guy started talking to Herbie. He wanted some money and he's giving Herbie a big fuckin' story and a lot of crap. Herbie cuts in and says, "Listen, man, please don't tell me any more—money talks and bullshit walks." Anyway I got my money.

I met this guy Francisco Rabo de Vaca—the tail of the cow.[7] He used to rent apartments to the Ricans or, naturally, to anybody else he could. I got my apartment in the Bronx through him. Then I went to Alexander's and bought a living room set and a bed on credit. I had a two-room apartment setup and even had an air conditioner. I had to work like a son of a bitch to pay it off, I was hacking seven days a week. This was a period in my life when I spent a lot of my free time blasting. I would grab some woman in the cab and take her to my nice apartment.

Rabo de Vaca, the Cuban, was never a good pal of mine, but I

---

7. *Rabo de Vaca* is a pejorative name given to someone who is not highly esteemed; literally, it means "cow tail," but probably translates better as "ass hole," the tail being close to that area.

stayed connected to him. One day he said to me, "Benjy, you come into business with me." He couldn't speak English and needed me for that. The Cubans, as I have said, are very smart. So I stopped hacking for a while and started getting into the apartment business. Immediately I was making more money than I had in the cab—150, 200 bucks a week. So what happened? One day a man from the D.A.'s office walked in and said, "There has been a complaint against you." I said, "What is it?" He said, "You guys took some woman for three hundred dollars." Such-and-such address. I looked at my records and couldn't find anything about it. He said, "All right, just a minute," and brought the woman in. She looked at me and said, "No, this is not the man." She was a Rican. My friend, the tail of the cow, had been stealing money from the Puerto Ricans. I think they gave him about six months, and I went back to hacking.

There was another cab driver, an Italian, who lived downstairs. He was married to an Irish woman named Rose. She must have been about twenty-eight years old, from South Carolina, and she was the super of the building.

I lived on the top, I think it was the fourth floor, and she lived on the floor below. From my window I could look into hers. She used to keep her venetian blinds open in such a way that I could see her there naked all the time. So I was always looking at her, and one day I caught her looking up at me—in other words, she had been doing the whole thing purposely.

Well, that was the start of that. She used to come up to my apartment in the morning. I really got myself into a terrible mess that time. I knew her husband and didn't want to get into trouble with him. I kept saying to myself, Why's she doing this to him? We live in the same building, he could walk in any time! I tried to cool it, but she kept coming around, bringing me food, jumping into bed. I would see her husband around, and he would say hello all friendly and tell me his wife was bringing me some food that day, and stuff like that. Man, I felt bad. Really lousy. I even took off for a while on a ship. When I came back, there she was, hotter than ever. Goddamn, I don't know how I got into things like this.

During this time I met Junior's mother at a Rican party. I worked it out to shack up with her. That wound up with a kid. She got pregnant, I got scared. I never loved the woman, it was just that I went with her to blast. She was one of those fucked-up Puerto Ricans on welfare. If I stayed with her and the kid was born, I was gonna be tied up. I didn't love the woman, I didn't like the woman. I didn't want to get married anyway, that just ties you up. If you have some sense of responsibility, you end up saying "Well, I have to get some steady job. I have to do it, I have to do it." And you end up a dishwasher or a house painter, something like that.

I had a lot of other girls, like I said. Sometimes I was seeing three, four at a time. I just couldn't think about the marriage deal—not yet.

I always kept a balance in the bank, anywhere from five hundred to a thousand dollars. I never wanted to get broke. When I saw my balance was going down, I would rush out and get into my cab for a week. But my life was slipping by. I said to myself, Benjy, you're finished, you're a fuckin' cab driver, you're gonna die a cab driver in New York, and what's more, you're gonna die young. Cab drivers always used to die young, from heart attacks at fifty or so, on account of the pressure of driving in New York traffic.

I almost gave up the idea that I could make anything of myself. I would be a cab driver to the end. So maybe I would have a few more women—I mean, this is a lousy life. I was in a world where I thought I would rot. I was beginning to realize that the average Rican has a job, goes to work, eats, drinks, and that's it. Nothing constructed. Nothing worth living for.

In the meantime there was my nephew. At the time I came out of the Army, he was about eight or nine, in elementary school. When I went to NYU, he was in junior high school. He went all the way through university. When he was a little kid, I used to recite quotations to him, and he would always laugh and listen. And my sister pushed him hard. He went to high school, then on to the University of Georgia where he got his B.S., then to Ohio University where he got his Master's, and then to Arizona for his doctorate. His doctorate, I think, was in the field of art or something like that. I lost track of him later on, but he was there.

— 19 —

Turning Points (1955–1961)

IN MY APARTMENT, all fixed up, I was a regular New Yorker now. I was a working man and a bachelor. If I got depressed with my life in New York, I'd get on a ship for a trip to do sightseeing, among other things. I mean, how could I have gone to Europe or seen Alexandria, Haifa, Beirut, Piraeus, Barcelona, otherwise? And everywhere the women. . . . But I also saw how other people lived and thought in these countries—that was a product of NYU and Aaron Prep.

I noticed something strange in Piraeus. They had a "Puerto Rico Bar." And in Genoa they had a "Puerto Rico Bar," and in all those places there were "Puerto Rico" bars. A bartender explained to me once that sixty percent of the U.S. Merchant Marine was Puerto Rican, guys that had left Puerto Rico and gone to the States to work. American seamen—including the Puerto Ricans—were wealthier than other seamen. To get the Puerto Ricans to go to them these bars were called "Puerto Rico Bar" so the Puerto Ricans would feel at home.

During this period I started thinking about becoming a Negro in the United States. I met a steward on one of the ships. He was light but he was a Negro. We went to shore together, and he took me to a Negro place where there was a big party. This was a different world for me. He introduced me, "This is my friend," and the people were looking at me like I was a Negro and not a Puerto Rican. Not a stranger, not a Puerto Rican, not an American. Suddenly I'm getting the feeling that I was accepted with this group, that I was a *bravo* in there, that I was beautiful.

This started driving me crazy because all the girls looked at me like I was a king. I didn't say anything. They didn't hear my accent. The guy kept moving me on, I said, "Hello," and that's it. All these Negro girls were looking at me, Jesus Christ, like I were Valentino. After I left I started thinking about it. I said to myself, Goddamn, there I can make it, if I go there I'll be on top. I was a little light but I was a Negro, too. I could have lived three or four years in the Negro race in the United States. I never did that because I lost contact with that guy when they took me off that boat. But, man, I could have married one rich Negro woman, because some of those son of a bitches, they have money.

It was the late fifties, and I was living in the Bronx, hacking. Things were bad. I thought I was through, and I was really ready to quit. Then came a turning point in the shape of a guy just up from Havana. Somebody there had told him, "Listen, if you go to New York, you go and see this guy Frankie." I said to him, "Who are you?" And he said, "Oh, you don't remember me, but when you were in Cuba I knew all about you, about what a nice guy you were." The point is, he was only a kid, about twenty-two years old. I didn't know him but he knew me—and from six, seven years back. When you go to a poor country like Cuba, you can really make an impression on people, especially on young kids. They look at you and think, What a terrific suit, and a car with plates from the United States! In Havana I had been really something compared to the Cubans—in their eyes I was a big shot with a lot of connections.

At this time in Cuba, Fidel was in Mexico, but nobody was taking the revolution seriously, especially not me because Batista seemed so powerful.[1] Anyway Fidel had come to New York to collect money for the 26th of July movement. There was a party, and all the Cubans went, including this kid, who was mixed up with Fidel.

---

1. Fidel Castro attacked the Moncada Barracks 26 July 1953. He was captured and jailed shortly thereafter. Released on 15 May 1955, he then left for Mexico to continue his fight against the Batista regime. In autumn 1955 he traveled to Miami and New York to solicit support for his cause. He returned to Cuba in December 1956 and successfully fought the Batista government from the hills. He finally gained power 1 January 1959.

Anyway, he came to me and said, "I don't know what to do. I've got to talk to you." He was nervous, pacing back and forth. He wanted to join up with the revolution. They were looking for guys, and he was going to Mexico. He wanted me to go with him.

I told him not to be a fool. "Listen, go to work, you're here now, get a job, and start trying to make a few bucks, and when you get back to Cuba, start a little business. In no time you can be making fifty, a hundred bucks working in a restaurant." I figured that what was eating most of these guys in Cuba was there was no work. But in New York this one could get a job, make some money, and get himself some nice clothes and things.

When I said all this to him, he practically jumped up and down and said, "No! You're crazy! I want to get to the mountains, and I want you to come with me. I thought you were the kind of a guy who would go."

Meanwhile I was saying to myself, Goddamn, the guy's crazy, they're going to wipe him out. I didn't really believe that even if Castro won he would change anything in Cuba.

Anyway, that Cuban went off to the revolution, and there I was— a dull guy, driving a hack, shacking up with some lousy woman cheating on her husband.

I got a letter from José from Mexico. He invited me to go there with him. I don't know who wrote that letter for José, maybe he wrote it, maybe he learned how to write. He wrote me, "Listen, Frankie, come over here in Tijuana. There's a lot of women here, you don't have to worry about nothing." I started thinking of going to Mexico. I figured I had a few bucks, enough to take a trip. I started thinking that José was a good guy and everything, but if he gets me out there, I'd end up in the drug business, marihuana. Because he made a mistake in that goddamn letter. He said, "You can cross the border easy. You're American." That kept hanging in my mind. I said to myself, If I get down there I'm gonna be involved in crossing the marihuana back and forth, and I like the guy so much, and I may need the money, and I could get into the wrong line, and that will wreck me forever. I remembered what happened in '53 in that immigration deal when the Italian gave me a break, and immediately I saw the Italian guy with the two Irishmen in front of me, and I decided, No, I'm not gonna go.

I had given New York nearly fifteen years. Every time I looked around I had said, "This is the greatest city in the goddamn world. This city is so big, so powerful, it has everything." That's what they used to tell me, and that's what I myself used to say, but I never could find the means to break through to all those things they promised you in that place. And then I came to see how everybody was out to fuck you all the time. If you're a Rican in New York, you can't be a person, you're just a Rican, no matter what you do, you're treated so low.

I decided to go back and look at Puerto Rico. When I was a kid I hated the island because of how poor it was. I promised myself I would never come back. But now I wanted to take another look. People had been telling me that everybody was better off now, but I remembered how it had been when I left, and I wanted to see it with my own eyes. I got down here and looked up one of my sisters and, sure enough, I found she was really all right. Her husband was making good money, and they were living very nice. I decided to return.

Because of how I felt about New York, I started going *independentista*.[2] I said, "Goddamn it! Get rid of these goddamn Americans." And I thought there was a real chance that the people would rally for something that had all the arguments on its side. What you read in history books is that people always want to have their independence. And since I had a reason for wanting to get rid of the Americans, I thought everybody would feel the same way. Mari Bras[3] kept on saying that same thing: "It must be, it will be, it has to be, next year it's going to be."

I was living at my sister's house then, and I began going to demonstrations in San Juan organized by the *MPI*.[4] Antonio Corretjer[5]

---

2. A follower of the political movement favoring independence of Puerto Rico from the United States.
3. Juan Mari Bras (1925-), militant independence advocate, leader of the Pro-Independence Movement since 1959.
4. Pro-Independence Movement.
5. Juan Antonio Corretjer (1908-1985), militant independence advocate and well-known poet.

would be there, and I would talk with him. I had many talks with him. Then I met Landing.[6] He and Mari never got along. That's one thing I can't understand—why if people believed in something, and they were lawyers, educated people, why they had to fight among themselves. Still, I didn't give it too much thought at the time.

I never got too close to Mari. I would talk to him, but Mari was a very difficult guy to make friends with. Landing was different. I went to his office, and the guy tried to help me. He gave me summonses to serve, five summonses for twenty-five dollars. I began to hang around with Landing. I had a car, so I could get around to do my serving.

Then I got some other lawyers to work for. I began to feel better about myself. In New York I couldn't have talked to lawyers. It's hard for people who haven't had the experience to understand what such a thing can mean to someone. You have to have lived that dirty fuckin' life to understand how different I felt about myself when I talked to those guys. I met Prado, he was a lawyer too. We talked together like two men. I put my points, and he listened to me. He talked to me as an equal.

The husband of my sister was the vice-president of a company, and that, too, gave me a feeling that all the money in the world couldn't have bought me—you know, there were times in New York when I had plenty of money. The only other time I had had this feeling was when I went to NYU and had my gang who just accepted me.

Now I would talk to Corretjer or to a man like Perez—he was a senator in the *Partido Independentista*.[7] I even talked with Concepción de Gracia.[8] Inside of me I would say, Benjy, you can talk to those people, you could do a real job, you don't have to hack, you can make something of yourself regardless of all these things you got against you.

Then I started to feel I could even pass judgment on others. Mari, for instance. He was a lawyer and a leader, always posing as powerful.

---

6. Jorge Luis Landing, minor pro-independence leader, known for his participation in a 1948 student strike at the University of Puerto Rico.
7. The Puerto Rican Independence Party (*PIP*).
8. Gilberto Concepción de Gracia (1909-68); independence advocate and president of the *PIP* from 1948 to 1967.

If I didn't like the guy I could say, "Well, fuck Mari." I could even tell him so to his face. And what I could do to Mari I could do to anybody on the island. I didn't go around talking this way to others, but it was inside me. I didn't even express it myself in words.

This new sense of confidence meant I didn't have to be afraid like I was in New York all the time. In New York I was afraid I would make a mistake. I was even afraid of helping people. Sometimes in the subway I would see someone fall down, and I would have an impulse to go over and help him up. But I'd get scared that if I grabbed him, the cops would come over and grab me. "You fucked this guy in some way. Come on, let's go to jail." Such a thought stayed with me in New York, and I know it must have been that way with most Puerto Ricans. I can't speak for now, because they tell me that now Ricans do some crazy things.

So I walked around with these independence guys, and all the independence guys were leftists. One day Ferré[9] and the Cubans (the Cubans that lived in Puerto Rico were anti-Castro) paraded into San Juan and held a rally at the plaza, where they were denouncing Castro. I happened to be there and I started shouting *"¡Mercenarios!"*[10] I also shouted *"¡Viva Fidel!"* and stuff like that.

I don't know why I did it. I was inclined to the Cuban revolution, leave it at that. I'm not one to hope for the impossible—if something is impractical, I don't hang on, like a fanatic. But in those days I was for Castro the way I was for an independent Puerto Rico.

In any case when I said "Long live Fidel," the whole crowd of Cubans turned on me and started hitting on me with their placards. "Down with Communism," "Down with Castro," "Long live Kennedy," stuff like that. Then the cops arrived, and I was smart enough to melt into the crowd—there was a big crowd around the plaza that day. The Cubans didn't know who the heck they were hit-

---

9. Luis A. Ferré (1904-2003), a long-time supporter of statehood for Puerto Rico, was governor from 1969 to 1973. His father migrated to Puerto Rico from Cuba. In Puerto Rico, the family was often referred to as Cuban; in Miami, where his nephew, Maurice Ferré was mayor, they were often thought of as Puerto Rican.

10. Mercenaries; equivalent to "scabs."

ting, they just started hitting everybody. It got to be a free-for-all between the Cubans and the crowd. In the end the cops grabbed all of us. Down at the police station the Cubans kept telling the police that the rest of us were Communists and that they should beat us up. I couldn't get over it, this group of guys from another country telling our own people, our own police, to beat the hell out of us in our own jail!

And then I said, "Listen, I have the right to use the telephone." One way or another I got through to Landing and Prado, they arrived, and we went into court for the arraignment. The Cubans were there in the courtroom with their placards. The police testified as to what happened, and the judge asked one of the Cubans what happened. The Cuban said, "This guy is a Communist. We were marching and these people started shouting, 'Long live Fidel!' " Then he asked me what happened and I told him, "Well, listen, your honor, with the *venia* of the *tribunal*[11] [I learned that word because I heard the lawyers use it a lot], I was in the crowd and suddenly these guys turned on me and hit with those things they have there." He asked me, "Where you were born?" "I was born on Vieques." "Oh, you're a foreigner, too." Everybody in the courtroom laughed, the lawyers and everybody. Vieques is an island off Puerto Rico that's part of Puerto Rico. The Cubans kept shouting, and the judge said, "You quiet down." "But this guy's a Communist." The judge finally had to cite one of the Cubans for contempt because he wouldn't shut up.

The judge charged the Cubans with assault, and he let me go. When I walked out of that courtroom, I realized what it meant that this was a free country. That judge was saying I had a right to say, "Long live Fidel," whether the people here like it or not and whether the judge likes it or not. The FBI could watch me as a security risk, but that's not enough reason to take me to jail. As long as I don't violate the law, I'm free to use my mouth. But if you hit somebody, you're in violation of the law. This was something I really came to understand that day.

---

11. With the permission of the court.

Another guy I met whom I would never even have been able to speak to in New York was a media guy who started a school to teach other people how to get work in the newspapers, radio, TV, theater, and so on. We became good friends. He always tried to help me, so one day he told me, "Listen, Benjy, you're going to take care of the *matrícula,* the registration in my school." I kept the records for him, advised the students, told them what courses to take, things like that.

Some of the students came from the Barrio de Martín Peña, a shantytown. Their mothers must have made terrible sacrifices in order for their daughters to study theater and television and so on. One of those girls kept getting into my car and asking me for a lift to Stop 34—that's where Banco Popular now is. I would drop her off and go on to my sister's house. One day I went to have a drink with a friend of mine after school, and this same girl was there. After my friend left she came over to me and asked me to have a drink with her. She wasn't bad-looking and she was clearly trying to get me interested. We kept on drinking together, but I said to myself, *"¡Coño!* this is a very young girl. I ain't gonna do what I want to—she's much too young." So she got very mad at me and right there in the bar started screaming at me. I left.

A couple of days later my friend said to me, "Listen, they're looking for you, the police." That girl had charged me with a technical violation. I was innocent, but I was scared. Because now I wanted to be in Puerto Rico and I didn't want to fuck up. Even if I beat the charge, it would still be in the newspapers. That was a chance I didn't want to take. I had something to lose. This was my home and I didn't want any trouble with the law here. I wanted to be clean. This was the first place I had ever got to where I really cared about not dirtying it up. I decided to get out and return to New York. If I had to wait a year or two until the trouble blew over, well, I would wait. I might have decided the other way, to stay and face the charges. I was confident I could win—I had good lawyers now, and I was innocent. But I was afraid to gamble, so I got out. I sold the car and took the plane. I landed in New York about five in the morning. Before we landed I had looked out and seen all the lights and thought, Here's that big son of a bitch, that monster, again! Goddamnit! I had in mind to go back to the ships, and I took a room on 182nd Street, where I stayed holed up for nearly a month until I got my shipping card.

When my card came I went to a ship called the *Mormac Cape something*. I didn't care what job they had for me—a wiper, I didn't care, I'd clean all the engines. And I got on that goddamn boat and felt free. I stayed, made my trips. I got back with a thousand dollars in my pocket, and I didn't owe anybody anything. I called my sister in New York, and she told me, "In Puerto Rico they're still looking for you, the police." So I stayed right on the ship, didn't even go ashore, and waited for a new trip. Another month and I checked again.

In Puerto Rico there was still one detective nosing around. Today I could call the governor and have him put in jail. Now I know the boys, they drink with me, but at that time I didn't have the connections.

So I stayed on the boat, and the money was piling up. I was making eight hundred, nine hundred dollars a month with no expenses and nothing to do with it. I cheered myself up by thinking, Well, I've got money, and the time will come when I can go back to the island again. I remained on the ship month after month, and I kept checking on developments in Puerto Rico. I wanted to wait until everything died out.

This one detective had been specially assigned to my case. I found out that he was the brother of the first wife of my brother. My brother and she had two daughters, and afterward they divorced. By this time my brother had been married to another woman and had had another family. The point is that this detective who was after me was an uncle to my brother's two daughters just like me! So the son of a bitch kept after me and never let up. If not for him the case would have died and I wouldn't have had to put in all those years on the goddamn ship. I had to stay away until finally he got kicked out of the police.

— 20 —

My Exile from Puerto Rico (1961–1965)

SO MY SHIP became a prison and at the same time it became my home. It was a beautiful ship, that was a help at least.

In 1946 I had made two trips; in 1951, three; in 1953, six; and then I made two trips in 1957 and 1958. Add it all together, and it didn't come to a year at sea in a total period of fifteen years. This means that I had not really been a professional seaman. I was actually much more of a professional cab driver. But in the time I was staying away from Puerto Rico I put in something like four years in a row at sea. That's when I became a seaman.

I bought myself a tape recorder and a good two-hundred-dollar radio. This time I would have comfort. There were only two wipers living in the quarters, another guy and I. That was something else that made it easier. In other ships six or seven guys had to share one room. The ship was air-conditioned, too, except of course for the engine room and the deck, and had a nice mess room. It was almost like being on a passenger ship and at the same time being paid for it. At first, till my body got used to the work, I would drag myself to bed at night half dead. I took three books by Sartre with me, but I couldn't read, only sleep. But gradually I got stronger on the job. Certain hours of the day I would listen to Havana on my short wave radio to keep in touch with the revolution. The guys in the ship would ask me, "How come you're a wiper when you're so intelligent?" It was my exile from Puerto Rico.

I remained a wiper for a long time. My duties were to clean the engine room, sweep, and carry out the garbage. I liked the job. Not because I like to clean up, but because it was free. I got Friday in port and didn't work until Monday. The other duties paid more, and I could have had them. I had been an oiler before, they offered me the job many times. That was supposed to be like *un acenso,* a promotion, but I didn't want it. It paid maybe fifty dollars more, but still I didn't. I liked the freedom of being a wiper. And, besides, I found out how to make a little extra money.

The main point was my free weekends. Sometimes when a holiday worked out right I would have three, four, sometimes five days in a row to myself. And Jesus Christ, do you know what that would mean to me? Not in money, not even in getting to the whores—but in being able to travel around to places, like Rio in Carnival. I got to places and saw things you couldn't afford for thousands of dollars living in New York.

I started to know people in Rio and Buenos Aires and didn't need any guides or hustlers to show me around. I even met the chief of police of Buenos Aires. I had expensive clothes—even the captain of the ship didn't dress as I did—and so I mingled with this type of people. All the more reason the guys in the ship couldn't understand why I wanted to be a wiper. I never tried to explain to them why, because if I had they would be hurt and then become my enemies. But they were there because they were seamen and that's how they always made a living; and I was there temporarily and not because I had to be. I used to tour around, for instance—I went to see the Christ This, the Christ That, and once flew seven hundred miles out of Buenos Aires to see the *Cataratas del Iguazú,* the waterfalls between Argentina, Paraguay, and Brazil. It makes Niagara seem like nothing. The guys on the ship had been traveling all their lives on boats and they never saw it. The captain never saw it. When I got to the *Cataratas del Iguazú* then, I even chartered a small plane out of the airport and flew over the goddamn thing. What did it cost me? Two hundred dollars? Three hundred dollars? I could have never done such a thing in my life, but now I could do it because I was a wiper. Being the cleaner of the engine room made me see the world! It made me the best man on that ship!

On my third trip a new steward came aboard. The steward is the guy who takes care of all the food. This one's name was Charlie Meléndez. Anyway, we became good buddies. Now, the steward has the power to bring the provisions onto the ship. He and I figured out that in Argentina and Uruguay things were much more expensive than in the States. For example, a TV that sold for one hundred and twenty-five dollars in the States in those days sold there for five hundred. So we started a terrific little racket. We would smuggle televisions aboard with the steward's stuff. And when we got, say, to Buenos Aires, the customs would never find them, and we would sneak them off the ship at night—give the guy a little something—and have them hauled away by a guy from the shore.

Another thing I used to do was go to 14th Street in New York, I have a Jewish friend over there, and get clothing they needed in South America. In Buenos Aires and Montevideo they liked Lee pants, Levis, Wranglers, and I would buy boxes and boxes of them. I think I would buy them wholesale from my friend for two or three dollars a pair and sell them for ten dollars, a terrific profit. We even had credit already in New York, because the Jews don't want the money out of the bank. Sometimes I came to my friend with an order and didn't have the cash to pay him right away. He would say, "O.K., no problem, put it away, Lopez." I would fill all the orders in New York. I did that job so that Charlie would take over the dirty job at the other end. You weren't checked at the New York end, you were checked when you got off the boat.

I never fucked around with the United States government. I had already learned my lesson with those people. In South America anything could be done, but the only thing I ever smuggled into the United States was Fidel's record "The Second Declaration of Havana."[1] I bought it in Uruguay and just put it in a Sinatra cover and didn't declare it. Sometimes I also brought in lobster tail. In Brazil it cost fifty cents and in the States ten or fifteen dollars, but it was for me, not part of the racket.

---

1. The reference is to Fidel Castro's speech of 4 February 1962 calling for revolutions throughout Latin America.

I used to make five hundred, a thousand dollars per trip beyond my pay on this television business, so I had lots of spending money for South America. I could spend three hundred, four hundred dollars without even touching my salary. I put ten thousand dollars in the bank, man, in those four years. In New York I had a brand-new car on which I didn't owe a penny. I had about ten or fifteen suits, never less than $150 a suit. I had about twenty-five pairs of shoes. I had all that stuff and money in the bank at the same time. And I was living that way as a wiper!

I kept the ship very clean. Every time we got to New York the people from the company would come and say this is the cleanest ship they had ever seen in their lives. Once they got to know me, they never told me what to do. I arranged my work for myself. I used to have another wiper working with me, and in the four years there must have been about six or seven different guys. But all of them got along fine with me because I knew how to handle them. I would tell them, "Listen, you take it easy, you got nothing to do." Usually I would wind up with the guys taking the garbage up and loving it because it would give them a chance to get out of the engine room. I would tell them, "You take all the time you want. Look around, if you see the chief coming, you come down here. But if you don't see the chief coming, you can stay in the aft. Half an hour, an hour, whatever you want—just dump the garbage over the side and you stay there."

After a while I always wound up controlling the other wipers. Not because I played boss, but on the contrary, I always told them, "Listen, I'm nothing here. I'm only a wiper like you. You do whatever you wanna do." They found out right away that when they were goofing off I would never turn them in, so they trusted me. And after that I would always ask them, "What do you think? I mean, do you want me to take the garbage up or do you wanna take the garbage up?" And they would say, no, they would take the garbage up. I really liked that, because I didn't want to carry that fuckin' garbage. It was a five-gallon bucket and full it weighed maybe seventy-five pounds. With my back troubles from before I figured it was better to take a brush and paint. All the wipers that came to work with me ended up taking out the garbage. Every time there was something to get in the machine room: "Listen you go over there, don't worry, I'll do this." What the other wiper didn't like to do, I would do.

What I was doing, I was doing for pleasure. I was daydreaming. I would paint and I would dream. I remember when I was in NYU I studied a book called *Daydreaming in Psychology*. Just like in that book I learned how to work daydreaming. I would say, "All right, I'm gonna daydream now," and I had a kind of system. Say, I was painting a pump. I would do the job in two, three hours, there was no hurry, and I would remember something in the past, bad or good, or think about what I would like to see happen in the world. Stuff like that. You can't really make a mistake painting, you know, anyway not one you can't correct. So I freed my mind. The ship was white, I kept it white. Wherever there was a spot I painted it, and the officer would walk in and never dared say one word to me.

I used to make a lot of overtime at sea. If the chief likes you, it's easy. I had about three chiefs and four executives, first officers, in my four years, and they were all good to me. I remember one guy especially, he gave me as many extra hours as he could, sometimes even jobs that didn't exist, so I could make money.

One day I got mad at an officer who was in the engine room, and I almost hit the son of a bitch. The guy went over and told the chief, so the chief came to me. I said, "Well, listen, Chief, the only thing I can do is just get off the boat when we get to New York. You want me to go?" See, the officer didn't have any authority over me. The only man with authority over the wiper is either the chief engineer or the executive officer. The executive is the guy that is supposed to be in charge of the cleaning of the ship, and in the union arrangement the wiper doesn't have anything to do with the other officers. The chief engineer, the first chief, was a Spaniard. The second chief, the one I'm talking about now, was Norwegian, an American citizen but Norwegian, with an accent. He said to me, "Listen, I tell you one thing, Lopez, if somebody's gonna get off this ship as long as I am chief, it's him and not you. I'm not gonna lose you."

I had my lousy blows and I was still having blows, but they were easier to take. I was older, wiser. And now I knew that even if my job was only as a wiper, you can make a difference with any job. And if you're forced into it, you can do with any job what you want to do. So the man who was supposed to be my boss ended up saying to me, "If anybody goes, it's the other guy, not you." I looked around and said to myself, I'm the chief. I'm the chief now. After that I would sometimes go back in the aft of the ship and laugh at the sea.

— 21 —

The Waterfront Deal Was Dying for Me (1961–1965)

THERE WAS a famous whore in Brazil, I forgot her name, but I used to call her "*La Chuchua*," which in Puerto Rican ship talk means "the woman that's the best of the whores."

There was a guy, Gómez was his name, who had La Chuchua steady like. Every time we went to Rio, Gómez went with the Chuchua. But everybody knew her, she was a beautiful woman and nice to everybody. She did not go with any seamen, though, except Gómez. So the talk in the ship was about how everybody tried to get La Chuchua away from Gómez. I would go around with Gómez when he went to see the Chuchua, and she got to know me very well. Every month or so I would see her with Gómez and have a few drinks. The way it worked is the ship would go to Santos, which is the port that goes to São Paulo, about fifty miles or so inland. The ship schedules were in the newspapers, so when the ship sailed out from Santos to Rio, La Chuchua would be there waiting for Gómez.

Now, after my first year on the ship the waterfront bars, the whores—the whole waterfront deal—was dying for me. The waterfront was ending. I was only there to say hello when I got off the ship—one drink with the guys and then I was gone. Off to Copacabana or, in Buenos Aires, to Palermo. Some nights I would spend about three hundred dollars going to different places in Rio or B.A. One day Chuchua was with me. Gómez had stayed home on this trip, home with his family. Chuchua and I had a few drinks and danced, and she took me to her house. She had a beautiful house in Rio with another whore.

I slept in the living room and didn't go to her room. She spent the whole night going back and forth around the house, almost naked, and she was beautiful. But because she was a whore she didn't mean anything to me as far as sex was concerned. I liked her as a friend, that's all. When I got up in the morning, she brought me breakfast. It was a Saturday, so I could stay. The next day she gave me breakfast again, and then I went back to the docks and shipped out.

After that it was me she was always looking for. And this was fantastic—everyone wanted the Chuchua, even the captains. She was famous, she was the doll of the whores. She told me, "I have been going after you for a long time, six months. And you have been coming and sleeping in my living room for all that time and you didn't fuck me." In the end I stayed with her, and she became mine.

She had such a beautiful body and such a beautiful face, black hair and green eyes, she was a mixture of Portuguese and German. In Brazil you have all those kind of crazy mixtures, and because of that in Brazil you find the most tremendously beautiful women.

Chuchua was afraid her tits would be destroyed. She used to say, "Nobody can touch them. I don't let anybody play with them because once they go, I will go." I said, "Well, listen, do you want me to adore you alone without that?" "No, you are the only guy that is going to, I have been after you for so long a time."

I used to go to other places in Brazil, too—Pernambuco for one, that's the poorest place in all Brazil. The people there lived in the streets, like in India. You would walk at night in the streets and find you were stepping on women and kids. Girls ten, twelve years old were whores there. It was disgusting. I couldn't stand it.

Another place I went to was Salvador de Bahia. That's a beautiful place but it's poor, too, very poor. I think we went there two or three times, but I couldn't do anything there either. No woman, no restaurants, no connections. Not like in Rio where you can get a nice hotel, a nice woman, go to the best restaurants, and eat the best foods.

I was in Brazil when they had a coup d'état, in March 1964. I was in a bar in Copacabana, and they announced that Goulart[1] was under

---

1. João Goulart (1918-76) was president of Brazil from 1961 to 1964.

fire in Rio. He declared that the army was making a coup, and he was not going to surrender. Then he got on a plane to Brasilia, which is a long trip, and by the time he got there, it was all over. He just took off for Uruguay. Living through a coup d'état is something. Even if it's bloodless, like Batista's. In Brazil, too, there was no killing, no big fighting, but still the people were in panic. Nobody knew where to go, what to do, and nobody would talk.

If the waterfront in Brazil was dying for me, in Buenos Aires I had already been staying away from it for a long time. I found girls of a different kind, nice girls. And in Montevideo I had the daughter of a colonel. These people needed money. I would give a girl fifty, a hundred dollars sometimes. The other guys on the ship, even the officers, hung around the waterfront most of the time. But I knew guys who could introduce me to girls that had families. I would even meet their fathers and their mothers, and they used to write to me. It was an altogether different setup from the dirty whoring thing the other seamen had.

The Uruguayans and Argentineans are more like Europeans, they don't look like Puerto Ricans. I wanted to find out why, so I started reading history, South American history. I bought books about Bolívar and I read about Belgrano[2]—that's a big guy in Argentinean history—and Santander.[3] I read a lot about their struggles among themselves, their battles—the foolish battles these people had sometimes!

We used to make trips to South Africa, to Capetown. I knew that this was a very controversial place to go, especially for me. It was the same goddamn thing as I had found in Texas in '46. In Texas they said, "White or Colored." Here they said, "Europeans or No Europeans"—the whites in South Africa didn't call themselves whites, they called themselves Europeans. And compared with there, Texas didn't look that bad. On the streets you had to cross in different places; in the post office there were different lines! They put a man in jail if they

---

2. Manuel Belgrano (1770-1820), Argentine general and patriot.
3. Francisco de Paula Santander (1792-1840), general and politician in Colombia when it was New Granada.

found him with a woman of a different color. There were cases in the newspapers where Portuguese sailors were sentenced to five years just because they were found in the sack with a woman. Even if she was a prostitute it didn't matter.

There were a few Ricans on that ship who were friends of mine—Charlie, Gómez, another guy, and this guy that I used to call Mao because he always talked about Mao Tse-tung.[4] Not that he was a Commie, he probably didn't know anything about it. Mao was a black Puerto Rican, real black, he had a face like a violin. He looked like the kind of Puerto Ricans that lived in the *fanguito,* the ones who were cut and scarred and so on. I didn't want to have even a slight argument with that guy. But as time went by, it turned out he was the nicest guy on earth. It was during that period that Kennedy got killed, and I remember Mao was happy and came up on deck and said, "Well, they got the son of a bitch." We used to listen to Castro all the time on short wave radio, and it was always Castro against Kennedy. Castro was very attractive to people at that time.

Anyway, when we got to South Africa, I said to myself, "If I go to shore with all these Puerto Ricans, how are we going to get along in this goddamn place?" Like I said before, once a group of Ricans get together, everybody's Rican. If you're a single Rican, you can pass, especially light ones.

I didn't know which line I was going to play there. I decided to go ashore with another Rican that was a little lighter than I. We went around the town and landed in a place where nobody said anything. We had a couple of drinks. Then we came back to the ship. When we got back, there was a lot of talk on the ship about the bullshit going on on shore. The Ricans didn't know where to go. Should they go to the white side or the Negro side? Some Ricans went to the Negro side and didn't have any trouble, some went to the white side and didn't have any trouble.

Next day we went ashore to rent a car. Again nobody said any-

---

4. Mao Tse-tung (1893-1976), led the Communist Revolution in China. When the People's Republic of China was established in 1949, he became Chairman of the Party and the State, disastrously attempting to force China to industrialize.

thing. "What ship are you coming from? An American ship? Pay in advance, please." We hired a Ford with the wheel on the left side, like in England, for four, five days. I drove the car near the ship, parked it there, went to work, and then when two o'clock came, I went to town. My friend and I drove to the Negro side, we didn't have any trouble. We went to the Negro bars, no trouble. We went to the white bars, no trouble. When we got back to the ship, we talked to the bosun,[5] a white guy from Boston, and we said, "Listen, Bosun, we went to both sides, we saw both positions." He laughed his head off, "Jesus Christ, you guys are privileged sons of bitches because I can't go both ways."

In Capetown I saw something that struck me. I saw these tiny cars like they have in China. The passenger sits in the back, and the guy runs like a horse. They had a big Negro dressed like a tribal chief, and he would jump like a fuckin' horse. He looked like an animal, the fuckin' guy. The passenger would sit in the back, and the Negro gives him a whip so he can whip him. Then he will jump like a horse. I didn't take a ride on it, I just watched the guy a couple of times. I guess he made money with the tourists.

Another time we went to this national park where they had wild animals roaming around, lions and hippos and things I had never seen in my life. Driving back, I saw this Negro hitchhiking on a deserted road. First we went by him, but I said to my buddy, "Goddamn, let's stop and get this guy. If he has to walk, it will be two days before he gets anywhere." So I backed up and took him in. The guy tried to dump himself on the floor of the car. He was very humble. I said, "Man, sit up there, don't worry about it." So we rode and rode and rode and rode, for about fifty minutes, no cars. Then I saw a car coming from quite a distance, and we got scared, the other Rican and I. We knew you weren't supposed to give a black man a ride if you were white. My buddy said, "Well, listen, you better tell the guy to hit the deck again, man, because we don't want the cops jumping on us." So the guy lay on the floor until the other car passed us. The guy told me he wanted to get out. I couldn't under-

---

5. The boatswain.

stand his language, but he made signs, and we pulled over and got rid of him.

They had a lot of Indians from India in South Africa, and they were not considered white either. The Indians have good hair, and their features are not Negroid, but even so they can't fuck around like the Europeans. Pakistanis, too. I went to a bar, and the guy, an Indian or something, kept calling me "Pakistani." I told him, "Listen man, I'm Puerto Rican," but the guy couldn't understand. I tried to explain it to him. "Puerto Rico, that's in America, that's on the other side of the world." "No, man, you're a Pakistani." As if I was trying to be somebody else! He thought I was a Pakistani, and I didn't want to be a Pakistani. Like a Rican that doesn't want to be a Rican. "Don't be ashamed you're a Pakistani," that's what he was trying to tell me.

Like that time in Texas when I gave up and said, "All right, I'm a Mexican." But I could understand about their insisting I was a Mexican, because I spoke Spanish. Now I was saying to myself, Goddamn, I have to go around the whole fuckin' world and I still can't be a Puerto Rican! I can't be Rican in Texas and I can't be a Rican here either. I don't even know where Pakistan is. It's terrible, man!

They talk about discrimination in the United States and the discrimination in South Africa. But everybody discriminates whether they're white or not. You're not white, but you come among other people who aren't white, and you too discriminate.

We also went to Madagascar, to the capital Tananarive. We were there for four or five days. The more primitive the ports are, the longer the ship stays, because the facilities for unloading are so backward. You get to New York, man, and you're ready in two days to get out. The same in all these modern places—no matter how old the facilities—the ships unload fast and stay only two days, the most three days. But in this Tananarive it took us five or six days—first because the unloading equipment was bad, and second because the men who worked it were far from pros.

I would call the New York longshoremen the most professional in the world as far as handling the docks is concerned. They might be sons of bitches, they might be Mafiosi they might steal, constantly have strikes and all that stuff, but when they go to work they know their business. You take places like Madagascar, the guys who are unloading are Pakistani or whoever, it takes an hour to move the booms, and then the little truck comes over, and it's a tragedy.

The more you set out to talk against the Americans, the more you have to end up admiring them—the technology and efficiency of their country. This world is shit. Take the United States out of the world, and I don't know what would happen. It would cripple itself, go to pieces—you could just close down the whole world. I think even my old friend Mao knows this.

In Tananarive I made a date with this blonde girl, this French girl. I met her and I took her to dinner, and then she took me to her apartment. When I got there, I was feeling the woman up, and I shacked up with her, loving her up. Suddenly a dark-haired girl comes in. We talk and bullshit, and the blonde got cool in the loving setup. It got a little late, and I have to leave, and I went to one of those nightclubs to sing, "Begin the Beguine" and get drunk and then go to the ship. I found out later that the blonde was a lesbian. And I blasted her! She was a beautiful young girl about twenty; the other one was young, too—but about ten years older. They told me the older one, the dark-haired woman, was the *macho,* the man. The blonde was the woman I blasted, and it was good, too. You have these types.

My last trip I made as an oiler. I was sorry that I did, too, because it was a very bad trip. The oiler lives with the fireman and has the same watch as the fireman. The fireman on this trip was a guy from Trinidad. He was a regular, full-blooded black Negro, tall and muscular, and we started calling him "the Baboon." One day in the engine room, I don't know how come but I was talking to the guy and I referred to him as Baboon. He already knew that everyone on the ship called him that, so he got furious with me. One day on deck he told somebody he was going to beat the shit out of me and he was going to do some buttin' on me. It was only later I found out 'buttin' meant hitting with the head.

We slept in the same room. He kept the air conditioning very cold.

That night we got off watch, and I went to sleep. I took two blankets, and I was still shivering in my bed. I turned the thermostat up to seventy, and he put it back down. We kept on like that all night.

At four in the morning we were awakened to go to the watch. I decided I just couldn't take it any more from that guy, and I told him to cut out that shit. He made a face at me, that was his answer. So I said, "O.K." We came up from the watch at eight in the morning and had breakfast. I was watching him and when he got into the room, I went in and got myself a knife. I knew if I didn't set this guy straight, I would be fucked up the whole trip. I locked the door and said, "Listen, man, this is it, we're gonna have it out now." He said to me, "I know you Puerto Ricans cut, right?" The knife was in my hand. I said, "Yeah, the Puerto Ricans use the knife, and here's the knife." I was shitting in my pants, to tell you the truth, because I figured the guy to be six foot and I was thinking about that buttin'. I said to myself, If he comes with the buttin' I can punch him with the fuckin' knife. But then I saw he was turning yellow on me, and he calmed down. I didn't want to push it too hard either, so I quieted down, too, and put the knife away. You know what happened from then on? He became my best buddy. He used to talk all the time about Castro and how much he hated the Americans, how they used the Negroes, and how the Negroes were going to free Africa and all that. He wanted me to be a revolutionary on his side. Some revolutionary!

By this time the ship was supposed to go to Vietnam and become a shuttle. Being on a shuttle meant going back and forth between Saigon and, let's say, some port in the North, taking cargo, maybe for a year. It wasn't for me! They doubled your pay because that was a war area, but I wasn't interested in just the regular pay. On the other hand, that shuttle deal would've put my racket with Charlie out of business, too. So I said to them, "If you go to Vietnam, I don't go." Anyway, I found out that my situation in Puerto Rico had cooled, that the lieutenant who was looking for me had been fired, so the case was *archivado*.[6] Now I could go back home.

---

6. Filed away.

— 22 —

Even Inside Puerto Rico (1966)

WHEN I GOT BACK to Puerto Rico, I began working as a salesman for a company started by a friend of mine. It was a small company connected with a bigger company owned by my friend's father. I had ten Gs in the bank. I didn't need to pay rent, because I was living with my sister in Río Piedras. The only thing I had to pay for was my food and gas for my car, which I brought from the States, a brand new 1966, all paid.

I started selling. My friend did the organizing, "You go to this place and to that place." The father's company was worth millions of dollars, but the company of the son was worth nothing, it was new. So in the beginning I didn't draw any pay. As a matter of fact, I had to spend money. I had to take the "boss" for lunch, I had to drive him here and there, pay for the gas. He didn't have any money. I practically had to finance the whole goddamn business.

After two or three months of working that way, the old man said to his son, "O.K., give him a hundred and fifty, two hundred dollars a week." In the beginning the old man was sort of afraid of me. I was a seaman, a hackman—a tough guy, he thought. He never felt too comfortable, because I was not raised up like him. He must have figured I was some guy from the poor sections. I would tell him, "Listen, I want more money," and he would say, "O.K."

I bought a house on a big corner lot. I filled out the papers, you know, like a man with money in the bank and a regular job. The house was not finished, they were still building it. It had about a nine-hundred-foot lot—usually you have about three-hundred-fifty, four-hundred—three bedrooms, bathrooms, everything brand new. I was going to set up a nice bachelor's house, to duplicate what I would have done in New York. This was my plan, but it didn't work out that way because later on I got married.

Meanwhile during the time I was working as a salesman I developed swollen glands. I went to a doctor, and he gave me some medicine and said, "You got mumps, and you have to stay quiet in bed." There is a saying in Puerto Rico I think he was hinting at, that if you move too much, the thing will go to your balls and make them swell up.[1] I remembered when I was a kid I used to see men walking around the streets with big balls in their pants, and so I went straight home and got into the goddamn bed and didn't move an inch. One day went by, two days, three days. On the fourth day suddenly I had this tremendous pain in my back. This time something told me, "Benjy, move." I moved all right. I got up and said to my sister, "Take me to the hospital."

She took me. When I got there, the doctor who examined me found I had a blood clot on my lung. It happened because my legs got so stiff from my not moving. They called it an embolism. That happens a lot in people's legs. In my case it rolled up my body and went to my lungs. I almost kicked off right there. On account of trying not to have big balls, I was almost not going to have any balls at all! But anyway I got to the hospital in time. They rushed me into intensive care. I was between life and death for a few weeks. They gave me heparin, a medicine that breaks down blood clots. In the end I was lucky and came back to life.

When I came from New York, I didn't know anything about Puerto Rico. I've been away twenty years, straight. Actually I'm a foreigner when I got here. I got all kicked up all over New York. I'm pissed off and in trouble in the streets, treated like a dog, so I came over and I figured that the people wanted independence. I thought it was feasible. But, we are living in an age in which ideals don't mean nothing. I looked around for a little while and I found out that that bullshit didn't work, that the people over here didn't care. Ideal is only if it's

---

1. "*Si te baja para abajo los huevos se te ponen grandes.*"

reality, if it's practical. If I have an ideal and I see after I analyze the whole problem that it's impractical, unreasonable, that it cannot be done, then my intelligence tells me that I just can't be fanatic about it. I can't be yelling "That has to be, I believe in that, I believe in that!" when I know that it can't be done. Like a mathematical problem, when you check on the lines and the angles and you see it can't be, what is the sense then? So I say to myself, I'm not going to knock my head off for something that won't work.

But during this time the FBI seemed to be chasing me, and I didn't know why. They went to my sister's house and asked about me. But they never came straight to me. That burned the hell out of me because I figured if the FBI wanted anything from me they should come to me straight. In my sister's neighborhood everybody could see into one another's houses and into one another's lives. The people who lived on either side of my sister were from the *PPD*.[2] I leaned more to the *MPI*, and so did my sister and her family, more or less. We didn't vote. We didn't register. We weren't political. So when the FBI came around, the neighbors all knew. If they had opened their windows, they could even have heard the questions. So that really burned the hell out of me.

Anyway, they kept on that way. One day I came over to visit, and they were outside the house waiting for me, two FBIs. One of them called me, and I went over and got inside their car. "We want to talk to you." They started asking a lot of questions. "He was an *MPI*," the guy in the front said. I said, "Listen, you fuckin' guys are no fuckin' good anyway because the whole fuckin' system is no goddamn good." I told him I read a book called *The FBI Nobody Knows*.[3] The guy said, "You read too many books."

They were Americans, the two of them. And I said to myself, Goddamn it, even inside Puerto Rico these sons of bitches come and fuck me over, I can't get away from them. I pulled a trick on them, and they got scared, like cowards. My car was still in the street, fac-

---

2. The Popular Democratic Party which advocates the current commonwealth association between Puerto Rico and the United States.
3. A 1964 exposé of the FBI by investigative journalist Fred J. Cook (1911- 2003).

ing their car. I got in my car, put the lights on, and backed up more than seventy-five yards. They were parked by the entrance to my sister's carport. I started the motor, put it in first, gunned it, and the FBI guys started backing up. Instead of coming forward the way they were facing, they backed up the length of the whole goddamn street. When I got to the entrance to the carport, I slammed on the brake, made a sharp left, and pulled in. They backed up all the way.

That night I said nothing but made up my mind to go and see them in their office. So the next day I went there. As soon as I sat down, the boss walked in, his name was Anderson. He started, "Where were you these last twenty years? Tell me about you." "I was in the Army." "O.K., you were in the Army." The guy kept on looking at me and moving closer, closer, and closer, pushing me and putting his face close to mine. I started suspecting that the guy was a fag. But afterward I came to the conclusion that he was looking at my face to see if I was lying. Since I was clearly telling the truth, acting so natural, he was amazed. That must have made me an even greater liar in his eyes—just like the lousy FBI.

When I told the guy I worked with about all this, he said, "Let's go to the Civil Rights Commission."[4] He was very close to one of the members. We went and told the story to his friend. On the way back I started thinking about the bullshit the FBI would say, that I was a subversive and stuff like that, and since the big company had a federal license, I was worrying that they would give the old man some needle, and he would say, "Well, get this guy out of here, that's it." I didn't want to lose the job. I was just starting to feel I had escaped from the goddamn boats, away from the whole lousy battle. So I decided not to go to the Civil Rights Commission after all and to forget about the thing, but I was still pissed off at the FBI.

One day the FBI came to my office. "We're the FBI." I said, "Well, I'm Lopez." I knew the guys right away. "All right, you wanna talk, let's talk," they said. We left the office and walked down to the park-

---

4. A permanent Commission on Civil Rights was established by the Puerto Rican legislature on 28 June 1965.

ing lot, and I was walking in the middle, one on one side, one on the other. They were about a half-step or so behind me. We got to the FBI car, and one guy opened the door. He said, "O.K., sit down." The other guy went around to the wheel, opened the door and got in, and the first guy got in the back. I saw that guy open his jacket and undo the holster of his gun. He was sitting in the back with the gun, and I was sitting in the front trying to figure out how I have to play this thing. I decided not to cooperate. "I don't tell you guys anything. You want information about me, you look for it. Work your asses off."

I don't know if the SS[5] was that good, and I don't know if the NKVD[6] in Russia was that good, and I don't know if Fidel's outfit is that good. In those systems they have the right to come and grab you by the neck. But over here we are supposed to be in a free country. If they want to investigate somebody, they should investigate the guy secretly, you know, without anybody knowing it, and if they don't really have any goddamn thing on the guy, they don't have to come around and fuck him over. You know, cost him his job, make him go hungry in the streets, and maybe he is even innocent.

They started claiming that I came from Cuba, that I came in a submarine. Then I told them everything about myself the same as I told Anderson, but they didn't believe me. "No you're a liar. You come from a submarine in Cuba." "Man, how was I in Cuba? I was on the *Mormac Cape,* for four fuckin' years." "No, from 1960 on you disappeared and you were in Cuba. We know it. You're lying to us, you are a liar." They said they went to the hospital, and I didn't have a record there. They checked in New York, and I wasn't in the Army.

Suddenly I figured out why they couldn't find my records. It happened that the Army wasn't fussy about papers before World War II. My uncle, my father's brother, used to tell me that his name was de Lopez, so when I was lying to get into the Army and they asked me my name, I said it was de Lopez. So that is how I was registered in the

---

5. SS, abbreviation for 'Protective Squadron,' the Nazi military organization under Hitler responsible for many of the crimes perpetrated during World War II.
6. NKVD, abbreviation for 'People's Commissariat Internal Affairs,' the Soviet secret police organization responsible for political repression during the Stalinist era

Army and how my name appeared on my discharge papers, and from there to the merchant marine, the Veteran's Hospital, and so on. All over the United States I'm de Lopez. But in Puerto Rico I went back to Lopez because people here don't like the de Lopez shit.

So I realized that's where they got fouled up, and I started laughing like a madman in the car. I had my seaman's certificate with me, and I pulled it out. I said, "Listen, man, you're full of shit, look at that." When they grabbed the papers and saw "Benjamin de Lopez," they said, "SHIT!!! God, no, no, no!" I said, "Yeah, see what'd I tell you, you're full of shit. You're no good. What kind of investigator are you? You steal money from the government, you don't know how to investigate. I was one of the ten most suspected fellows in Puerto Rico, and I've been in the payroll of the United States all my life!" I got out of the car, and the guys sat there for a minute, and then they drove off like a bullet, and I never heard from them again.

— 23 —

If I Keep on Thinking . . .

WOULD I DO IT OVER AGAIN? Go to New York? If I had known what would happen—no, man, I wouldn't want to face it. From the Army I would have come straight back to Puerto Rico or maybe gone to some other place, to Brazil, but not New York. I wouldn't want to go through that shit.

But everyone takes it. Everybody wants to go to the United States—from all over the world—because of the economics. But if they had a chance to live through what I lived all those twenty years in New York, a lot of them would rather live in a hut some place.

It took me a long time to find out what that world is all about. I had to go through all these women, I had to go through all the suffering on the ships, I had to go through everything to find out in my forties what the world was all about. Because I was raised in ignorance.

When I see one of those big rich guys—I don't care if he's George Romney[1] and you know, I met him—to me he's just like the guy that's gonna cut my grass. I look at the guy and I say, "How do you do, man, you gonna run for president of the United States? I'm Benjy Lopez, how's everything, have a drink." Now if Nelson Rockefeller[2] was standing in front of me, I wouldn't think I was looking at a god. I would just be seeing a human being that's got a lot of money. It took

---

1. George W. Romney (1907-1995) was president of American Motors, governor of Michigan, candidate for president of the U.S. and a cabinet member in the Nixon administration. His son Mitt Romney was governor of Massachusetts.
2. Nelson Rockefeller (1908-1979) was governor of New York, candidate for president of the U.S. and vice president of the U.S.

me all those years to find that out that everybody's the same, that's it. There's no more kings. The rich characters here, I treat them just the same and they mix with me. There might be a little difference between us—they got three or four million dollars that I don't have—but that's another matter.

It's a tremendous advantage to think this way. Imagine if you were twenty years old and didn't feel inferior to anybody or better than anybody—what an advantage! When you learn to treat everybody the same, people open up to you. Everybody's open to me. I don't make enemies, because I don't have anything against anybody. Besides, if you play everybody equal, you can learn a lot more than if you try to push somebody. He gets like a rat in a corner and tries to hide or fight you. My way, nobody tries to fight you off and if anyone has any flaws, they show up immediately. That's the tremendous advantage I have: I talk to everybody, and right away I know the guy that's going to try to fuck me. I can see it all, because I'm not trying to protect myself against the guy. Actually to learn all this takes a long time. New York taught me a lot.

New York taught me other things. The greatest school for bureaucracy is the United States. Everything is, "Fill the papers, you get some money." You could be right, but if the papers are wrong, you're fucked. If you need some money and you go to the bank, you could be the best guy, the most truthful guy, the best paid, but if your papers are wrong, you get nothing. If you're bad and your papers are right, you get whatever you want. I was sick in the ship. It isn't the idea of getting yourself cured; it's the idea of you having a right to it because it's the law. You're supposed to get fifty or seventy-five or four hundred or five hundred dollars compensation. If you're really sick and you don't do the papers right, you don't get the money. If you're just a little sick and you know how to do the papers, you get all the money you want. It's the same thing in the Army. The Army is a tremendous school for learning how to work the goddamn papers.

In Puerto Rico people are not so advanced as in the United States, especially they didn't used to be when I was younger. In the last ten years Puerto Rico has started to catch up, but it's still behind. If you know how to work the system, you can get along a lot better than most of the people who live here do. It's like when you testify in court, you learn to say only as much as is within the law, and that's it. However good your story is, if it doesn't go straight with what the law says, it doesn't count. The technicalities can set you free.

If I keep on thinking and digging into my past, I'm going to wind up saying, "Goddamn! There was a lucky side to New York." It was the kind of thing that plays both ways. Actually my life would never have been the same if I hadn't gone through all that. I wouldn't be the way I am now, Wouldn't think the way I do now, I might be just like all the other people. Things that people who stayed never think about, I think about immediately now.

Back here in Puerto Rico the people who live around me are not the same as me anymore. They can't think like me. Never. I can see more than these people do. I go to places here and I walk in, everybody thinks I'm a lawyer. Or sometimes I'm with a doctor and everybody thinks I'm the doctor and the other guy is not. I go to the hardware store and I buy a few things, cement, stuff like that, to do some little work, and I say, "Listen, this, that, put it in the truck, send it over." The guy says, "You don't have to pay, you're a lawyer." I think that's the splash that I got in those ugly days in New York.

It goes back to what I said at the beginning, *Salpicar,* the splash. And the splash, you get more of it or less. I met this guy, he's a lawyer. I started talking to him. O.K., he's bright, he has a lot of education, he went to the States and got a law degree. But even though he lived in the States for three years, he didn't get that much of the splash. No matter how much they teach guys like that in school in two years, three years, they don't get to understand the American society. They get a degree from Yale, from Princeton, but still they don't understand the society. Me, I lived twenty years in the jungle. And I got the splash. New York for me was a tremendous ordeal—but it has helped me tremendously, too.

But a lot of the people that are from New York itself, they never get much of the splash—the ones that were raised there and never left. Someone from outside is like a great enigma for them. They just stay in the same place and don't move, and their brains don't move either.

I know the Puerto Ricans. I was like them until I came out of the Army. I know the Neoricans, too. I know their ways. I understand them and why they think the way they do. The Neorican has a lot of complexes. I know the Americans. I started to understand them in the Army and then in New York. I went to school with them. I walked with them. So I can live like an American. I can think like one, too. And on the ships I also got to know a lot of other people—Germans, South Americans. . . . I even read their histories. Don't forget the Cubans either. I can fit in with them perfectly—as good as with the Ricans, as good as with the Americans. The end of all this is that I am not a Rican. I am not an American, I am not a Neorican. I'm a fuckin' international—an international who's been splashed!

I may be an international, but I have to say the splash I got in the goddamn streets of New York. That New York school is so big—it's a whole university, not just a four-year college. I learned that if I was up to something and found out it wasn't going to work, why kill myself? Find another way. There's no other way for a human being to live. There's always something new to do in this world.

I never get tired of something that produces. If it doesn't produce, it's no good. And I don't care what's going to happen tomorrow. Somehow I'm always going to make it. As easy as that. The seeds of this idea started developing in New York, in the cab and in the ship.

It's the same thing with women. What's the sense of living with a woman about whom you don't feel good, you don't feel right. Somewhere you are going to run into the right one. Sometime. Take me, for example.

My first wife was Marta. The second woman who was the mother of my kid was another. I had never found a woman to whom I could say, "I tie myself up to you, one woman for all the time." For forty, forty-five years I couldn't find a woman in this world. Thousands of women, and I couldn't find one! Suddenly I ran into this woman by accident, and it was a blitzkrieg. This was it! Somewhere in this world there's always that woman for a man.

Sometimes men and women don't take the steps they should, and they get stuck. She gets stuck with a husband that is rich, three cars, money, clothes, nothing, no happiness. And they grow old, get gray, and lead a lousy life. They should have broken it off. Why do people stay tied up and remain unhappy?

It's very expensive to worry about security. The idea is to live like a rich man without being rich. When I used to live in New York and drive a cab, at the end of the day I put on my $250 suit, put $150 in my pocket, and went downtown. I don't know why I did it, but I always wanted to do it like that. Something pushed me to do it. "Benjy, you gotta dress and you gotta spend two hundred and fifty bucks on a goddamn suit." I feel good, and I put my money in my pocket, and I go downtown. I walk around, walk inside some bar. Nobody knows who I am in a big town like that, that I'm just a cab driver who'll be taking them home tomorrow. I would go over to the East Side and walk around, or go to the Copacabana. With $150 in my pocket, for half an hour I am richer than Frank Sinatra!

Stuff like that I did, the other Ricans didn't do. I don't know, maybe the splash has been with me since the day I was born. Which all comes back to the point that everything is in the person himself. Each brain is a separate brain, each life is a separate life. I must have been born with the splash.

AFTERWORD

Changing the Story*

MOST TRADITIONAL SOCIOLOGISTS and anthropologists regard actors as products of the social world. They hold a kind of "plop and pop" conception of the relation between the actor and society. According to such a view, "plop" the actor into a culture, and "pop," into his heart and mind go the values and definitions of the place in which he happens to be. The social world is viewed as massive and monolithic with minted actors lockstepped into conformity. Chinese children, accordingly, become Chinese, and Eskimos, Eskimos. Such an assertion incorrectly envisions a society of unreal power and authority that determines an actor's thoughts and actions, creating not individuals but "cultural dopes," to use Anthony Giddens's striking phrase.[1] Effectively integrated and programmed, according to this view, the actors are vital if a culture directs them to be vital and meek if a culture directs them to be meek. The problem with this idea is that the concept of socially produced vitality is, at best, oxymoronic, and, at worst, a contradiction in terms.

When social scientists approach the terrain of the literary artist, the connection between social determinism and vitality becomes more troublesome. The medium here is the testimonial, the life history, sometimes called the personal document or the first-person sociology. In a testimonial, a person relates the events of his life and the social conditions surrounding it. When the protagonist lives through periods of great social change, such first-person sociology becomes a vivid, if not a vivacious, eyewitness social history.

---

* The notes accompanying this essay begin on page 203.

Anthropologists have used the testimonial to articulate the lives of primitive and traditional peoples; sociologists, to portray the lives of ethnics, deviants, the poor, and inhabitants of the Third World.

Around the time first-person sociology initially became popular, works spelling out the methodological assumptions of this new medium began to appear.[2] One author, John Dollard, argued in 1935 that "the problem of the life history is . . . [to show] how the new organism becomes the victim or the resultant of this firm structure of the culture;"[3] the life history, he continued, "is thus an account of the socialization of a person."[4] For him, social science differs from art in that social scientists are not simply articulating the social drama of human life as much as they are demonstrating that this or that life is a product of these or those social circumstances. The badge of social determinism, in fact a retrospective determinism,[5] was to distinguish social science from art. Unfortunately, these studies typically perceived their protagonists not as activists but as products of their cultures—victims, to use Dollard's infelicitous term.

The differences between traditional sociology and modern literature have become even more marked as areas of the latter have become radically vitalistic. A new spirit lit up American literature after World War II.[6] A. J. Guerard, introducing Bellow's *The Adventures of Augie March*—the classic example of the new style—characterized this attitude as "activist."[7] That term is not political. It announces an author's or a protagonist's vision of "energy, vitality, sheer activity as moral goods."[8] The new activist fiction, then, is unsymbolic, rich, crowded, adventurous, and picaresque. Little justification is offered for the commonplace, the apathetic, the compliant. The ordered, dull, and defeated are bypassed in favor of mobility, novelty, and "racy toughness."[9] "Life remains free, unpredictable, undetermined."[10] Agency, autonomy, and vitality struggle to surface in a world of chance and transience.

The heroes of such works are incorrigibly vivacious and have an irrepressible will to live life to its fullest. Crudity, roughness, opportunism do not ruffle them. They are the owners of their spirits; have aware, alert, and willful consciousnesses; hold playful attitudes about the capricious nature of fortune and fate. They repudiate mediocre living. For them life is to be confronted, not avoided; willed, not accepted; "encountered, not shunned."[11] Augie March, for example, is an urban wanderer, travels up and down the social structure, accepts no social location, has no specific role. A rogue and a *pícaro*,[12] he is "a man of fundamental good nature though capable of amorality and even minor crime."[13] He refuses to give in, settle down, or be willing to specialize. His attitude is "not to rebel but to be in opposition to fixity."[14] He is in constant search of sense in a world of casual flux. He is, in his own words, self-dedicated "not to lead a disappointed life."[15]

Benjy Lopez had many of the characteristics of these activist literary heroes, and his story reads much like one of these novels. To me, he was a Puerto Rican Augie March, and this book, a sociological parallel to activist fiction, a kind of activist nonfiction,[16] a picaresque sociology, a sociology of vitality in the face of social structure. I trust that such an idea is at most merely oxymoronic, and not a contradiction in terms.

Lopez saw life as a series of episodes. He had a great sense of the contingencies of life and made few assumptions about continuity. Life involved deals, bargains, angles, short-term and long-term schemes, and projects. Life was discontinuous; what kept it together, what gave it the semblance of continuity, was the central role that he played. Clearly, it was he who was the agent of happening. It was he who gave it meaning and importance; it was he who organized it and who got himself through life's events.

This style of his was a conscious critique of lower-middle-class virtuosity where actors would willingly play the game, religiously following the rules and settling for but minor shares of the rewards. Lopez critically viewed the struggle of running a *bodega* in one of New York's Spanish neighborhoods, for example, to be an unjust and senseless urban version of cutting sugarcane in the fields. Why do it when it was so routine, so devoid of variation, so physically tiring, and so meager of reward? But his style—that of episodic man —was also a critique of middle-class bureaucrats who steadfastly, if not mindlessly, organized their lives around the long tunnel of the career. Whereas for the bourgeois middle class, adventures were often confined to one's private life (and understood as intimate escapades, if not transgressions), for Lopez most of life had a structure of adventure.

As was proper for a person who cultivated his imagination, Lopez was both greatly fascinated with others' lives and well able to marvel at the oddities of everyday life. In his spotting of odd conventions and styles and his comment on them, he rivaled the more interesting social cataloguers. Listening to him relate his observations of American life, I often felt that I was hearing an anthropologist reporting on a quaint United States. In his culturally expansive life he witnessed and catalogued a whole series of variations on life's themes. He saw everything from strange animals to alternative sexual styles. Lopez celebrated relativism, but one tempered by his own unfinished attempts at developing a standard. On the island, he compared things with their analogues off the island; away from Puerto Rico, he compared things with like happenings in Puerto Rico.

Lopez liked to uncover the ambivalences of social life; he saw two sides, if not more, to every story. He spotted the inconsistencies in arguments and the exaggerations in declarations. To deal with the dualisms of the social world he would often evoke a kind of dialectical logic and pile irony upon irony. He could take an argument to its logical extreme, develop it to its fullest, and then, without warning, show you the reverse. His language reflected this multiple vision: saying something was "tremendous" might mean it was bad; modifying something with the American intensive might mean that it was good.

The Lopez I knew saw himself as heroic, as someone who could successfully find a way to triumph over adverse conditions. This self-image was in part a consequence of his own deliberate construction, for he was an expert in the short con,[17] the ability to underpresent one's capacities so that success appeared to be that much more dramatic a recovery. He would use his identity tactically, and simultaneously both refuse to internalize an assigned negative Puerto Rican self-image as well as play at such an identity if it would get him out of a tight situation. When confronted by adversity, he would concurrently acknowledge its presence while seeing through the images and definitions that tried to legitimate and confirm that adversity.

Lopez rejected conformity, but his deviance was strategic rather than decadent—decadence was often a surprise to him. As far as I could gather, for him this book was not an attempt to show the reader that he conformed to anyone's expectations, nor was it an *apologia pro vita sua*, an attempt to excuse himself for something he possibly should not have done. Rather, it was an attempt to convince the reader of the value and the ingenuity of the way he did things—perhaps differently, maybe even better, the result of a man who rejected foregone conclusions.

Yet Lopez did care about the image he presented to the world. On the one hand, that image was important in terms of his capacity to manipulate that world; on the other hand, it was important because he often judged himself in terms of comparative advantage. However, no conventional self-image was as valuable in his eyes as the capacity to manipulate that world freely or to gain that comparative advantage.

When Benjy Lopez was younger, there was a kind of violence in him that he was later to overcome. Some of his tougher moments were with women in New York whom he treated as objects. But even then, in the midst of such indelicate moments, Lopez was capable of recognizing the human quality of man/woman relationships. Once that violence dissipated, Lopez saw victory less in conquest than in a social relationship where he could get the other to listen to and understand him. His encounters became verbal, with little, if any, trace of the physical. For Lopez believed that there was something that he could teach and something the listener could learn. The nature of his social encounters, which he once thought naive, and then thought callous, came to be clearly dominated by the wit, will, and words that characterized his style.

In many ways Lopez was a *pícaro*, a rogue, in and out of scrapes, exposed to the world, searching to make sense of it, all the time aware of his struggle. He developed strategies for achieving his goals, directly or indirectly. He knew how to persuade, to outwit, to operate. He could play into the norms or play without them. He could be charming, indeed ingratiating, and empathic to a fault. He rejected subordination and declared himself equal. He claimed to have a better understanding, after many trials and tribulations, of what made the world go round. He manifested a particular zest in his way of doing things and was excited about his style of life. He was free in the sense that he was able to resist getting caught up in everyday routine and remained ready to innovate.

Inconvenient Individuals

Traditional sociology, which wants to conceive of the individual as a product of society, admittedly has a difficult time dealing with inconvenient individuals such as Lopez who are hard to contain within the concepts of normality, social control, and programmed deviance. One way sociologists explain a style such as his is to argue that it represents one form of resistance by the powerless who, not having made it in the taken-for-granted everyday world, would try to make it elsewhere. They regard rejection of the conventional as a reaction to a feeling of being denied access to the means of achievement in society. According to this view, proof that such a style is but an adaptive strategy for dealing with one's exclusion is found in the assertion that if an actor were given access to the standard opportunities in society, he would be more likely to adopt a more conventional view of life. The problem with this explanation is that it pictures an actor who, though not a product of the conventional world, is a product of his not being a product of that world. What happens to this theory should the actor *not* prefer the conventional opportunities?

It could just as easily be asserted that the conformist does what everybody else does because he does not have the internal strength necessary to veer creatively from that path. This argument holds that all actors have the potential to be creative, and that if for some reason they cannot be, then they follow the conventional. In the case of Benjy Lopez, whose creative potential was obvious, he did not accept the social world as a demanding authority telling him what to do or what it would allow him to do. Rather, he saw that world as a field of opportunities open for his selection and development (which opportunities he often spotted before anyone else even realized their potential benefit).

Disappointment with what he had not been able to realize might have influenced him to embrace wholeheartedly what he found. Instead, he held onto his skepticism and nagging sense of irony and used these faculties as guides through the marginality that his existence encouraged. Benjy Lopez had longed for but then no longer expected to achieve a community he thought one day might be his. It is not clear that had he been presented with any more of the conventional opportunities of Puerto Rican life, he would have been any more conventional than he was; I suspect he would simply have followed his style from a much more secure base. Lopez toyed with but ultimately rejected any effort to change his society to conform to his own ideals. That would never have happened, since for him the system was upstairs, and he thought of himself as downstairs trying to take advantage of it. Some may lament this, though I surely doubt that *he* ever did—for any disappointment had not been total, and his hopes had found other outlets.

Thus Lopez's story was not one of despair and resignation[18] but rather a picaresque adventure in which the hero worked his way through and around the labyrinth of race, ethnicity, class, and bureaucracy in the cosmopolitan world of New York City. Lopez hustled hard in New York; but he did so with sufficient role distance[19] to allow himself to be both reflective and calculating. His was the story of a man who never gave up. Although close to it at times, Benjy Lopez never gave himself the excuse of feeling that he was without alternatives, without additional plans to pursue. Lopez never gave in to the unreasonable demands of a witless and unconsidered reality. This final resistance reflected a basic refusal to lead a disappointed life. As long as he could, he intended to will his way.

The United States' most successful immigrants have nurtured an eminently practical approach to life. Outside the U.S. status system, they have had no commitment to it and have had no illusion about social standing in the States. Not embracing the rules of society, they have made their own. Lopez partook of this "no-illusion" practicality. Ultimately, he was anti-ideological. More proximately, he was constantly calculating: forever weighing ends and means to obtain the most for the least. In contrast to the attitude of other immigrants who took the United States too seriously, Lopez took from the Americans rather than ape them. "Americanization" for Lopez meant becoming America-smart, meant being aware of and taking advantage of opportunities of an American character—opportunities that had not normally been available to Puerto Ricans on the island. Such opportunities and experiences set him apart from those who did not have them. Yet he took such opportunities and had such experiences very much in his own way. Lopez did not so much become

"Americanized" as he had become multicultural, half outside each of at least two different social worlds.

Given Lopez's marginality, a question arises as to the representativeness of his story. It has been argued that since their protagonists must be articulate, testimonial literature in general is not specifically typical of the populations from which it is drawn.[20] How then do we interpret this book? Personal memoir? Rogue adventure? Social history? Though it recounts the experiences of one man migrating, the world he experienced was shared by many. Therein lies its sociological importance: by letting him tell his story we get a chance to be exposed to a world common to many Puerto Ricans. His reactions to that world, told from his perspective, were his own and shared in various degrees by others.

The Sad Tale of the Puerto Rican Testimonial

Unhappily, the testimonial literature about Puerto Rico and Puerto Ricans has conformed to the genre's customary methodological pessimism; and, as a consequence, it has not been faithful to the Puerto Rican experience—witness titles such as *Nobody's Hero, A Criminal Addict's Story, A Puerto Rican Family in the Culture of Poverty, A Welfare Mother,* even the seventeenth-century *Infortunios de Alonso Ramírez*.[21] The Puerto Rican was presented as a person unable to take advantage of the world he lived in, unable to use it for his own purposes. Denuded of his vitality, the Puerto Rican was made to look like a mere product of his world, rarely portrayed as a producer of that world. There were virtually no protagonists in this genre who actively and heroically and effectively counter-managed the world in which they lived. Benjy's odyssey of self-creation is here presented as a deliberate alternative to the typical Puerto Rican testimonial.

Reflecting on the convulsive changes that have taken place on the island since 1940 by virtue of Puerto Rico's unique political circumstances—the attempt to industrialize the island and the emergence of the Puerto Rican circuit—one must be impressed by the sheer enormity of their effect. Whether one considers the Puerto Rican economy as dependent or balanced, fully developed or only partially so, energized or stalled, substantial changes have taken place in the island's society and economy. Yet when authors discussed these changes, the Puerto Rican personality was rarely invoked. There was no equivalent to the ascetic Protestant who fueled the emergence of modern capitalism in Western Europe and its English-speaking outposts, or to the dedicated worker of Japan and Southeast Asia, or to the hoped for new man of socialism who some romantically suggested would guide Third World countries on their path toward modernity.

The only discussion that I can recall concerning the role of the Puerto Rican personality amidst all the change on the island was that of Henry Wells who, in *The Modernization of Puerto Rico*, depicted the Puerto Rican as docile.[22] Puerto Rico modernized, according to Wells, because the governor, Luis Muñoz Marín, decided to impose United States welfare values upon it. Wells found nothing ascetic, dedicated, or even hopefully new about the Puerto Rican personality—and certainly nothing heroic.

Thus, the picture of the Puerto Rican drawn in the testimonial—as rural worker, as urban slum dweller, as immigrant to the mainland—was of the Puerto Rican as loser. And while in the very end we are all losers to the processes of biology, it is not true that we are all losers to the processes of society. Given all the changes in Puerto Rico, one would have expected to encounter portraits of individuals more vital than those portrayed in these testimonials. Clearly, there have been biases in their selection.

Perhaps the most significant reason for the dismal state of the Puerto Rican testimonial has to do with the way social change has been introduced into Puerto Rican society. It has come from above. Thus, the socioeconomic changes on the island obviously could not be understood as having been initiated or propelled by changes in the actions and attitudes of the typical Puerto Rican. Yet even in top-down processes of social change, there needs to be a human infrastructure below to activate such changes. For these changes to be effective, actors in such a system have to either do what is required of them or be smart enough to take advantage of the changes going on around them. Social change stimulated from above does not eliminate heroic possibilities and personalities from those efforts. Rather, the hero is the intelligent personality oriented in search of opportunities—one who can spot possible advantage, chance it, pursue it, and develop it.[23] Anybody who knows Puerto Rico knows that it has its share of such personalities. Puerto Rican society is not a playing field for losers. Concentration on the way social change has come about in Puerto Rico, however, has often obscured that reality.

Given the repeated calls for vitality from the intellectual left in Puerto Rico, one might have expected that it had located sources of such vitality. Obviously, the left would not have found it in the reigning socioeconomic system. Advocates of the independence of the island, they criticized the "Americanization" of the economy and the creation of the Puerto Rican circuit as processes making Puerto Rico dependent on the United States. For an individual to take advantage of the possibilities created by such processes—at the expense of working for Puerto Rico's political transcendence—represents to the left not a heroic mentality but a colonial one. Thus, the left found vitality not in beating the system but in resisting its oppressive encroachment and, while denying the docility of the Puerto Rican, could not quite celebrate his actual social circumstances either.

Another bias relates to the intellectuals' vision of the bourgeois middle class: according to this vision, the lives of the middle class are too prosaic to be interesting. What the bourgeois are willing to calculate is limited by what already is, not by what might be. To the extent that their roles are adequate to modern circumstances, they are minimally heroic, devoid of poetry, divested of systematic adventure. Nor are their lives tragic. Thus, social scientists perceive them neither as losers nor as active winners, and their lives rarely are selected for social science testimonial.[24]

Moreover, there are cultural prohibitions in Puerto Rico against acknowledging as heroic an activist personality. Taking advantage of a situation is often confused with taking advantage of another person. Within the context of the moral imperative to respect others (*respetar*) lie restrictions on how one is supposed to deal with them.[25] In an encounter with another person, one must not violate the ceremonial code of behavior but must express deference to and protect that other. He or she must not disturb the other's self-presentation nor malign his or her self-image. With proper signaling Puerto Ricans can suspend the rules of *respeto* and engage in *relajo* ("joking around"). But even within *relajo* one must be careful not to become abusive or offensive, for such behavior would indicate *una falta de respeto* ("a lack of respect").

Within such a moral climate the "aggressive" individual seeking to maximize possibilities is often criticized as *un listo* ("an overly clever one") or, worse, as *un atrevido* ("an audacious, even impudent, person who dares to do what others would never even think to attempt"). This is not to say that within Puerto Rican culture there are no surreptitious or even open attempts at countervailing socialization. Puerto Ricans acknowledge, for example, the value of noncooperation in *jaibería* and the *pelea monga* (*jaibería* refers to goldbricking strategies to avoid authority; *la pelea monga* is a "relaxed fight" in which one challenges others without letting them know it).[26] And, as in all societies, open countervailing pressures confront the Puerto Rican. Thus, while he is told not to be *un listo*, he is also told not to be *un bobo* ("a fool"), not to be *un pendejo* ("a schmuck") —not to let things get by him. He is told to conform and not disturb the mutual ceremony but also told *not* to conform if it means getting the short end. Nevertheless, the social climate is overwhelmingly pro-*respeto*; and in that ambiance it is understandable why the individual who hustles and refuses conformity, avoids resignation, and attacks opportunities has not gained officially acknowledged heroic status.

This respect for respect had historical roots in an agricultural Puerto Rico. If that attitude was first challenged in urban Puerto Rico, it came into open assault with the hostile reality of the migration to the States. New York, Chicago, Philadephia were uncaring receptacles of unsophisticated settlers. Cold, heartless, and amoral, if not actively immoral, the urban mainland was waiting to devour those who came from the island. Were the migrants to retain any original virtue they would appear to be hopelessly naive; were they to give in to the urban anomie they would appear to be helpless victims. So the migration itself made it difficult to see heroic possibilities. Early on there was no mythological respect for the achievements of the venturers, no mythology describing courageous and valiant efforts to "do" the migration.

To the extent that the heroic is equated with success achieved in an American context, this has presented an additional dilemma for observers of Puerto Rican society. In such a circumstance, personal success takes on the character of a political statement promoting the annexation of Puerto Rico.[27] The successful Puerto Rican in America risks looking like a *vende patria*, like a sell-out turning his back on his own country.[28] It is intellectually taxing to present the *pitiyanqui*—the 200% American who is more American than the Americans—as heroic. How can you have a heroic suck-up? And yet in a post-racial, multiethnic-trending America, you can, indeed, perhaps *need* to be able to avoid the negative smack down of assimilation and focus on the subtleties of becoming America-smart.

For some observers, the development of the two centers of Puerto Rican life, on the island and on the continent, seemed to have created an irreparable fissure in the Puerto Rican community, so that island Puerto Rican and mainland Puerto Rican shared no common purpose. If Puerto Ricans in New York were disparaged and looked down upon by many Americans, many Puerto Ricans who returned after spending time on the mainland were looked down upon when they came back to the island. Neorican, Nuyorican,[29] sometimes simply *un americano*, has been used not just to identify mainland Puerto Ricans but to stigmatize the returnees. Benjy Lopez was such a returnee. However, I would submit that the lives of individuals such as his, when told in testimony, do not make up as sad a tale as the lives recounted in past Puerto Rican testimonials and, in fact, change the nature of the Puerto Rican story itself.

Notes to the Essays

Introduction: Reflections on a Puerto Rican Life
(pages 1–12)

1. Puerto Rico's unique political relationship with the United States has presented both opportunities and costs for its compatriots while causing confusion for some and advantages for others. Spain ceded Puerto Rico to the U.S. in 1898 at the conclusion of the Spanish-American War. Puerto Ricans were given U.S. citizenship in 1917 and then, in 1950, the right to draft their own constitution. Since 1952, Puerto Rico has been a commonwealth or "freely associated state" of the United States. The U.S. takeover profoundly influenced the economy. Coffee had been the principal crop; soon thereafter sugar was raised to prominence as U.S. businessmen rationalized production and organized it around large plantations for export. Puerto Rico's rural workers thus became vulnerable to fluctuations in the world economy. But Puerto Rico's relationship with the ethnically distinct U.S. also created the possibility of an economic strategy to take advantage of that relationship.

Despite 110 years of American political dominance, Spanish cultural influences remain today in ways beyond the obvious use of the Spanish language. The legal system is based on Spanish civil code but functions within the U.S. federal system of justice. On the island's highways, speed limits are marked in miles per hour, while distances are indicated in kilometers. Lopez's interest in reading the great books stems from the influence that the classics, mediated through Spanish philosophy and literature, had on university and intellectual life on the island.

The confusion inherent in the relationship with the U.S. is manifest in the ironic titles of two recent books about the island: *None of the Above: Puerto Ricans in the Global Era* (Frances Negrón-Muntaner, ed. [New York: Palgrave Macmillan, 2007]) and *Foreign in a Domestic Sense: Puerto Rico, American Expansion, and the Constitution* (Christina Duffy Burnett and Burke Marshall, eds. [Durham: Duke University Press, 2001]). Bureaucratic confusion is visible in many instances; for example, U.S. levels for food stamps were applied to Puerto Ricans despite their very different socio-historical experiences. That was not the first time Puerto Ricans were bureaucratically transposed into an American context for policy purposes. During World War II, Puerto Rican GIs received additional "overseas" combat pay all the while they remained billeted on their beloved island. Nobody had to go anywhere to be put into an American context.

The first serious post-World War II attempt in Latin America to combat poverty by encouraging export capitalism was initiated in the early 1950s by Luis Muñoz Marín, the island's first native governor. Operation Bootstrap invited U.S. capital to come to the island to create jobs via a series of inducements such as tax incentives, inexpensive labor, and inclusion within U.S. tariff walls. The results were impressive. Puerto Rican export capitalism brought electricity and water to mountain villages, boosted life expectancy, and reduced illiteracy.

The relationship also created the Puerto Rican circuit, the possibility of unlimited migration between two societies, unencumbered by customs, passports and visas, creating what some have called a "commuter nation." The Puerto Rican influx to the U.S. has been called "the first great airborne migration" (Joseph P. Fitzpatrick, *Puerto Rican Americans: The Meaning of Migration to the Mainland* [Englewood Cliffs, N.J.: Prentice Hall, 1970] p. 2). The trek to the mainland began years before World War II but did not gather speed until after the war. In 1940, some 70,000 Puerto Rican-born residents were living on the mainland. A jump came in 1946, at about the time of Lopez's arrival in New York. In that year, 40,000 Puerto Ricans journeyed to the U. S., which then housed approximately 135,000 Puerto Rican-born residents, 85% of whom lived in New York City. By 1950, the total number of Puerto Rican-born residents surpassed 225,000. (Migration statistics can be found in "The Puerto Rican Exodus: Development of the Puerto Rican Circuit," in Barry B. Levine, *The Caribbean Exodus* [New York: Praeger Publishers, 1987] pp. 93-105).

As of 2006, according to Census Bureau estimates, some 3.7 million Puerto Ricans resided on the island and 4 million Puerto Ricans (by birth or parentage) lived on the U.S. mainland. If we assume, conservatively, that one half million were return migrants living once again in Puerto Rico, then at a minimum 54% of all Puerto Ricans have had significant life experience on the U.S. mainland. This total is based on 2006 U.S. census estimates (http://factfinder.census.gov), but assumes that 5% of the residents on the island are not Puerto Rican. Rivera-Batiz and Santiago calculate that there were 158,175 return migrants between 1980-1990, and an additional 130,335 circular migrants who traveled back and forth during the same period. Uncounted are commuter migrants (Francisco L. Rivera-Batiz and Carlos E. Santiago, *Island Paradox: Puerto Rico in the 1990s* [New York: Russell Sage Foundation, 1996] pp. 59-62). The number of return migrants is an estimate since there is little hard data to confirm it. The point is that the return migrants augment the significant mainland life experiences of Puerto Ricans. See also Jorge Duany, *The Puerto Rican Nation on the Move: Identities on the Island and in the United States* (Chapel Hill: University of North Carolina Press, 2002); Edna Acosta-Belén and Carlos E. Santiago, *Puerto Ricans in the United States: A Contemporary Portrait* (Boulder: Lynne Rienner Publishers, 2006); Carmen Teresa Whalen and Víctor Vázquez-Hernández, eds., *The Puerto Rican Diaspora: Historical Perspectives* (Philadelphia: Temple University Press, 2005), Elizabeth M. Aranda, *Emotional Bridges to Puerto Rico: Migration, Return Migration, and the Struggles of Incorporation* (Lanham, Maryland, 2007); Virginia Sánchez Korrol, *From Colonia to Community: The History of Puerto Ricans in New York City* (Berkeley: University of California Press, 1994); Clara Rodríguez, *Puerto Ricans Born in the U.S.A.* (Boulder: Westview Press, 1991).

2. *Jíbaro* is the Puerto Rican term for "peasant" and connotes a person who lacks sophistication. At the same time, the *jíbaro* is also credited with astuteness. Thus the phrase "'*Para un jíbaro, otro, y para los dos, el demonio*,' which means, 'To get the best of a *jíbaro*, employ another, and to catch both, Satan himself must take charge of them'" (from *Uncinariasis in Porto Rico* by Drs. Ashford and Gutierrez, cited in Fred K. Fleagle, *Social Problems in Porto Rico* [Boston: D. C. Heath & Co., 1917] p. 13).

3. Agriculture organized for export production floundered. A high birth rate and high population density further undermined the economy. The living standard was low, poverty abounded. Rural life offered little opportunity for advancement; a significant urban economy had yet to be created. Work in the needlepoint trades or employment as a domestic provided for a bare urban subsistence. One commentator characterized the Puerto Rico of the thirties as "an island of sick, starving, and superfluous people, without land, without work, without hope. . . ." (David F. Ross, *The Long Uphill Path: A Historical Study of Puerto Rico's Program of Economic Development* [San Juan: Editorial Edil, 1969] p. 18).

4. Given Puerto Rico's economic malaise at the time, where, then, could individual Puerto Ricans look to find economic opportunities? Industry initiated and owned by the Puerto Rican government helped some; federally sponsored emergency relief projects provided a stopgap solution for others. Offers by labor contractors to work overseas was yet another. Still others in search of work, such as Lopez, enlisted in the federally funded National Guard, which upon being called into federal service for World War II became an active component of the United States Army. The Army had an important, if unintended, economic impact as dependents' benefits, GI benefits, and federal spending on the island for military expenditures were critical economic stimuli, and it became the institutional prototype par excellence of the United States employer. Some 76,000 Puerto Ricans did military service during World War II; about half remained in the states when the war was over. It was in the Army during the 1940s that many Puerto Ricans received their initial training in modern nontraditional urban skills. Certainly this was the case for Lopez.

5. "Strategic leniency" is a term coined by Peter M. Blau (1918-2002), an American sociologist, to describe apparent permissiveness in certain authority situations which actually functions to strengthen authority over subordinates (*Bureaucracy in Modern Society* [New York: Random House, 1956] pp. 70-74).

6. Lopez was not alone in believing that migration might be an effective means to escape from poverty. Migration is the kind of opportunity that requires choice; the person who chooses to emigrate must perceive its potential value and have both the capacity to risk seeking the reward and the motivation to take the risk. Those who initially take such an opportunity can be expected to be either less insecure economically, having been able to take advantage of previous opportunities, or to be more adventuresome, or both. They are among "those best prepared for rescue" from poverty (John Kenneth Galbraith, *The Nature of Mass Poverty* [Cambridge: Harvard University Press, 1979] p. 138). Members of this non-accommodating minority are the first to spot the opportunity. They demonstrate the feasibility and effectiveness of the adventure, and others who so choose soon follow. Indeed, the first Puerto Rican emigrants played such a role. A 1947 study reported that Puerto Ricans in New York had higher incomes than Puerto Ricans on the island, that they were more urban, skilled, and educated and had a more stable record of employment than those who had not emigrated. The rural proletariat had not yet begun to emigrate. Once the

forerunners were established, others less prepared and less daring came to perceive migration as less risky (C. Wright Mills, Clarence Senior, and Rose Kohn Goldsen, *The Puerto Rican Journey: New York's Newest Migrants* [New York: Russell & Russell, 1950] chap. 2). Analyses of Puerto Rican immigrants during 1957-61 demonstrate that about 35% of those people migrating who were in the labor force were farm laborers as compared with the few rural immigrants found by the 1947 study. A comparison of the 1950 and 1960 censuses with the 1947 study shows that an ever-increasing proportion of unskilled to skilled workers were emigrating until finally they came to form the bulk of the total emigrating population (Stanley L. Friedlander, *Labor Migration and Economic Growth: A Case Study of Puerto Rico* [Cambridge: MIT Press, 1965] p. 102).

7. For a glimpse of what it is like running a *bodega*, or grocery store, in the 1950s and '60s, see Richard M. Elman, *The Poorhouse State: The American Way of Life on Public Assistance* (New York: Pantheon Books, 1966) pp. 217-30. The role of the *bodega* on the mainland has been well commented upon. See, for example, Oscar Handlin, *The Newcomers: Negroes and Puerto Ricans in a Changing Metropolis* (Cambridge: Harvard University Press, 1959) p. 71; Christopher Rand, *The Puerto Ricans* (New York: Oxford University Press, 1958) p. 7; Nathan Glazer and Daniel Patrick Moynihan, *Beyond the Melting Pot: The Negroes, Puerto Ricans, Jews, and Irish of New York City* (Cambridge: The M.I.T. Press, 1963) p. 112.

8. Witness, for example: "Puerto Ricans are not born to be New Yorkers. They are mostly crude farmers, subject to congenital tropical diseases, physically unfit for the northern climate, unskilled, uneducated, non-English-speaking and almost impossible to assimilate and condition for healthful and useful existence in an active city of stone and steel" (Jack Lait and Lee Mortimer, *New York: Confidential* [Chicago: Ziff-Davis, 1948] p. 126). Clarence Senior, *The Puerto Ricans: Strangers— Then Neighbors* (New York: Anti-Defamation League of B'nai B'rith, 1961) chap. 4, has chronicled the prejudiced reception given Puerto Ricans.

9. Valuable discussions of the different forms that race prejudice took on the island and on the mainland are found in: Joseph P. Fitzpatrick, *Puerto Rican Americans: The Meaning of Migration to the Mainland* (Englewood Cliffs, N.J.: Prentice-Hall, 1971) pp. 101-14; Ruby Rohrlich Leavitt, *The Puerto Ricans: Culture Change and Language Deviance* (Tucson: University of Arizona Press, 1974) pp. 169-71; Eduardo Seda Bonilla, "Social Structure and Race Relations," in Stanten W. Webster, ed., *The Disadvantaged Learner: Knowing, Understanding, Educating* (San Francisco, Calif.: Chandler, 1966) pp. 104-17; Gordon K. Lewis, *Puerto Rico: Freedom and Power in the Caribbean* (New York: MR Press, 1963) pp. 280-89; C. Wright Mills, Clarence Senior, and Rose Kohn Goldsen, *The Puerto Rican Journey: New York's Newest Migrants*). Most academic discussions about the role of race in Puerto Rico and on the mainland center on the facts that (1) North Americans classify people into two races, whereas Puerto Ricans classify people into additional categories; and (2) North Americans identify race by the presence or absence of Negro

blood, whereas Puerto Ricans do so by physical appearance. For an articulate account of some of the conflicts race prejudice has caused Puerto Ricans in the U.S., see the autobiography of Piri Thomas, *Down These Mean Streets* (New York: Alfred A. Knopf, 1967).

10. *Neorican* typically referred to New York Puerto Ricans—that is, Puerto Ricans influenced by both Puerto Rican and American cultures. It is not clear who first used the term. "Neo-Rican Jetliner," a poem and an article by Jaime Carrero, discusses the complex set of attitudes a Neorican must hold (*San Juan Review* [April 1965] 2[3]: 8-12).

11. Puerto Rican poet Lola Rodríguez de Tió (1843-1924) described Cuba and Puerto Rico as two wings of the same bird. In a similar vein, Luis Muñoz Marín once wrote his wife that "the Cuban is a happy Puerto Rican and a Puerto Rican a sad Cuban" (6 May 1945). Notwithstanding such statements, the fact that Cuba—but not Puerto Rico—gained independence from Spain earned Puerto Rico a lesser status in many Latin American eyes. Puerto Ricans were not generally seen by many Cubans as men of action and were often stigmatized as surrogates of the United States politically, as nonaggressive economically, and as unmotivated socially. In turn, many Puerto Ricans stigmatized Cubans as pushy and disrespectful.

12. Aim-rational action, according to the German sociologist Max Weber (1864-1920), is that in which an actor calculates ends, means, and side effects to maximize personal gain and minimize loss. It is also called "purpose rational" or "instrumentally rational" and refers to action "determined by expectations as to the behavior of objects in the environment and of other human beings, these expectations . . . used as 'conditions' or 'means' for the attainment of the actor's own rationally pursued and calculated ends" (Guenther Roth and Claus Wittich, eds., *Economy and Society* [New York: Bedminster Press, 1968] p. 24).

13. While the emigration was in process, the Puerto Rican economy was undergoing great changes. Not only were Puerto Rican workers traveling to the United States for jobs created by U.S. capital, but U.S. capital was invited to come to Puerto Rico where it created jobs for Puerto Ricans. The Puerto Rican Government focused on the possibility that its political tie with the United States might provide the source for the development of its own economy. In a sense it generalized from its experience with the United States Army and embarked upon an intense program to attract U.S. institutions to the island, providing a variety of jobs. Operation Bootstrap offered incentives to entice U.S. capital. Puerto Rico went from a society that was largely agricultural to one that was urbanized and industry-oriented. In 1940, the gross national product of Puerto Rico was $287 million. By 1965, around the time Lopez returned to the island, its GNP had jumped to $2,748 million; per capita income, which was under $120 in 1940, rose to $889 in 1965, and family income went from $611 in 1940 to $4,292 in 1965. Between 1940 and 1970, the economy grew at a rate near 10% per year. Job creation in industry, public administration, and trade, in con-

junction with emigration, absorbed population increases during those years. Agricultural employment declined from 45% to 16% of all employment on the island, losing 100,000 jobs in the interim. Manufacturing, commerce, and the public sector, which provided 24% of all jobs in 1940, increased to 51% in 1965, adding 200,000 positions. During this period 1,000 factories opened, providing 70,000 jobs. Government bureaucracy emerged to become the principal employer on the island. The ratio of unskilled to skilled members of the labor force, five to one in 1940, declined to two to one in 1965. In 1940, there were 500 medical doctors and 6,300 teachers; in 1965, there were 2,700 of the former and 18,600 of the latter. In those 25 years, registered motor vehicles climbed from 27,000 to 319,000; telephones from 17,000 to 195,000; annual electric energy production from 166,000 thousand kilowatts to 6,652,000 thousand kilowatts. Urbanization increased from 30% of the population to over 50% (and to over 58% in 1970). Agriculture continued declining: by 1977, only 5% of the jobs were in agriculture.

Between 1973 and 1977, growth slowed dramatically (the rate of growth fell to zero in 1974 and was negative 2% for 1975), in part because of the oil crisis and the ensuing world recession, but, more important, because the island was becoming less competitive. Unemployment doubled, rising wage rates and higher minimum wages slowed the growth in manufacturing employment. Agricultural jobs continued to decline. The major employer became the public sector. During the 1970s, Operation Bootstrap generated only about 18,000 new factory jobs, while population increased by one-half million persons. Yet, curiously, per capita income continued to rise: 1977 per capita income was reported at $2,472. Puerto Rico's GNP per capita was $6,010 in 1989, higher than all but 35 nations and territories. At that time, the world average was $3,760, that of Latin America and the Caribbean, $1,990 (Population Reference Bureau, *1991 World Population Data Sheet* [Washington: Population Reference Bureau, 1991].

How could that have happened? An enormous increase in the amount of transfer funds from the Federal government to the Commonwealth was largely responsible. When Operation Bootstrap began, the island received about $150 million per year from the Federal government. By 1982, that figure surpassed the $3.4 billion mark, roughly $1 billion of which came from food stamps. U.S. law simply refused to acknowledge sufficient differences in the island and mainland economies and used similar formulas to allocate benefits to both. The application of the United States Food Stamp program to Puerto Rico illustrates the consequences of this logic. The Federal Food Stamp program was developed to fight poverty. But what is "poverty" in one place is not "poverty" in another. Despite manifest differences in economic activity and social history, food stamps were made available in Puerto Rico using standards intended to apply to the mainland. In a flash, 70% of the island's residents were labeled poor—10% of the U.S. program got diverted to an island that constituted only 1.5% of the total national population (*cf.* Barry B. Levine, "Puerto Rico—Cashing Out Food Stamps" [*The Journal / The Institute for Socioeconomic Studies,* Vol. VII, No. 3, Autumn 1982] pp. 47-58). It was this same logic, allowing the island to benefit from American largesse regarding federal grants, that operated with respect to wage demands and minimum wages.

Puerto Rico's special link to the United States was beneficial to its industrialization, and by virtue of that link, the island was on the verge of becoming one of the Newly Industrialized Countries (NIC). But island governments chose an easier road, also by virtue of the link to the United States. When offered more and more benefits from the United States, they chose not to resist in the name of some theoretical benefit to accrue from austerity. But by becoming a transfer economy, Puerto Rico self-generated a brake on its own progress. The more it integrated into the United States, the more benefits it received bureaucratically, and the less it was able to maintain comparative economic advantage (cf. Barry B. Levine, "Las economías caribeñas de transferencia en Puerto Rico y Cuba," in Barry B. Levine, *El desafío neoliberal: el fin del tercermundismo en América Latina* [Bogotá: Editorial Norma, 1992]). Should the island choose statehood, all comparative advantage would be dissipated. The fatal error in Puerto Rico politics was the linking of independence to a socialist future rather than to a capitalist agenda and the creation of a national bourgeoisie. In opposition to a socialist independence, the political parties favoring bourgeois capitalism thus ended up competing with each other to prove which one could generate more transfer payments from the United States. Rivera-Batiz and Santiago (*Island Paradox: Puerto Rico in the 1990s*) summarize the crisis: Puerto Rico no longer represented the vanguard of export-led development given competition from NAFTA and other countries in the hemisphere as well as the success of the NICs in East Asia; the United States and the island were at cross purposes with respect to critical policy issues such as the application of federal minimum wages to the island and the extension of Section 936 federal tax immunity (the basis of Puerto Rico's economic engine); and continental Puerto Rican communities developed interests not always in sync with the island.

I am working on another testimonial, *The Impermanence of Industry: Lessons Learned from the Last Great American Garment Maker,* in which I annotate, inter alia, how the Puerto Rican economy began to decelerate about the time that Benjy Lopez returned to the island, paradoxically by virtue of its relationship to the U.S. A vivid example is the way American unions were able to unionize Puerto Rican industrial workers and press for the elimination of any differential in minimum wages—as a consequence Puerto Rico lost its comparative economic advantage in wages and was less able to bring in significant investment for labor-intensive industries.

14. The growth of the Puerto Rican urban economy increased the number and quality of jobs available to Puerto Ricans. For some who had migrated to the States, return to the island became a practical economic alternative to remaining on the mainland. As in the case of the original emigration, there were many reasons for a decision to return. Some returned to accept better work, some because of the "decreasing demand for blue collar workers performing repetitive and routine jobs" on the U.S. mainland (José Hernández Alvarez, *Return Migration to Puerto Rico* [Berkeley: Institute of International Studies, University of California, 1967] p.7). Others returned to find jobs that, although paying less than had their jobs in the States, would have more status. Some, such as Lopez, returned for more existential reasons. Life in New York was unpleasant and often undignified. The problems of

living in the city were daunting: drugs, discrimination, language, the persistent hassle of everyday life—all made it difficult for one to create a meaningful life. For some Puerto Ricans it meant that they could rejoin family and friends; for others, that they could bring up their children properly; for still others, that they could satisfactorily deal with health problems. For many, Lopez included, return meant that they could start to think in terms of building a better life in their own country.

Beginning around 1965, the phenomenon of the return migration began to gather momentum. As in the emigration from Puerto Rico, the first to return were both more skilled and better educated than those who stayed on the mainland. And the return migrants were better educated, more skilled and more urban than those who had not emigrated and against whom they would compete for opportunities back home. Furthermore, those who were returning were better skilled than those who were leaving the island for the mainland during the same period (Friedlander, *Labor Migration and Economic Growth*, p. 102). The net result during at least the initial stages of the return migration was to make the island labor force look more like the labor force of the mainland. As the return migration grew, however, the characteristics of the returnees became less selective; educational and skill levels of later returnees are notably lower than those of returnees who came back before 1960. During the time the Puerto Ricans on the mainland had been pressured to "Americanize," the Puerto Rican economy also was responding to similar "Americanization." Thus, when "America-smart" migrants returned to an "Americanized" Puerto Rico, they brought a whole host of skills and tastes that they had acquired in New York; in this sense, the mainland economy for a long period served as a vast training ground where returnees could learn both formal and informal skills relevant to the urban environment that had developed in Puerto Rico. Many returned not only with specific skills and new ways to do things but also with knowledge of how to capitalize on these new ways.

A 1964 study compared successful and unsuccessful returnees. Successful migrants "represent a middle-class element, bordering on the Island's educational, occupational, and financial elite. Many have taken advantage of opportunities becoming available as a result of modernization, resuming life in Puerto Rico under favorable circumstances—as professionals, white-collar workers, and highly skilled technicians. . . . That many started life in rural areas and ultimately settled in San Juan suggests a fair degree of social mobility" (Hernández Alvarez, *Return Migration*, p.2). Given their economic self-assurance, the subjective reasons they offered to explain their return most frequently had less to do with earning a living than with the social conditions that could allow them to live such a style of life. On the other hand, those who were unsuccessful on the mainland felt an economic compulsion to return. Having lost a job or having had a job "only once in a while" or not having ever had a job, such a Puerto Rican returned to the island for sustenance and maintenance by family and friends until he or she could find employment. And such a person was most likely to return to his birthplace, frequently a rural area or a small town—neither one a strong base for social mobility (Hernández Alvarez, *Return Migration*, p.104).

The exodus to the mainland and the economic growth on the island created a kind of migration equilibrium—or circuit—for Puerto Ricans. Individuals thus have the option of going from one place to the other in search of economic and social opportunities. Puerto Ricans who want to work in industry, for example, can do so on the mainland or on the island, and those who want to lead a particular style of life can choose to do so in San Juan or in the States. Some will alternate, "migrating and returning at various intervals and for various lengths of time." The more successful may "alternate periods of work in the United States with their main occupations on the Island . . . [and even] become scheduled commuters . . . [while the less successful may] drift from having no fixed employment to having no fixed residence in a pattern of almost aimless search for small job advantages" (History Task Force/Centro de Estudios Puertorriqueños, *Labor Migration under Capitalism: The Puerto Rican Experience* [New York: Monthly Review Press, 1979] p. 141). See also Jorge Duany, *The Puerto Rican Nation on the Move*, especially chapter 9.

What happens to those Puerto Ricans who will no longer have to return to their island to regain lost status—for example, when they achieve merited status in the United States as well as increased income? Perhaps it would have been more satisfactory had Puerto Rico been able to offer this segment sufficient income so that they didn't have to migrate in the first place; perhaps it would have been better had Puerto Rico been able to grow economically to the extent that it had hoped to, so that people could return and maintain class and status rankings. But as the economy flounders and as the possibilities for personal status recognition overcome discrimination on the mainland, then more and more of the better prepared are not going to come back home, seeing the United States, either enthusiastically or begrudgingly, as their new home. For some, the Puerto Rican circuit is but an expanded field for those potential voyagers who think in terms of ever greater, often varied, economic and social opportunities not hemmed in by mere geography and habit. If those returning are not as adventurous, entrepreneurial, or educated as those who stay, then this will have an effect. It is not quite a question of a brain drain but of a leak in the process so that opportunities gained on the mainland that otherwise might be transformed into benefits at home on the island will no longer be achieved at the same rates. Not even migration will help the island then.

15. See the work of Oliver Sachs, especially *An Anthropologist on Mars* (New York: Vintage Books, 1995).

Afterword: Changing the Story
(pages 183-194)

1. Anthony Giddens, *Central Problems in Social Theory* (Berkeley: University of California Press, 1979).

2. For example, John Dollard, *Criteria for the Life History, With Analyses of Six Notable Documents* (New Haven: Yale University Press, 1935); Gordon W. Allport,

The Use of Personal Documents in Psychological Science (New York: Social Science Research Council, 1942); Louis Gottschalk, Clyde Kluckholm, and Robert Angell, *The Use of Personal Documents in History, Anthropology, and Sociology* (New York: Social Science Research Council, 1945).

3. Dollard, *Criteria for the Life History*, p. 16.

4. Ibid., p. 188.

5. Reinhard Bendix, *Force, Fate & Freedom: On Historical Sociology* (Berkeley: University of California Press, 1984) pp. 55ff.

6. Fueled by works by Saul Bellow, J. P. Donleavy, Jack Kerouac, Ken Kesey, Philip Roth, and others.

7. Albert J. Guerard, "Introduction" to Saul Bellow, *The Adventures of Augie March* (Greenwich: Fawcett Publications, 1967), p. vii. *Augie March* was first published in 1953. The introduction by Guerard first appeared as an article, "Saul Bellow and the Activists: On *The Adventures of Augie March*," *The Southern Review* (Summer 1967) 3 (3). A similar argument to Guerard's is David L. Stevenson, "The Activists," *Daedalus (*Spring 1963).

8. Guerard, "Introduction" to *Augie March*, p. vii.

9. Ibid., p. ix.

10. Ibid., p. x.

11. Ibid.

12. A *pícaro* is an adventurer known for his cleverness and playful teasing of conventional reality. The *pícaro* became central to the picaresque novel, a genre first prominent in Spanish literature, in which the escapades of the rogue-hero were portrayed with a deafening realism and a biting satire. *Pícaro* derives from *picar*, "to prick." Alejo Carpentier defined the *pícaro* as: "The man without a job who looks for ways to survive. The man without a job who will do any job—because he has no job. The man who goes from one extreme to another: living it up in a palace today, down in the kitchen serving a fallen gentleman tomorrow, as he doesn't have anything else to do, musician, actor, medicine salesman, etc, etc., ... a man who makes a living out of whatever comes his way" ("Habla Alejo Carpentier," in Salvador Arias, ed., *Recopilación de textos sobre Alejo Carpentier* [Havana: Casa de las Américas, 1977] p. 34; author's translation). The first modern picaresque novel is generally thought to be *Lazarillo de Tormes*, published anonymously in Antwerp and Spain in 1554.

13. Guerard, "Introduction" to *Augie March*, p. xii.

14. Ibid.

15. Ibid., p. viii.

16. Frank Rich discusses a journalistic equivalent to this genre, "nonfiction 'novels.'" *Esquire* and *Harper's* magazines helped legitimate such works by Tom Wolfe, Hunter S. Thompson, and Norman Mailer. "How to Cover an Election," *The New York Review of Books* (29 May 2008) LV (9) pp. 9-10.

17. The concept of the "short con" is elaborated in Ned Polsky, *Hustlers, Beats, and Others* (New York: Doubleday, 1969) p. 42. Polsky discusses the concept in relation to the poolroom hustler who needs to feign "less competence than he has" in order to get others to shoot pool with him for money. The hustler's cardinal rule is "don't show your real speed."

18. Puerto Ricans' sense of resignation is believed to be expressed in their frequent use of the term ¡*Ay bendito!* (the phrase derives from the Catholic expression *Bendito sea Dios*, "Blessed be God," and roughly translates as "Oh my gosh!"). This story is not, however, an ¡*ay bendito!* tale. While Lopez does express lamentation, the attentive reader soon discovers that it is a kind of functional lamentation the storyteller/protagonist has designed to win over the reader rather than to bemoan his own lot.

19. "Role distance" is a term coined by Canadian sociologist Erving Goffman (1922-1982) to describe action that one performs but from which one's self is kept apart (*Encounters* [Indianapolis: Bobbs Merrill, 1961] pp. 85-152).

20. Cf. Juan F. Marsal, *Hacer la América: Autobiografía de un inmigrante español en la Argentina* (Buenos Aires: Editorial del Instituto, 1969) p. 41.

21. The first Puerto Rican testimonial was written many years before the social scientists captured the genre. In 1690, Carlos de Sigüenza y Góngora recounted the tale of a poor Puerto Rican carpenter's son who, at thirteen, left San Juan to travel the world. Perhaps, anticipating future testimonials, the title referred to the protagonist's "misfortunes" or "misadventures," rather than to any heroism on his part (*Infortunios de Alonso Ramírez* [San Juan: Instituto de Cultura Puertorriqueña, 1967]). Nearly three centuries later, Sidney Mintz published the life history of Don Taso, a rural proletarian. During the initial stages of the changes uprooting Puerto Rico, Don Taso helped establish the reform-minded Popular Democratic Party in the countryside. Later he turned away from party activity and converted to a Pentecostal religious sect. Contemplating his protagonist, Mintz concluded that "perhaps the reader will see the waste I think I see: the waste of a mind that stands above the others." The profundity of the changes occurring in Puerto Rico was not matched by a conversion to the Pentecostal faith, which carried with it a great sense of inadequacy (*Worker in the Cane: A Puerto Rican Life History* [New Haven: Yale University Press, 1960]).

In the same decade, Oscar Lewis came to Puerto Rico to prove the worth of his "culture of poverty" concept. *La Vida* was about a family typical of "the subculture of poverty," which Lewis presented as living proof of how that internal force prevented people from escaping from poverty. He claimed that "culture of poverty" life was harsh and brutalizing, spontaneous and tolerant. But it was clear that Lewis came to Puerto Rico to find losers. His protagonists did not confront modernity successfully; nor did he expect them to (*La Vida: A Puerto Rican Family in the Culture of Poverty—San Juan and New York* [New York: Random House, 1966]). Susan Sheehan took the culture of poverty concept to New York. *A Welfare Mother* was about Carmen Santana, her husbands, lovers, and children. One child became an addict, another, pregnant. Her life was "a series of accidents." To demonstrate that Santana was not a welfare chiseler, Michael Harrington argued in the introduction that she was not "a woman playing the system for all she can get." He thus pictured her as yet another Puerto Rican "unable to cope with the demands and complications of life in present-day America" (New York: New American Library, 1977).

Lloyd Rogler's *Migrant in the City: The Life of a Puerto Rican Action Group* (New York: Basic Books, 1972), a study of a Puerto Rican civic action group in Cleveland, could have presented contemporary Puerto Ricans in roles appropriate to the modern context as well as potentially successful. But it, too, turned out to be a story of the unsuccessful and of self-defeat. Another sad tale is that of Manny, a young Puerto Rican on the mainland, who lived as gang member, heroin addict, minor racketeer, criminal, prison inmate, and parolee (Richard P. Rettig, Manual J. Torres, and Gerald R. Garrett, *Manny: A Criminal Addict's Story* [Boston: Houghton Mifflin, 1977]). Manny is similar to two autobiographies published around the same time: Piri Thomas's *Down These Mean Streets* (New York: Alfred A. Knopf, 1967) and Lefty Barretto's *Nobody's Hero—A Puerto Rican Story* (New York: New American Library, 1976). Thomas's poignant story tells how he grew up in Spanish Harlem trying to overcome race prejudice and ethnic discrimination. He was involved in drugs, caught in a robbery, and spent time in prison. Lefty Barretto also went down the addict-criminal-prisoner path. There was hope that the protagonist would be successful, for he was the author; but the title, *Nobody's Hero—A Puerto Rican Story*, once more described the Puerto Rican as devoid of heroic possibilities.

At most these books showed Puerto Ricans learning lessons rather than teaching them. Eugene Mohr has suggested that these stories have contributed to the growth of a "literary genre defined as a narrative, possibly autobiographical, about a Puerto Rican male growing up in El Barrio and coming to grips with poverty, discrimination, gang warfare, drugs, crime, and sometimes imprisonment" (*The Nuyorican Experience: Literature and the Puerto Rican Minority* [Westport: Greenwood Press, 1982] p. 61). Héctor Varela's self-published *Affinity for Trouble—A Puerto Rican Story* (Florida-Boricua Publishing, 2006), not as downtrodden and not in El Barrio, nevertheless again flashes a negative title.

New York Times columnist David Brooks relates a postscript to the sad tale of the Puerto Rican testimonial: the Chicago neighborhood once occupied by Augie March deteriorated as its Jewish residents assimilated and moved out. Puerto Ricans moved in. To combat the worsening situation, a community organizer, José E. Lopez (no relation) professed a radical anti-colonial ideology to promote ethnic pride. Much was accomplished. "But stubborn problems remain. Eighty-five percent of the students who come to the area's Roberto Clemente High School are unprepared for high school work, and most will drop out. There is not a single male student, or a single black or Hispanic boy or girl, who tests above grade level. . . .[M]ost students don't even think about their long-term futures. Instead, many join gangs and go to jail, and once they have felony convictions on their records, they find it very hard ever after to find jobs." Brooks concludes that the "biggest difference between the neighborhood in Bellow's day and now is that then, the path to success was through assimilation, whereas now it is through ethnic self-determination." He adds: "I much prefer the assimilationist model. Instead of encouraging people to spend their lives around the same few streets, it opens up the wide possibilities of America. But nobody in the neighborhood believes in that model anymore, and the more immediate problem is that so many kids in the neighborhood are raised without any model, either Saul Bellow's or José Lopez's. They live without any idealism, and hence without any sense of the universal eligibility to be noble" ("Looking Out, And In," *New York Times*, 20 September 2003).

22. Henry Wells, *The Modernization of Puerto Rico* (Cambridge: Harvard University Press, 1969). The vision of the Puerto Rican as docile is central to the essay by René Marqués, "El puertorriqueño dócil," *Cuadernos Americanos* (January-February 1962). Roots of the discussion of docility can be found in Antonio S. Pedreira, *Insularismo: Ensayos de interpretación puertorriqueña* (Madrid: Tipografía Artística, 1934).

23. To even search for such heroic personalities, it is necessary to unlink any determinist vision of society from the individuals supposedly produced thereby.

24. When I asked Oscar Lewis why he abandoned his study of middle-class Mexican families, he replied that it was too boring. In Puerto Rico, one work, *The Sober Generation,* portrayed middle-class lives. It was a story of twenty Puerto Rican high school and college students; neither reactionary nor progressive, they simply wanted to get along, "content with the imperfection and instability of human events, seeking no happiness beyond the tranquility of rational and realistic expectations." Compared with those who lost on the streets, these youngsters were not losers; but somehow the capacity to cope competently, without an element of existential challenge, left them short of success (R. Fernández Marina, U. von Eckardt, and E. Maldonado Sierra, *The Sober Generation: Children of Operation Bootstrap—A Topology of Competent Adolescent Coping in Modern Puerto Rico* [Río Piedras, Puerto Rico: University of Puerto Rico Press, 1969]). Eugene Mohr adds: "People who adapt successfully may be less interesting to write about than people who ostentatiously fail to adapt" (Mohr, *The Nuyorican Experience*, p. 21).

25. Anthony Lauria, Jr., "'Respeto,' 'Relajo' and Interpersonal Relations in Puerto Rico," *Anthropological Quarterly* (April 1964) 37: 53-67.

26. Kal Wagenheim, *Puerto Rico: A Profile* (New York: Praeger, 1970) p. 214.

27. This particular dilemma never confronted Jews who migrated to the U.S. and who, having no country of their own, sought refuge hoping to escape their political circumstances. Not all refugees, of course, are happy to leave their country.

28. Pedro Juan Labarthe's self-published *The Son of Two Nations: The Private Life of a Columbia Student* (New York: Carranza, 1931), while auto-proclaiming success, demonstrates this problem. It is not simply that self-publication leads to self-congratulation, but also that commercial publication may encourage negative sensationalism (see Mohr, *The Nuyorican Experience*). There are emerging examples of a trend away from negative life histories, without the self-indulgence. Interestingly, these are by women authors such as Judith Ortiz Cofer, Nicholasa Mohr, and Esmeralda Santiago.

29. "Nuyorican" can be used positively as when referring to the New York Puerto Rican intellectual movement of the 1960s and 1970s. Or it can be use pejoratively as when an island Puerto Rican wants to put down a mainland Puerto Rican as being bereft of island culture.

Acknowledgments

During the writing of this book I shared *Benjy Lopez* stories with many of my colleagues at Florida International University. Their comments and reactions proved energizing to me, and I wish to acknowledge my appreciation. This book thrived at FIU in the days when the University promoted an interdisciplinary intellectual conversation. To my previous colleagues at the University of Puerto Rico, I also owe a great debt—it was there that my love of things Puerto Rican first developed.

I am especially thankful to Peter L. Berger, who "discovered" *Benjy Lopez: A Picaresque Tale of Emigration and Return* and urged me to proceed during a time when the project was at a standstill; to Antonio Jorge, who persistently assured me that even picaresque heroes have faults; and to my brother, David L. Levine of St. Johns College, Santa Fe, who long ago reminded me that social roles were not the biggest things in life. Many thanks also to Juan de la Rosa for the design of the cover.

The book is dedicated to three families: the Lopez family, the Wagenheim/Jiménez family, and my own. The first edition was published before my own family began. Like Lopez, I too learned that it is more meaningful to take on the world with co-conspirators. I trust that my wife Rosario, and our sons, Harris and Nathan, know that I love them dearly.

> Barry B. Levine
> Barry.Levine@fiu.edu

www.ingramcontent.com/pod-product-compliance
Lightning Source LLC
Chambersburg PA
CBHW032252150426
43195CB00008BA/418